Christina Stoddard

Light-bearers of Darkness

By Inquire Within

ⒸMNIA VERITAS.

Christina Stoddard
(Inquire Within)

For some years a Ruling Chief of the Mother Temple
of the Stella Matutina and R.R.et A.C.

Light-bearers of Darkness

First published by Boswell, London, 1930

Published by Omnia Veritas Limited

© Omnia Veritas Ltd – 2024

ⒸMNIA VERITAS.

www.omnia-veritas.com

As the three grades of ordinary Masonry included a great number of men opposed, by position and principle, to every project of social subversion, the innovators multiplied the degrees of the mystic ladder to be climbed. They created occult lodges reserved for ardent souls... shadowy sanctuaries whose doors were only open to the adept after a long series of proofs calculated to test the progress of his revolutionary education.

Louis Blanc — *French Revolution*

In all he did, in all he taught, he kept this aim in sight:
To get the deeds of darkness done,
disguised as works of light.
He spread his poison, slow and sure,
through many a specious sect,
And made the evil seem the good,
bamboozling God's elect.

The Coming of Lucifer By X.

CHAPTER I

THE OVERSHADOWING POWER

This book is an attempt to show, by means of actual investigations, of documentary evidence, and personal knowledge of the inner workings, that this present movement for World Revolution leading to World Domination is but an age-long and culminating, fanatical effort on the part of some Overshadowing Power working through many secret illuminised sects.

Whatever his ideas on the Messianic era and the true destiny of man may have been, the following account of mysticism and magic, written from 1823-25 by Hoëné Wronski, might well be an actual picture of world conditions to-day under the influence of similar mystic and secret societies — far more numerous and influential than the public imagine — through which the Invisible Centre is again seeking to direct and dominate the nations and the world.

In his *Traité méthodique de magic Pratique*, Papus. the well-known occultist and cabalist, Dr. Gerard Encausse, writes:

> "A learned initiate and encyclopaedist, Hoëné Wronski, in a work which is almost unobtainable today, *L'Apodictique Messianique*, has given an analysis of magic and its origins, as well as its results, which merits a close study on the part of serious inquirers. We hope therefore to render service to such by reproducing the whole of the section devoted to mysticism and magic."

Briefly, Wronski states that the aim of Mystic Associations is *"Participation in Creation,"* and the physical end is *"Direction of the Destinies of the Earth."* This mysticism "consists of the mystic limitation of the absolute reality (universal life-force or energy), forming in general the neutralisation of this negative and positive energy," a form of magnetic polarisation, creating the etheric link; for this reason these societies cultivate supernatural sentiments and arts such as… *"Hermetic Philosophy, Alchemy, the Great Work or Stone of the Philosophers, the Panacea, Magnetic-healing, Regeneration, etc.,* and certain mysteries of physical generation, etc." Being unable to discover scientifically, by reason, the destinies of the earth, they profess to foresee it by a *"Cabalistic interpretation* … of the traditions of the Holy Scriptures"; then they seek to direct these destinies by means of special missions given to chosen men in all ranks of society.

Secret Societies. He says:

> "As the supernatural efforts made by the Mystic Association to take part in creation can neither be practised nor discussed publicly … and being equally debarred from openly directing the destinies of the earth as Governments would oppose it, this mysterious association can perforce only act through *Secret Societies.* Thus actually it is in the heart of mysticism that all secret societies, which have existed, and still exist, on our globe, are born, and which, controlled from this mysterious source, have dominated and, notwithstanding Governments, continue to dominate the world. These secret societies, formed when needed, are detached into groups distinct and apparently opposed, professing respectively and in turn the most contrary opinions of the day, so as to direct, apart and with confidence, all parties, political, religious, economic, and literary. They, in order to receive common direction, are again united to an unknown centre, where this powerful source is hidden which seeks thus invisibly to control all earthly sceptres … and without doubt all these secret societies are themselves, through the skill of certain of their chiefs, controlled and directed according to the ideas and orders of an Unknown Supreme Committee who governs

the world."

Freemasons, Applied or Political.

"Pure or speculative masonry is properly only the great nursery from which all mystic associations choose their high chiefs (*epoptes*)... Also the grades of initiation are so arranged that the great part of Freemasons, far from doubting the aim of their affiliation, see in it only an object of mutual pleasure and good-will. Only those who have been tested are admitted into the higher grades, and it is from among the latter that the different branches of applied Freemasonry are formed, whose aim is manifestly to realise, by deeds and according to circumstances, the liberal mystic speculations of Freemasonry.Thus in our day have been successfully *formed the Nocturnal Chapters of Ruel and Passy, the Lodge of the Contrat-social, the Philadelphes, the Carbonari, the Tugend-Bund, the Burschaften, the Comuneros, etc.*" (This does not apply to British Masonry.)

Reciprocal Influences between the Visible and Invisible World. (Etheric Link) The Illuminati (Illuminism).

"The name Illuminati (not·Wissende) ... appears to have been introduced only about 1775 by the secret society which was founded by Weishaupt, and developed, it is said, by Baron Knigge. But ... it must have existed from the greatest antiquity. And actually the mystic affiliations under the Pyramids of Egypt, the esoteric sect of Pythagoras, the astrologers or mathematicians of Rome in the time of Domitian, the House of Wisdom of Cairo, the Ismailis or Assassins, Companions of the Old Man of the Mountain, the Templars, the Rose-Croix ... appear to form but an uninterrupted chain of these superior affiliations ... under the name of Illuminés."

Also their branches of *"Stricte Observance,* or preparation for Illuminism," including "eclectic Lodges or Egyptian Masonry, such as the Lodges *St. John of Melchisédeck, the Souffrants,*

Royal Priests, Masters of the Wise, and the Chercheurs." The *Asiatic Brethren,* either with these or the Illuminés.

The *Directing Power — the Invisibles or Earthly Beings* (Masters working on the Astral).

> "Once only have these Invisibles shown themselves to men, that was when, at the terrible Secret Tribunal — seeing that all the powers of earth, ministers, princes, and even sovereigns themselves begged the favour of being admitted to this formidable affiliation — these invisible Chiefs believed that at last they had conquered the earth, and they dared, so to say, to give away the secret by openly showing the way in which they intended to govern the world... These earthly beings do not appear today but it is they who form the Supreme Committee from which emanate the orders which rule all secret societies, and·in this Committee the ancient Book of Records ever remains open..." (Here we have the "Supreme and Invisible Hierarchy of Cabalistic Jews.")

Here is the Oath administered to the Illuminati:

> "In the name of the son crucified (the Pentagram, the illuminised man), swear to break the bonds which still bird you to your father, mother, brothers, sisters, wife, relatives, friends, mistresses, kings, chiefs, benefactors, and all persons to whomsoever you may have promised faith, obedience, and service. Name and curse the place where you were born, so that you may dwell in another sphere, to which you will attain only after having renounced this pestilential globe, vile refuse of the heavens! From this moment you are free from the so-called oath to country and laws: swear to reveal to the new chief, recognised by you, what you may have seen or done, intercepted, read or heard, learned or surmised, and also seek for and spy out what your eyes cannot discern. Honour and respect the *Aqua Tofana* as a sure, prompt, and necessary means of purging the globe by death of those who seek to vilify the truth and seize it from our hands. Fly from Spain, Naples, and all accursed land; finally fly from the temptation to reveal what you may hear, for the thunder is no prompter

than the knife, which awaits you in whatsoever place you may be. Live in the name of the Father, Son, and Holy Spirit. (This is the Trinity of Illuminism-Cabalistic and Gnostic. The Father — the generating fire; the Holy Spirit — the Great Mother Nature, reproducing all things; the Son — the manifestation, the vital fluid, the astral light of Illuminism. It is a perversion of Christian symbolism.)"

The reason for Wronski's exposure of these sects was to show the appalling spread of Illuminism at that time and its diabolical plan of destruction.

Mrs. Nesta Webster, in her *Secret Societies* and *Subversive Movements,* tells us how about A.D. 872, an Ismaili, Abdullah ibn Maymün, brought up on the doctrines of Gnostic Dualism, a pure materialist, formed a sect known as the Batinis, whose project was thus described by Dozy in *Spanish, Islam.*

"To unite in the form of a vast secret society with many degrees of initiation, free-thinkers ... and bigots of all sects; to make tools of believers in order to give power to sceptics ... to build up a party, numerous, compact, and disciplined, which in due time would give the throne, if not to himself, at least to his descendants... The means which he adopted were devised with diabolical cunning... It was ... not among the Shiites that he sought his true supporters, but among the Ghebers, the Manicheans, the pagans of Harran, and the students of Greek philosophy; on the last alone could he rely, to them alone could he gradually unfold the final mystery, and reveal that Imams, religions, and morality were nothing but an imposture and an absurdity ... but he took care to initiate devout and lowly souls only in the first grades of the sect. His missionaries, who were inculcated with the idea that their first duty was to conceal their true sentiments and adapt themselves to the views of their auditors... In the presence of the devout they assumed the mask of virtue and piety. With mystics they were mystical, and unfolded the inner meanings of phenomena, or explained allegories and the figurative sense of the allegories themselves... By means such as these the extraordinary result was brought about that a multitude of men of diverse beliefs were all working together for an object known only to a few of them..."

Here we have the system not only of Weishaupt but of all secret subversive societies of today, as later we hope to make plain in this book.

Again, in 1090 Hasan Saba, called "the Illuminator," founded the sect of the "Assassins" at Alamut in Persia on the Caspian Sea. He adopted the methods of Maymün, adding to them wholsale assassinations of those who opposed him. He also used as his ground-work the organisation of the Grand Lodge of Cairo. His was a "system of organised murder on a basis of religious fervour." As von Hammer said, "Nothing is true and all is allowed" was the ground of their secret doctrine, which, however, being imparted but to few, and concealed under the veil of the most austere religionism and piety, restrained the mind under the yoke of blind obedience." Their secret doctrines were eventually revealed by the leaders themselves. And von Hammer again said:

> "In the annals of the Assassins is found the chronological enumeration of celebrated men of all nations who have fallen victims of the Ismailis..."

And again:

> "Poison and the dagger prepared the grave which the Order had opened for so many,"

and so Hasan and his Grand Masters in turn assassinated by their next-of-kin (Mrs. Webster, *ibid.*).

As will be shown later, the Templars' self-appointed rôle was,

> "We shall be the equilibrium of the Universe, arbiters and Masters of the World."

In the March issue of the occult *"Revue Internationale des*

Sociétés Secrètes, began a French translation of the two most important collections of the original documents relating to the Bavarian Illuminati of Weishaupt — i.e.:

"(I) Einige Originalschriften des Illuminatenordens. Munich, 1786.

"(2) Nachtrag von weitern Originalschriften, welche die Illuminaten-secte ... betreffen en 2 parties.Munich, 1787."

Speaking of the occultists of Haute Maconnerie of the eighteenth century, the R.I.S.S. writes:

> "These Illuminés were in fact the secret rampart of the Sect. The Illuminés of France, with Martinez Paschalis, the unknown philosopher, Pernetty, and the whole school, which has left such deep roots in Lyons and its surroundings; the Illuminati of Bavaria, with Weishaupt and his accomplices. It was in these secret Lodges that the French Revolution was conceived and prepared; today it is in the Temples of the same Order, cabalistic and satanist, that the World Revolution has germinated and ripened... The plans of yesterday will better assist us to grasp the intention and methods of today."

The documents are thus described:

> "Some Original Writings of the Order of the Illuminati which were found at the House of Zwach, former Councillor of Gouvernment, in the domiciliary visit carried out at Landshut, October II-12, 1786."

> "The present collection has been published by the Supreme order of His Highness the Elector in order to convince the public of this and foreign countries of the undoubted falsity of the reasons given for the ceaseless outcry from the Illuminati against the injustice, violence, and prosecution to which they are subjected in Bavaria, and also at the same time to put them on their guard against this epidemic sect, and against all other such illegal and clandestine societies. For

these merely set themselves to deceive credulous people and get money out of them — and in place of spreading truth and morality, as they profess to do, absolutely ruin the latter and suppress or completely falsify the former. If anyone doubts the authenticity of this collection, let them present themselves at the secret archives of this town, where orders have been given to show the originals. Munich, March 26, 1787."

In one document Zwach speaks of the proposal to form a woman's order, to consist of two classes, each constituting a separate society, each remaining unknown to the other: one class of virtuous women, a means of obtaining money, secret information, and benefits fo the real Order; the other of light women, to satisfy the passions of F.M. so inclined. "Both should be kept in ignorance that they are directed by the men's Order."

Of their camouflaged and supposed aim Spartacus-Weishaupt-writes:

"As in the past, the future aim of the Order remains to interest man in bringing to perfection his mind and moral character; to develop humane and social sentiments, to oppose wicked designs in the world to fight against injustice, to help the unfortunate and oppressed, to encourage men of merit who a useful to the Order, and to spread knowledge of the sciences; and they are faithfully and solemnly assured that this is the real and not merely the supposed aim of the society. That it is vain to hope to gain greater power and riches by entering this Order."

The scheme of this Order is apparently to form a united machine absolutely controlled by the Superiors, who alone know its true aim. For this purpose there must be complete harmony among its members, no hatred, no jealousy, no unworthy egoism; having one spirit, one consideration, and one will! To help to bring about this desired orientation, a special list of books is prescribed upon which the members must build up their outlook. "The society cannot use men as they are; they must be shaped according to the use that is to be made of them." Here we have the same sinister methods as found in all similar societies of to-day!

Weishaupt further writes that the adept must learn the art of dissimulation, observing and probing others. Discovering secrets he must disclose them to the Superiors, who in turn promise not to make use of the information unless permitted by the informer! "The Order exacts complete submission in whatsoever concerns the affairs of the Order. They must practise perfect circumspection and discretion with regard to the world outside. Silence and secrecy constitute the soul of the Order," and even the Frater's grade is kept secret, save with equals, among whom there are signs for recognition.

As to the true aim of this Order, a document drawn up by Zwach shows its political progress for one year in Bavaria — Jesuits removed from all professorial chairs, and entirely cleared out of Ingolstadt University; penetration by F.M.of the Church, control of German schools, charitable societies, and other university chairs.

"On the recommendation of the Fratres, Pylade has become treasurer of the Ecclesiastical Council, and in this way the Order has the revenues of the Church at its disposal." Thus it was able to assist the Fratres and save some of them from the clutches of money-lenders!

Again:

> 'The widowed Duchess has organised the Institute of Cadets absolutely according to the plan indicated by the Order; all the professors are members of the Order … and all the pupils become adepts of the Order.

> 'We will draw to us all the young priests of the Bartholomew endowment … there is every chance that we may in this way be able to provide all Bavaria with instructed priests.'

Also among the documents were various recipes — 'One for

Aqua Toffana, a poison imperceptibly slow but deadly.' Another to bring about abortion; and yet another concerning herbs having deleterious properties.

The Initiation took place after one, two, or three years of probation. In the *Revers de silentio,* a form signed by the candidate before the initiation, submission and silence is promised, and he is assured that there is in the Society nothing contrary to 'State, morals, or religion.' Before the Oath is administered it is said — a sword pointed at the breast:

> "Shouldst thou become a traitor or perjuror, let this sword remind thee of each and all the members in arms against thee. Do not hope to find safety; whithersoever thou mayest fly, shame and remorse as well as the vengeance of thine unknown brothers will torture and pursue thee.'

> Then in the Oath which follows he swears 'eternal silence, and faithfulness and everlasting obedience to all superiors and regulations of the Order. I also renounce my own personal views and opinions as well as all control of my powers and capacities. I promise also to consider the well-being of the Order as my own, and I am ready, as long as I am a member, to serve it with my goods, my honour, and my life… If I act against the rules and well-being of the Society, I will submit myself to the penalties to which my superiors may condemn me…"

He received a classical name, by which he was henceforth known in the Order. He was required also to keep all things appertaining to the Order in a special place, having a label attached with the address of his superior, to whom the box had to be sent in case of his sudden death. In one of the recipes is found the description of such a box which, when opened by an uninitiated person, would at once burst into flames! To such an extent was secrecy and silence demanded!

After the breaking up of his Order Weishaupt and his followers still secretly carried on their intrigues, for by 1789 the 266

Lodges controlled by the Grand Orient Freemasonry were all Illuminised unbeknown to the large majority of the members, and a few months later the French Revolution of that date eventuated.

In 1794 the Duke of Brunswick, Grand Master of German Freemasonry, issued a Manifesto to all the Lodges showing how Masonry had been penetrated by this International Sect, and suggesting, for a time, suppression of all Freemasonry until it was freed from this unseen cancer. It says:

> "A great sect arose, which, taking for its motto the good and happiness of man, worked in the darkness of the conspiracy to make the happiness of humanity a prey for itself. This sect is known to everyone: its brothers are known no less than its name. It is they who have undermined the foundations of the Order (Freemasonry) to the point of complete overthrow; it is by them that all humanity has been poisoned and led astray for several generations. The ferment that reigns amongst the peoples is their work. They founded the plans of their insatiable ambition on the political pride of nations. Their founders arranged to introduce this pride into the heads of the peoples. They began by casting odium on religion… They invented the rights of man, which it is impossible to discover even in the book of Nature, and they urged the people to wrest from their princes the recognition of these supposed rights. The plan they formed for breaking all social ties and of destroying all order·was revealed in all their speeches and acts. They deluged the world with a multitude of publications; they recruited apprentices of every rank and in every position; they deluded the most perspicacious men by fasely. alleging different intentions. They sowed in the hearts of youth the seed of covetousness, and they excited it with the bait of the most insatiable passions. Indomitable pride, thirst of power, such were the only motives of this sect; their masters had nothing less in view than the thrones of the earth, and the government of the nations was to be directed by their nocturnal clubs. This is what has been done and is still being done. But we notice that princes and people are unaware how and by what means this is being accomplished…"
> (Mrs. Webster, ibid.)

Later, a law was passed, as a result of all this, by the English Parliament in 1799, prohibiting all secret societies with the exception of Freemasonry. To-day, it is said, these secret societies are still illegal, and although some call themselves semi-public, an oath of secrecy is still required by their chiefs, concerning the most important and secret teachings, relating, more especially, to contact with the mysterious controlling power on the astral plane.

According to Monsignor Dillon, 1885 (Mrs. Webster. ibid):

> "Had Weishaupt not lived, Masonry might have ceased to be a power after the reaction consequent on the French Revolution. He gave it a form and character which caused it to outlive that reaction to energize to the present day, and which will cause it to advance until its final conflict with Christianity must determine whether Christ or Satan shall reign on this earth to the end."

Was Weishaupt not merely the tool of another and more formidable Sect? Of this 'Overshadowing Power,' which is the life, as it were, of Illuminism, we are told, in *The Victories of Israel, by Roger Lambelin:*

> "Joseph de Maistre who was, one knows, a Freemason of fairly high grade, noted the influence exercised by the Jews. In 1811, examining the causes of the French Revolution, in a letter written to his King from St. Petersburg, he says: "The power of this *sect oriented by Jewry,* to bewitch Governments, is one of the most terrible and most extraordinary phenomena that have been seen in the world."

Again, Bernard Lazare, the Jewish writer, affirms:

> "It is certain that there were Jews even at the cradle of Freemasonry-Cabalistic Jews, as is proved by certain existing rites; very probably during the years which preceded the French Revolution they entered in still greater numbers into the councils of the society, and themselves founded secret societies. There were Jews round Weishaupt; and Martinez

de Pasqualis, a Jew of Portuguese origin, organised numerous illuminised groups in France, and recruited many adepts, whom he initiated into the doctrine of reintegration (regeneration). The Martinist Lodges were mystic, whilst the other Orders of Freemasonry were rather rationalist, which proves that secret societies represented the two sides of the Jewish mind-practical rationalism and pantheism; that pantheism which, while a metaphysical reflection of a belief in the One God, ends at times in a Cabalistic Theurgy."

And of the Jewish aspirations he writes:

"The Jew is also a builder: proud, ambitious, domineering, he tries to draw everything to himself. He is not satisfied with de-Christianising, he Judaises; he destroys the Catholic or Protestant faith, he provokes indifference, but he imposes his idea of the world, of morals, and of life upon those whose faith he ruins; he works at his age-old task — the annihilation of the religion of Christ!"

And M. Roger Lambelin adds:

"They are the ferments of revolution in all ethnic groups foreign to their race."

Further, Rabbi Benamozegh says:

"Is it surprising that Judaism has been accused of forming a branch of Freemasonry? What is certain is that masonic theology is only theosophy at bottom, and corresponds to that of the Cabala.

… Those who will take the trouble to examine with care the connection between Judaism and philosophic Freemasonry, theosophy, and the mysteries in general … will cease to smile in pity at the suggestion that Cabalistic theology may have a rôle to play in the religious transformations of the future… It contains the key to the modern religious problem."

In an interesting book, *Les Juifs et le Talmud,*[1] by M. Flavien Bernier, we find some light thrown on this Pantheistic creed of the Cabalistic Jews and the "Deified Man" of Illuminism. He writes, 1913:

> "Now the dominating philosophic doctrine among learned Chaldeans ... was absolute Pantheism. In the vast Temple which is the Universe, the learned Chaldeans suppressed the Creator... Everything was cause and effect; the world was uncreated and itself became its own God. Even the idea of Divinity was confounded with Universal Harmony which regulated all things, and with each of the things it regulated. God was therefore in turn, and as a whole, Earth nourisher of man, the dew which fertilised it, the Sun which gave light and heat, the wind which carried the fertilising pollen of vegetation; God was·the life principle which perpetuated the species, human and animal; which caused plants to germinate, grow, die, and spring into life again, which manifested even in apparently inanimate bodies. Identified as a kind of breath of Nature, uncreated and eternal. God emanated from the world not the world from God.

> "It is realisable that such a system, which bears the imprint of a bizarre but undeniable poetry, would, in all ages, have the power to seduce the human mind. It would seduce it all the more that the system had, as immediate result, the increase of human pride in the cult of the 'Deified Man.'"

> "In effect, if no Supreme Being as distinct from Nature was imposed over the latter by right of creation — if all things had in some manner an intelligence or soul, and if God was merely the sum of all these conscious or unconscious souls of the Universe, a hierarchy would necessarily exist among these souls of which each was a part of God, but which could only contain God in a very unequal manner. The divine

---

[1] *Les juifs et le Talmud : morales et principes sociaux des Juifs d'après leur livre saint : le Talmud – 1913*, Omnia Veritas Ltd, www.omnia-veritas.com.

principle would find itself distributed in less abundance in a stone than in a tree, which lives, breathes, grows, and dies; in a tree than in an animal, which thinks, perceives, and acts; in an animal than in a man who meditates on the past and future, solves the problem of Nature, corrects the latter's imperfections by his labour and ingenuity, and seeks to perfect himself indefinitely. At the summit of the ladder of beings Man, much more perfect and more intelligent than any of the others, evidently absorbed the greatest amount of the divine essence of which the universe is composed. Having emptied the heavens of any being superior to himself, he was in truth God of the World, where all were apparently inferior and subordinate to him."

In a footnote the author adds:

"Those of our readers who are familiar with the works of Hermetic Freemasonry will at once recognise the favourite ideas of the pontiffs of that sect, ideas which they have inherited from the alchemists of the Middle Ages, who held them from the Cabalistic Jews. The same may be said of the cult of the 'Deified Man,' which was the basis of Chaldean Pantheism, and which bas remained that of Occultism, ancient and modern.

"Certain traditions give to Zoroaster, a Jewish Prophet, as Master... But, on the other hand, Chaldean thought acted powerfully upon orthodox Judaism and determined the growth of a sect in its midst which was to transform Israel... This sect was that of the 'Pharisees'... What they borrowed (from the Chaldeans) in fact ... was the essence of the Pantheistic doctrine... It was then that was formed from these borrowings that Kabalah of the Pharisees which was for long transmitted orally from Master to disciple, and was, 800 years later, to inspire the compilation of the Talmud, and found its completest expression in the 'Sepher ha Zohar.'... This religion of the 'Deified Man,' with which they were impregnated in Babylon, was only conceived as benefiting the Jew, superior and predestined being.

... The promise of universal domination found in the Law by the orthodox Jew was not interpreted by the Pharisees in the sense of the reign of the God of Moses over the Nations, but in the sense of a material domination which would be imposd by the Jews over the Universe. The expected Messiah ... was to be a temporal King, all bloody from battle, who would make Israel master of the world and trample all peoples under the wheel of His chariot."

Have we not here the basis of the teaching in all these Orders and groups, mystic and occult, of the present time — the cult of the life-force, the I.A.O., the "Serpent Power" the all-pervading ether? And have we not also the key to the Cabalistic Jews, in these Pharisees of old and of to-day; these so-called "Divine Guardians'working behind and through these secret Orders, who profess to teach the doctrine of the deification of the adept, but who in very truth create Illuminised slaves controlled by the Cabalistic Jew, who claims to be the "Deified Man"—as M. Bernier says, 'the God-people' rather than the 'People of God.'

In the *Patriot*, March 7, 1929, we find some interesting material in connection with Secret Societies and the French Revolution; it says:

"In 1910 there was published a very remarkable book, enitled *Marie-Antoinette et le Complot Maçonnique.*[2] It was written by M. Louis-Dasté, an erudite historian, who had spent a great deal of time in examining published and unpublished documents throwing light on the part played by secret societies in preparing the French Revolution... The extracts show, among oher things, how anti-Christian and revolutionary ideas were circulated by bodies ostensibly engaged in educating the French people. Behind these bodies was French Freemasonry, which was and is, unlike our own

[2] *Marie-Antoinette et le Complot Maçonnique*, Omnia Veritas Ltd, www.omnia-veritas.com.

Freemasonry, anti-Christian, political, and revolutionary."

We quote the following extracts showing their methods:

"At the beginning of the eighteenth century France was still fervently attached to her religious and political traditions; at the end of that century she broke — or rather a secret influence made her break — with all of them. What was this secret influence? It was in every case the influence of Freemasonry... For more than half a century the Freemasons had, in fact, been secretly preparing the mine, whose explosion in 1789 wrecked the old France... From 1750 onwards Reading Societies were started in most of the towns in France. Like the Free Thought Societies of the present day, they were under the control of Freemasons... Members of these societies who had been the most easily caught by the Masonic bait, and who, in addition, possessed literary talent, were admitted into groups of a higher degree, the societies called 'Academic.'... Like the Reading Societies, the Academic Societies were secretly directed by Freemasons ... who provided the money spent either on prizes given for anti-Christian pamphlets or on the printing and publishing of them... Finally, above the Reading and the Academic Societies were the so-called Societies of Action, which were neither more nor less than exteriorisations of Masonic Lodges... The work which the Reading and Academic Societies did in conjunction with the Lodges controlling them was as deadly as it was simple. Under the influences of these groups of Masons and their helpers, luke-warm Catholics gradually became unbelievers, and finally fanatical anti-Christians... Freemasonry first infected the King's ministers and the high functionaries; then magistrates of every kind, lastly the Church of France itself... Thanks, therefore, to their ignorance of the Masonic danger and to their semi-complicity with the enemy, the two d'Argensons, Maurepas, and St. Florentin allowed the Freemasons of the eighteenth century to destroy the Christian monarchy of France..."

In the *Revue Internationale des Sociétés Secrètes* there was an article on 'Revolution, Terror, and Freemasonry,' which explained the connection of Grand Orient Freemasonry with the French Revolution and its present-day aim at a 'World Republic' — Universal Freemasonry (see Patriot, August 16, 1928).

> "In 1789 the revolutionary crimes were prepared by the Committee of Propaganda of the Lodge *Les Amis réunis*, and the plan of 'The Terror' is due to one of its most influential members, the Jacobin Freemason, Adrien Duport (who when questioned as to his plan said)... "Now, it is only by means of terror that one can place oneself at the head of a revolution in a way to govern it... It is therefore necessary, whatever repugnance you may have, to resign oneself to the sacrifice of some marked persons."

> ... Instructions in conformity with the plan were given to the principal agents of the department of insurrections which was already organised, and to which Adrien Duport was no stranger; execution followed quickly. The massacre of de Launay, de Flesselles, Foulon, and Berthier, and their heads paraded on pikes, were the first effects of this philanthropic conspiracy.

> "In 1922 the Orator of the Grand Lodge (France) said: 'My brother Masons, my hope is that Freemasonry, which has done so much for the emancipation of men, and to which history owes the national revolutions, will also know how to make that greatest revolution, which will be the International Revolution.''

Speaking of subversive propaganda at that time, Arthur Young, in his *Travels in France and Italy* (Young, in Paris at the opening of the French Revolution, was one of the acutest observers of the eighteenth century) writes (see Patriot, February 2, 1928):

> "June 29, 1789. Will posterity believe that while the Press has swarmed with inflammatory productions that tend to prove the blessings of theoretical confusion and speculative licentiousness, not one writer of talent has been employed to refute and confound the fashionable doctrines, nor the least

care taken to disseminate works of another complexion?"

Does the above not apply equally to the present "World Revolution," engineered by the same hidden and "formidable Sect?" How many dare or will publish the bedrock truth?

Let us now study the present aims of Grand Orient Freemasonry as shown by their own records. It is a Judaeo-Masonic body, political and revolutionary, working for World Domination.

In *"La Dictature de la Franc-Maçonnerie sur la France,"* M. A. G. Michel exposes some of these machinations:

> "It is the duty of universal Freemasonry to co-operate absolutely with the League of Nations in order that it may no longer have to submit to the interested influences of Governments" (Convent. Grand Orient, 1923).

> "The principal tasks of the League of Nations consist in the organisation of peace, the abolition of secret diplomacy, the application of the right of peoples to self-determination, the establishment of commercial relations inspired by the principle of Free Trade, the repartition of basic matters, the regulation of transport, restoration of normal relations between national devices, and the creation of an International note; the development of international legislation of labour, and especially the participation of an organised working-class in international councils; the spread of a general pacifist education based notably on the extension of an international language (Esperanto!); the creation of a European spirit, of a League of Nations patriotism — in brief, the formation of the United States of Europe, or rather World Federation' (Convent of the Grand Lodge of France, 1922).

> "Affirms that this Assembly (League of Nations) must evolve in a democratic sense and rapidly admit representatives of all nations; declare that the new establishment must assure equality of nations; report with satisfaction the creation of a Bureau of International Labour as a permanent organ of the

League of Nations.' (Convent. Bull. Off. Grand Lodge of France, 1920).

"The Commission demands that the Convention should unanimously vote that in all manner of cases the League of Nations shall henceforth have supreme authority to decide between peoples and Governments" (Convent. Grand Lodge of France, 1923).

"Further, it demands that the League of Nations, in order to assure the execution of its decisions, should be endowed with a permanent armed force placed under its sole authority, diminishing by so much the different national armies" (Convent. Grand Orient, 1923).

"The Federal Organisation of Peoples implies the establishment of an Over-State, or super-national State, invested with three powers — executive, legislative, and judicial; that is to say, possessing the three organs indispensable to all constituted society — a Government, a Parliament, and a Court of Justice. The Court of Justice must be furnished with a penal code, civil code, and a code of international procedure. The international authority must be sanctioned by an army or international police. To disarm separate States and arm the Federation of United States, these are two phases of the same progress" (Bull. Off. Grand Lodge of France, 1922).

"Studies through the League of Nations to create an International Bank based on the mobilisation of invested (foncière) property, public or private" (Bull. Off. Grand Lodge of France, 1922).

Leading to a programme of Universal Masonic Dictatorship:

I. *Policy of Destruction* (*Solve* of Illuminised Masonry): Destruction of the Church. Revolution.

II. *Reconstruction of a new regime (Coagula* of Illuminised

Masonry): (a) Economic and social; (b) financial and fiscal reform; (c) socialisation of individuals.

III. *Universal Masonry:* "This International Revolution is for tomorrow the work of Freemasonry" (Convent. Grand Lodge of France, 1922). "Three Revolutions: 1789, 1871, 19—" (Bull. Hebd. 1922).

The Grand Orient penetration of many groups is explained by the following extracts from the same document:

"Masonry must be felt everywhere, but must be found no-where" (Convent. Grand Orient, 1922).

"We are forming a great Association, dumb to the outside world, whose sole endeavour will be to express ideas collectively and overrun the country with them ... we must earnestly endeavour to make our thoughts penetrate the whole mass ... but our whole satisfaction will come from that which our ideas germinate" (Convent. Grand Orient, 1922).

"An active propaganda is urgent, so that Freemasonry shall again become the inspirer, the sovereign mistress of the ideas through which democracy is to be brought to perfection... To influence social elements by spreading widely the teaching received within the Institution" (Convent. Grand Orient, I 922).

"Sports societies, Boy Scouts, art circles, choral and instrumental groups. All organisations which attract Republican youth to works of education, physical and intellectual. There are so many fertile fields where Masonic propaganda ought most usefully to be exercised. Everywhere add to these adult courses, wherever there is any chance of them being taken up and frequented, libraries, etc." (Convent. Grand Orient, 1923)

"Freemasonry is not exactly international, it is universal; it is a society non-national, a society of 'humanity' not a society of international brotherhood, but a society of Universal Brotherhood" (Bull. Off. Grand Lodge of France, October 1922).

The Grand Orient was founded in 1772, formed a coalition with the Grand Chapter in 1786, and became a body both subversive and dangerous. By 1789, we have seen, it was illuminised just previous to the Revolution. It is therefore illuminised esoteric masonry, largely dominated by Jews, and its aim is political power. Their god is the Creative Principle, and they look upon God the Creator as a myth. On the other hand, the British masons are exoteric, non-political, and philanthropic, and they believe in God as the Great Architect of the Universe. For these reasons in March 1878 they broke off relations with the Grand Orient.

Many of these secret and pseudo-public societies, which are to be discussed later, are affiliated directly or indirectly to the Grand Orient, and are, as it will be seen, subversive.

Anyone who has at all considered the matter must realise that no movement such as the present World Revolution, with all its intricacies, could gain the proportions which it has very evidently done unless there was a means of cohesion and a powerful central mind directing the whole. What the late Bishop of Dijon has said of the Jews in his book *Les Pharisiens d'autrefois à Ceux d'aujourd'hui*, might well be said of the above movement. He writes:

> "But, in order that these colonies of Jews, so widely scattered as they are among such different races, under such dissimilar rule, buried among hostile masses, and without any apparent link, should have nevertheless succeeded in preserving their original characteristics, always the same ideals, everywhere the same mentality, the same ideas, a perfect similarity, it is indispensable that they should have some invisible uniting link, a common mind, a head, in a word a central government, and that government can only be an occult government."

In a footnote to the same book, and speaking of Grand Orient

Freemasonry, he says:

> "In the Lodges the discussions are not for the purpose of getting at the truth, but their aim is action. What matters is not a connected and real opinion corresponding to the convictions of each as a whole, but a collective and practised opinion, the result of a prearranged understanding for an interested end. They do not search for it by means of study as the philosophers do; they suggest and impose it… One is not forced to enter Masonry, but once in, the adept must take on the spirit of Masonry—it is 'initiation.' They set themselves to infuse him with it in order to orient him. But if each mason is personally oriented, so also is each group, unbeknown to themselves, by the higher groups, in such a way that, because of the impossibility of seeing what leads them or where they are being led to, they believe themselves free, whereas in fact they are oriented or directed by this '*Mysterieux Moteur Central*, known to us alone' says the author of that strange book *The Jewish Peril*."

The same secret system will be found in all illuminised secret societies of to-day, which are all ruled and directed by some mysterious hidden centre. Speaking of his own system, Weishaupt says that he forms his ranks "out of men who would submit to be led blindly onwards by unseen directors." He says:

> "One must show how easy it would be for one clever head to direct hundreds and thousands of men. I have two immediately below me into whom I breathe my whole spirit, and each of these two has again two others, and so on. In this way I can set a thousand men in motion and on fire in the simplest manner, and in this way one must impart orders and operate on politics" (*Mrs. Webster, Secret Societies and Subversive Movements*).

This is Weishaupt's system, but what of the mysterious central power?

It is not this book's purpose to prove or disprove "the Protocols of the Learned Elders of Zion," which have been somewhat unconvincingly pronounced by Philip Graves, in *The Times* of August 16–18, 1921, and again in 1923 in his book *Palestine the Land of Three Faiths*, to be plagiarised in parts from Maurice Joly's revolutionary pamphlet, *Dialogues aux Enfers* and in part supplied by the Okhrana or Tzarist secret police. What interests us, however, is that Mr. Graves admits that the same ideas and methods as expressed in the Protocols and the aforesaid pamphlet underlie all revolutions: "The French Terrorists, the Napoleons, the Turkish Chiefs of the Committee of Progress and Union, Lenin and his adherents." And of the Jews he says:

> "Do not these facts sufficiently explain why the Eastern Jews have been to a great extent the driving force of the Russian Bolshevik Revolution, intensifying its fanatical bitterness against Tzar, Church and Capital, but supplying it with greater brain power, greater continuity of policy and persistence, than could be found among the Russian masses or among the Communist fraction of the intelligentsia."

Here and there we quote these Protocols, comparing them with the work of these many secret societies solely to show that these same revolutionary ideas and methods still underlie the principles of these Jew-dominated secret and undoubtedly subversive movements of to-day.

CHAPTER II

ORIENTED BY JEWRY

B EFORE proceeding with the results of our investigations and research into some of the more magical and dangerous of present-day cults and societies, the conclusions arrived at by a learned French occultist may be of interest, as supporting and adding to some of our points.

But first we would explain that occultism is the knowledge and use of the dual sex or hidden creative forces in all Nature, and the Jewish Cabala, based on these same secret laws, is one of the most learned and powerful systems for gaining control over Nature and over the mind and actions of man, bringing into play and perverting these forces in order to attain power and dominion. It is polarity and a subtle method of suggestion. *The Revue Internationale des Sociétés Secrètes* has for some time been investigating and exposing the age-old source and hidden power of these secret societies, hoping also to assist other investigators, and supply a choice of weapons to those who are already fighting step by step against contemporary Judaeo-Masonry. M. Henri de Guillebert, "a specialist of first order in these matters," has taken a leading part in these investigations. We give a few extracts from his articles, "Studies in Occultism":

"The importance of the part played by secret societies in religious, social, economic, and political evolution is generally denied... There is no trace in the history of peoples of any international attempt to determine the origin, the vicissitudes, the aim, the claims, the doctrine, and discipline of sects, considered no longer as isolated phenomena, but as a permanent organisation, thus monstrously and solidly formed of a multitude of separate parts. It is therefore to a certain extent a novelty to show the action of occultism upon people in its successive phases by establishing what secret societies are; how they are linked together in time and space; where they come from and whither they wish to lead men; who constitutes them, and who directs them... In our time occultism can no longer be other than a material and human reality, a problem to be solved by recognised methods of criticism, a work analysable by means of investigations, capable of unmasking secret societies as a whole. To observe, analyse, classify, and compare all sects is a purely scientific work...

"*Judaeo-Masonry.* — This term can be used, making all reservations as to its correctness, to designate the organisation composed of Cabalistic Jews and secret societies, considered no longer as isolated phenomena in time and space, but as a whole, having a common doctrine and discipline, a common aim and methods... The method employed always consists of perversion of the traditions and institutions of Christianity, conforming them to the beliefs and organisations inspired by occultism... The destruction of the family, country, of authority, and of the Church is for occultism merely a means... The principle of the teaching minority is not only to keep the knowledge of the mysteries from the adept, but also to divide its teachings between twisting the mentality and perverting men in such a way as to destroy all obstacles to the establishment of its rule over the world, and to establish its tyranny over a land freed from all Church institutions. ... The final aim is the enthronement of the so-called world king, placing universal authority, by means of subordinate dupes, into the hands of the Grand Masters — all Jews; the subjection of all peoples to these men, by monopolising social offices, the transformation of man into a domestic animal, the exploitation of the masses by the Jew, once the heads of Christian control have been suppressed.

"The present revolution is the actual end. It is the

consummation, by a formidable convergence of efforts made everywhere and at the same time, of a permanent conspiracy, which failed, was taken up again, and pursued with a terrible tenacity, and with ever-increasing skill gained through long centuries of experience. Their aim, for ever inaccessible, would be the final domination of all peoples by the god-people, all esoteric religions having been but ethnological forms of the Cabala, transitory forms which vanquishing Judaism must get rid of… The sole force of Jewish cohesion lies in the submission of its scattered communities to the religious supremacy of a Patriarchate, whose social seat, constantly changed, remains unknown to the profane.

"The Jew looks upon himself as the sun of humanity, the male, opposed to which the other peoples are but the female, manifesting and assuring the coming of the Messianic era. In order to realise this sociological manifestation, the Jew organically extends his influence by means of secret societies, created by him in order to spread everywhere his initiating force … (hoping to realise) the 'Universal Republic' controlled by the god of Humanity, the Jew of the Cabala… The chief effort of these secret societies is to gather into their plans the religious traditions of all peoples.

"*Theurgy* — Theurgy has for its object the condensation in the theurgist of vital matter, by methods, in places and with aims, other than those possible through the limitations of organs. It results in the production of 'grand phenomena,' superhuman phenomena, that is beyond the powers of ordinary humanity. The realisation of 'grand phenomena' assures the multiplication of adepts and the glorification of the initiates. Theurgy places the 'diviner' (seer) higher than humanity, in a state of liberation which approaches the 'divine.' Also to attain this end, the theurgist recoils from no method permitting him to liberate, to his profit, the vital matter of which he has need in order to produce these 'grand phenomena'… Theurgists attribute surprising relations, which they claim to be able to establish with the phenomena of the universe by setting in motion a 'fluid' without the existence of which they recognise that their proceedings would be but jugglery... They claim to have the power to charge themselves with this fluid, and to project it at will upon organisms less strongly charged than they, and to put themselves thus in a state physically and physiologically of condenser and distributor of natural energy, rendering themselves capable of stunning and dominating by means of claimed fluidic exchanges" (hypnotic control as practised in these orders).

It is the force spoken of in the 'Protocols':

"We put Freemasons to death ... they all die when it is necessary, apparently from a natural death."

The celebrated occultist and cabalist "Papus," in his book on *Practical Magic*, gives the following simple explanation of magic: "A vehicle, a horse, and a driver, this is the whole of magic if one only knew how to look at it." He says the driver cannot set the vehicle in motion without a motor, which is the horse, which at the same time is stronger than the driver, but he controls and uses the brute force by means of the reins. The driver represents the intelligence and above all the will which governs the whole system — it is the "Directing Principle." The vehicle represents matter, which is inactive and which is the "Passive Principle." The horse represents "Force," obedient to the driver, and acting upon the vehicle the horse moves the whole system; it is the "Active Principle," and at the same time the intermediary between the vehicle and the driver, the "link" which unites the material basis and that which directs it, that is, between matter and will.

In practical magic the driver is the human will, the horse the "Vital Force," that dynamism carried by the blood to all the organs and to the brain itself. The vehicle is our body, the driver our will, and the reins the nervous system. The mind cannot act directly upon matter, it acts upon the intermediary, which again reacts upon matter; this intermediary is the astral plane, the life-force in nature and in man, that which continually modifies matter. This organic life-force of man can be projected by him

LIGHT-BEARERS OF DARKNESS

and can act at a distance: and this is the hyperphysical force used in magnetic healing and hypnotic control. As Papus said: "Among the ancients magic could be defined as the application of the will to the forces of nature, for the student learnt to control heat, light, and electricity." It is always the two contending forces united by a third producing manifestation.

All these many secret and pseudo-public occult societies — be they esoteric Masons, Rosicrucians, Illuminati, or merely calling themselves Universal Brothers — are, we believe, consciously or unconsciously, linked up with the Central Group which is acting behind the Third International of Moscow. Many of these orders outwardly appear antagonistic to each other, and each would, in fact, seem to believe that it and it only knows the WHOLE TRUTH. The craft of this lies in that members breaking away for various reasons almost inevitably seek for another, preferably opposed to the one they have left. These groups and orders are varied, so as to appeal to the many and different types of humanity. Many, if not all of them, are nominally working for "the Service of Humanity," but this appears to have resolved itself into the service and rights of the so-called workers of the world, and, although their watchword is said to be Love and Unity, it appears to mean class-hatred.

The *Great White Lodge* is apparently the centre of instruction, and many are looking for a "Messiah," be he a Christ or Christian Rosenkreutz. To us this spells invisible world domination by means of illuminised puppets or tools—Light-Bearers as they are called in some of these Hermetic Orders. It is no doubt the same secret organisation which earlier and on a less ambitious scale worked behind the French revolutions, the Balkan risings, and even the rising of the Lollards in our own country, all of which were merely experiments in preparation for the Great World Revolution of to-day. This secret movement is a plague generated in the hidden vaults and subterranean places of the world, which only rises to the surface when the hour of consummation appears to approach. Who can tell where this plague begins and where it ends, and who is immune from its deadly taint?

OK

Illuminism or so-called spiritual development is, we believe, the key to the movement, and the link which unites the whole organisation, and one and all of these various groups are but bodies built up for the purpose of preparing instruments, and the methods of arriving at this condition are briefly these:

I. *Orientation.* — Thought direction. by means of selected meditations upon writings said to be inspired by these Masters of the Great White Lodge.

2. *Polarisation.* — Direction of the currents of the dual sex-forces by thought and will-power uniting them with the forces directed by these Masters from without. Reciprocal vibrations — the action of one mind upon another.

3. *Illumination.* — Illuminism by means of the astral light; produced by, and leading to hypnotic obsession by, these same Masters.

To quote *The Great Work*, a publication of the Sadol Movement, in California: "In truth it is that principle in Nature which impels every entity to seek vibratory correspondence with another like entity of opposite polarity." In the same work we are told that, analogous to a farmer passing an electric current through the soil, at the root of the stalk, in such a manner as to touch the vital processes, thus multiplying their activity and intensity, so,

> "through ages of experimentation and study, the School of Natural Science (White Lodge) has wrought out and discovered a definite and scientific method whereby the intelligent student may supplement, facilitate, and intensify the process by which Nature evolves and unfolds the spiritual and psychical faculties, capacities, and powers of men..."

This is simply a hurry-up system producing illuminism, and leading to all sorts of unbalanced results.

These orders almost invariably culminate in communications,

teachings, and instruction from these masters or so-called spiritual beings — this Central Group of occultists and black magicians who, no doubt, from their many 'experimentations' upon unsuspecting humanity, have acquired a most profound knowledge of these hidden laws of nature. Who can put a limitation to the powers of the human body, its brain and nervous system, as a mechanism for receiving and transmitting these mysterious forces so little understood?

Further, this book tells us:

> "With a natural adjustment of economic, sociological, and ethnical relations, the opportunity will come to all who are ready and willing to develop their spiritual and psychical powers equally with the physical... The solution has already been wrought out by the Great School and when the time is right, it will be given to the world through channels which will ensure its recognition and adoption."

We will now study the doings and sayings of some of these illuminated and subversive "channels."

THE THEOSOPHICAL SOCIETY

In *Le Théosophisme René* Guenon gives much well-documented information on the Theosophical Society, showing its gradual growth into an instrument in the hands of some "inner Government of the World," an Invisible Power.

Mme. Blavatsky, the real founder, was born in Ekaterinoslav in 1831. In her many early extraordinary wanderings she apparently came under the influence and teachings of Paulos Metamon, a magician or conjuror; of the revolutionary Joseph Mazzini and the Carbonari; of Michel, a mason, mesmerist, and spiritist, who developed her mediumistic powers. These influences probably accounted not a little for her "phenomena."

On October 20, 1875, a society was founded in New York, said to be for "spiritualist investigations"; Olcott was President, Felt and Dr. Seth Pancoast Vice-presidents, and Mme. Blavatsky Secretary. Among other members were William Q. Judge, Charles Sotheran, one of the high dignitaries of American Masonry, also for a short time General Albert Pike, Grand Master of the Scottish Rite for the Southern Jurisdiction U.S.A., who was said to be author of the rituals of the thirty-three degrees — received from the Arabian member of the "Great School."

We are further told that George Felt, Vice-president, gave himself out as Professor of Mathematics and Egyptology, and "was member of a secret society usually called by initiates 'H.B. of L' (Hermetic Brotherhood of Luxor) … now this society … is officially opposed to spiritualistic theories, *for it teaches that these phenomena are due not to spirits of the dead, but to certain forces directed by living men*." It is said that Felt persuaded Mme. Blavatsky and Olcott to become associates of the H.B. of L. On November 17, 1875, the society's name was changed to "Theosophical Society," although Felt would have preferred the name "Egyptological Society." Shortly after this Felt suddenly disappeared. As René Guénon remarks, "no doubt his mission was accomplished!"

In November 1878, Mme. Blavatsky and Olcott left for India, and in 1882 founded the Theosophical centre in Adyar, near Madras; there she initiated her "esoteric section," and contacted the so-called 'Mahatmas', and her phantastic phenomena multiplied prodigiously. These 'phenomena,' precipitated letters, astral bells, materialisations, etc., were in time suspected and exposed·The matter was taken up by the "Society for Psychical Research," which in December 1885 reported her as "one of the most accomplished, most ingenious, and most interesting impostors." She herself affirmed the need of such phenomena in order to maintain her hold over some of the members, and in certain Theosophical circles they largely contributed to keep the society and its chiefs alive.

In conclusion René Guénon sums up:

"From all we have exposed, it is legitimate to conclude that Mme. Blavatsky was above all a 'subject' or instrument in the hands of individuals or occult groups sheltering behind her personality, just as others were in their turn instruments in her hands! This explains her impostures, without excusing them, and those who believe she invented everything herself and on her own initiative are almost as much mistaken as those who, on the contrary, believe in what she said concerning her relations with pretended 'Mahatmas.'"

It was after this, in 1887, that she compiled and published her *Secret Doctrine*, which is still the book of books to many Theosophists. This exposure, to a certain extent, broke Mme. Blavatsky, but did not break the Theosophical Society. There were many resignations, and some lodges, such as the 'Isis,' in Paris, of which Papus was a member, closed down only to be reformed under another name. Papus and some of his school, Martinists and Illuminists, remained members until 1890, when they either resigned or, as was said, were expelled on a charge of "black magic."

Mrs. Besant was presented to Mme. Blavatsky in 1889 by the Socialist Herbert Burrows (who was also member of the Stella Matutina), and she immediately succumbed to Mme. Blavatsky's irresistible magnetism and formidable power of suggestion. Mme. Blavatsky died in London May 8, 1891. Mrs. Besant was elected President in 1907. From 1910 to its consummation one of her chief works, assisted by Leadbeater, was to train Krishnamurti as Messiah, or as he preferred to be called, "World Teacher." On February 19. 1922, an alliance between Mrs. Besant's Co-Masonry and the Grand Orient of France was celebrated at the Grand Temple of the Droit Hutnain in Paris. Her present work is wholly political and subversive, "to build up India into a mighty self-governing community." But of her political activities more will be said later.

Charles Sotheran, the above-mentioned American mason, wrote to Mme. Blavatsky, January II, 1877.

"In the last century the Illuminati taught "peace with the cottage, war with the palace" throughout the length and breadth of Europe. In the last century the United States was freed from the tyranny of the mother country by the action of the Secret Societies more than is commonly imagined."

Mrs. Besant wrote in *India Bond or Free*, September 1926:

"Really, the awakening of India is ... part of the World Movement towards Democracy, which began for the West in the revolt of the American Colonies against the rule of Britain, ending in 1776 in the independence of the Great Republic of the West, and in the French Revolution of 1789!"

Again quoting from *Le Théosophisme*, we find much curious information on the production of this expected future "Messiah." René Guénon writes:

"Here we find the method by which, according to the Theosophists, the manifestation of a 'Great Teacher' is produced, or even sometimes that of a 'Master' of less importance; in order to save such an "evolved" being the trouble of preparing a 'vehicle' for himself, by passing through all phases of ordinary physical development, it is necessary that an 'intiate' or 'disciple' should lend his body when, after having been specially prepared by certain tests, he renders himself worthy of this honour. It would be from that moment that the "Master," making use of his body as if it were his own, would speak through his mouth in order to teach the "Wisdom religion."... It must be added that living 'Masters' are able in a similar fashion to make occasional use of a disciple's body... The 'Master'could only enter in, as Leadbeater says, "when this body was enfeebled by long austerities."... The Great Head of the department of religious instruction, said Leadbeater, the Lord Maitreya, who has already taught the Hindus as Krishna and the Christians as Christ, has declared that he will soon return to the world in order to bring healing and help to the nations, and to revive spirituality (psychic), which the earth has almost lost... One of the greatest works of the Theosophical Society is to do all in their power to prepare men for his coming… A single forerunner announced his coming formerly; now it is a society of 20,000 members spread over the whole earth who are given this task" (*Occultism in Nature*).

"Such is, therefore, the task which they assign to-day to the Theosophical Society, which Mrs. Besant declared years ago had been chosen… 'to be the link pure and blessed (etheric) between those above and those below'" (*Introduction to Theosophy*)

"The rôle which the Theosophical Society attributes to itself is not limited to announcing the coming of the 'Great Teacher'; it has also to find and prepare … the chosen 'disciple' in which he will incarnate when the time arrives. To tell the truth, the accomplishment of this mission has not been without failures; there was at least a first attempt which failed piteously… It was in London, where a kind of Theosophical community existed in St. John's Wood. There they brought up a young boy, sickly in appearance and not very intelligent, but whose least word was listened to with respect and admiration, because he was no other, it appears, than "Pythagoras reincarnated."… Some time later the father of this child, a retired captain in the British Army, suddenly withdrew his son from Mr. Leadbeater's hands, who had been specially charged with his education (Soleil, August I, 1913). There must have been some threat of scandal about this, for Mr. Leadbeater was in 1906 excluded from the Theosophical Society for reasons concerning which a discreet silence was kept… It was only later that a letter written by Mrs. Besant was made known, in which she speaks of methods, 'worthy of the severest reprobation' (*Theosophical Voice, of Chicago*, May 1908). Reinstated, however, in 1908, after 'having promised not to repeat these dangerous counsels' (*Theosophist*, February 1908) previously given to young boys, and reconciled with Mrs. Besant, whose constant collaborator he became in Adyar, Mr. Leadbeater played yet again the principal rôle in the second affair, much better known, and which had almost the same wind-up…

INQUIRE WITHIN

"In 1911 Dr. J. M.Nair had already published in his medical Journal (*Antiseptic*) a very caustic article against Theosophy, and he did not hesitate clearly to accuse Mr. Leadbeater of immoralty. In consequence of these attacks, and after a considerable time of reflection, three cases were filed in December 1912 against Dr. Nair, Dr. Râma Rao, and the Editor of the *Hindu*. All three were lost by the Society and its president... All this ended in upsetting the father of Krishnamurti and Nityânanda... He demanded at the Madras High Court that his sons should be returned to him. In giving judgment for the father, Judge Bakewell said: "Mr. Leadbeater agrees in his deposition that he has had and continues to have opinions which I can only specify as being unquestionably immoral and of a nature completely disqualifying him as tutor for young boys..." (*The Madras Lawsuit*).

After an unsuccessful appeal in Madras, Mrs. Besant was successful in London, May 5, 1914. Thus we saw Krishnamurti in 1926, the year appointed, presented by this society as the World Teacher or New Messiah!

Concerning the auxiliary groups again we quote René Guénon:

"... For the moment we wish to point out only a few of these auxiliary groups (of the Theosophical Society), and first of all "The Order of the Rising Sun," organised at Benares by Mr. Arundale, afterwards converted, January II, 1911, into the "Independent Order of the Star in the East," with Alcyone (Krishnamurti's astrological pseudonym) as nominal chief and Mrs. Besant as 'Protector,' 'in order to group together all those who, whether within or without the Theosophical Society, believed in the coming of the Supreme World Teacher.' It was hoped 'that its members would he able to do something on the physical plane to prepare public opinion for the idea of this coming by creating an atmosphere of sympathy and reverence, and that they would be able, by uniting together, to form an instrument on the higher planes which the Master would be able to make use of.' This Order 'excludes no one and receives all who, no matter what form their beliefs may take, share the common hope'; the acceptance of the following principles is all that is necessary in order to be admitted:

1. We believe that a great Teacher will soon appear in the world, and we wish so to live now that we may be worthy to know Him when He comes.

2. We shall try therefore to keep Him in our minds always. and to do in His Name, and therefore to the best of our ability, all the work which comes to us in our daily occupations.

3. As far as our ordinary duties allow, we shall endeavour to devote a portion of our time each day to some definite work which may help to prepare for His coming.

4. We shall seek to make Devotion, Steadfastness, and Gentlenes; prominent characteristics of our daily life.

5.·We shall try to begin and end each day with a short period devoted to the asking of His blessing upon all that we try to do for Him and His Name.

6. We regard it as our special duty to try to recognise and reverence greatness in whomsoever shown, and to strive to co-operate, as far as we can, with those whom we feel to be spiritually our superiors."

"Concerning the connections of the Order with the Theosophical Society, here is what Mr. Leadbeater said in the presence of Alcyone, at a meeting of the Italian section at Genoa: 'Whilst the Theosophical Society *demands* recognition of the brotherhood of humanity, the 'Order of the Star in the East' *commands* belief in the coming of a Great Master and submission to its six principles. Apart from that, the principles and precepts of the Order can be admitted without accepting all the teaching of the Theosophical Society. The initiation of the Order has shown us that, all over the world, there are people who are expecting the coming of the Master, and thanks to it, it is possible to group them together... The work of the Order and that of the Theosophical Society are identical: to enlarge the ideas of Christians and of those who believe that there is no salvation outside their own little Church; to teach that all men can be saved... For a large number amongst us the coming of a great Teacher is only a belief, but for others it is a certainty. For many the Lord Maitreya is only a name, although He is a great being to certain amongst us who have often seen and heard Him" *(Le Théosophie,* October 16, 1912).

"A little later these declarations were contradicted in certain points by Mr. Arundale affirming in the name of Alcyone that the 'Order does not indicate who the Supreme Teacher is for whose coming it was founded'; that no member had the right to say, for example, that the Order awaited the coming of Christ or of the Lord Maitreya,' and that·it would be prejudicial to he interests of the Order and those of the Theosophical Society to regard the aims of these two organisations as identical" *(The Daybreak,* August 1913).

Yet in a small pamphlet called Mrs. *Besant's Prophecy,* a lecture, given by R. F. Horton, D. D., August 6, 1911, and published by the "Order of the Star in the East," he (Dr. Horton), besides quoting the six principles, says, speaking of Mrs. Besant's prophecy concerning the World Teacher:

"But while she does not attempt to determine where the World teacher will appear, or under what conditions. She leaves her audience in no doubt as to who that World Teacher will be. In the most explicit terms she says that He is the One whom we Christians know as Christ ... and He who was Christ as known as the Lord of Love ... and there is no question in her mind that the great World Teacher who is coming is also the same Lord of Love."

Nothing seems more definite yet contradictory to Mr. Arundale's statement as quoted above.

René Guénon continues:

> "We again read elsewhere that "if some members believe that the World Teacher will make use of such and such a body it is only their own personal opinion, and not the belief to which the other members adhere." It is probable that it might have been otherwise if things had turned out better. In any case, here is a very clear example of the way in which the Theosophical chiefs know how to bow to circumstances and modify, to suit the occasion, appearances so as to enable them to penetrate into varied circles and from them recruit auxiliaries in order to realise their plans."

Again:

> "At the time of his first visit to Paris (he returned May 1914) Alcyone was sixteen years old; he had already written, or at least they had published under his name, a little book called *At the Feet of the Master,* for which Theosophists have shown the greatest admiration, although it was scarcely more than a collection of moral precepts without much originality."

These moral precepts are common to all illuminised orders, where the 'vehicle' being prepared, must be set apart, letting go its hold upon material life, living in the ideal, more often false, seeking self-abrogation and muting of personality, so that the Master, so-called, may take possession, as in the case of Krishnamurti.

Speaking on all neo-spiritualist movements René Guénon writes in *his Introduction to the Study of Hindu Doctrines, 1921*:

> "For those who do not rely on appearances there would be some very curious and very instructive observations to be made, there as in other domains, on the advantage to be extracted sometimes from disorder and incoherence, or from that which appears to be such, *in view of the realisation of a well-defined plan and unknown to all those who are its more or less unconscious instruments. These are political means of*

a sort, but the politics are rather special…"

Continuing in *Le Théosophisme*, René Guénon says:

"Organisations have been created so adapted as to reach each of the desired circles… There are some also which apply themselves especially to the young and even to children. Thus alongside of the "Star in the East," another association was founded called the 'Servants of the Star,' having as 'protector' Krishnamurti and as chief Nityânanda (Krishnamurti's young brother, who died November 13, 1925, on his way out to India); 'All the members of this Order, except honorary members, must be under twenty-one years of age, and the youngest child desiring to serve can join it' (*The Daybreak*, October 1913). Previously there already existed two other organisations of the same kind the 'Golden Chain' and the 'Round Table.' The 'Golden Chain' is a 'group for spiriual training,' where children of seven years are admitted and whose aim (at least the avowed aim) is expressed in the formula which the members must repeat every morning: 'I am a link of gold in the chain of love which surrounds the world; I must remain strong and bright; I wish to try to be gentle and good to all living creatures, to protect and aid all those who are feebler than myself, and I will try to have none but pure and beautiful thoughts, to speak none but pure and beautiful words, to do none but pure and beautiful actions. Then all the links will become bright and strong' (article by Mme. I. de Manziarly, *Theosophist*, March 1, 1914).

"If there is openly no talk of the coming of the 'Great Teacher' in the 'Golden Chain,' there is likewise none in the 'Round Table,' which can be joined as 'Associate' at the age of thirteen, as 'Companion' at fifteen, and as 'Knight' at twenty-one (it is scarcely necessary to point out the analogy, certainly intended, between those three grades and those of Masonry), and whose members must take a formal oath of secrecy. Here it has to do with following the great King which the West has named Christ and the East Bodhisattwa; now that hope is given to us of His near return the time has come to form Knights who will prepare His coming by so serving Him from now; it is required of those who would enter into the League to think each day of this King and to do each day a deed in His service (*Theosophist*, August 1, 1913). To sum up, it is above all a recruiting centre for the 'Star in the East,' which pretends to be the kernel of the 'New Religion,' the rallying-point of all those who expect the 'Coming of the Lord.'"

In New Zealand Dr. Felkin, late head of the "Smaragdine Thalasses," used what he called the "Order of the Round Table" as a cover and also a preparatory Order for the RR. et A.C. It is for men and boys from fifteen years and over, and there appear to be also three grades, "pages," "squires," and "knights." The aim is said to be service, and Dr. Felkin claimed to be the forty-first Grand Master of that particular "Round Table."

A despatch from Chicago on August 31, 1926, describes "the third day of the Convention of the 'Theosophical Society' and the first meeting of the Round Table" as follows:

"With upraised swords and swinging banners, the Knights of the Order of the Round Table entered the auditorium of the Hotel Sherman to-day. The young white-robed knights, with red and blue shields shining on their breasts, led their protector, Dr. Annie Besant, and the honorary knight, Krishnamurti, to the altar, and then stood to attention...

"Mr. Krishnamurti gave a brief talk on purity and nobility of conduct: "You do not carry swords of Damascus or Toledo steel, but you do carry rapiers, and they must be ever in the service of the right. You must be knights at heart-always courteous, gentle, and strong. You must not grow old emotionally or mentally, but keep ever the enthusiasms of youth, with its freshness, faith, and love. You must always be the ideal knight: never raise your hands against the weak nor take unfair advantage of another. You are knights, that is a great responsibility." The closing ceremony was picturesque and impressive, as the little ones, with hands on heart, pledged their service to the King (Krishnamurti as 'World Teacher'!) (*Patriot*, September 23, 1926).

Further, an article in *the Herald of the Star* of that month, entitled "The World Federation of young Theosophists," says:

> "The young Theosophist may be said to deal with the life of Theosophical youth while the 'Knights of the Round Table' deals more with the ceremonial aspect of the form side. Such a fellowship King Arthur planned in the early days of English history, and it was to revivify this noble·idea that the Modern Order was formed... The supreme governing body of the Order is the Council, composed of the Chief Knight in each country where the Order is working, and with the Protector, Dr. Annie Besant, and the Senior Knight at its head. Lieutenant Whyte was the first Senior Knight, and remained so until his death in Palestine in 1917, when Bishop Leadbeater accepted that office. The following are Knights of Honour: Bishop and Mrs. Arundale, Mr. Jinarajadasa, and the Rev. Oscar Kellerstrom. There are ceremonies written by the Protector, the Senior Knight, and Bishop Arundale for initiations, and other ceremonies for those Tables that care to use them, but the real spirit has to be translated into personal service! The motto is 'Live pure, speak pure, right wrong, follow the King,' in whose name all service, great or small, is performed."

Thus we see the highest ideals and the finest of our British legends perverted to help forward Mrs. Besant's now discredited scheme — the coming of a New Messiah.

Mrs. Besant's Co-Masonry was derived from the Mixed Masonry founded in France in 1891 by Maria Deraismes and Dr. Georges Martin, and known as "Droit Humain." Maria Deraismes had been initiated in 1882, contrary to the constitutions, by the Lodge "Les Libres Penseurs" of Pecq, for which the Lodge, was put into abeyance and the initiation declared null by the "Grande Loge Symbolique Ecossaise." At first the "Droit Humain" only practised three degrees, but later introduced the 33 degrees of Scottish Rite, and in 1899 the "Suprême Conseil Universal Mixte" was formed and became the directing power. This Masonry spread to England, Holland, Switzerland, and the United States, and on September 26, 1902, the first English Lodge was formed in London under the name of "Human Duty." In this Mrs. Besant was initiated and rapidly rose to the highest grades and offices. Then she founded the Lodge at Adyar under the name of "Rising Sun"; became Vice-president of the 'Suprème Conseil' in France, and a national delegate for Britain and her dependencies.

She then organised the English branch known as "Co-Masonry," and having obtained certain concessions from the "Suprême conseil," she, under the pretext of adaptation to Anglo-Saxon mentality, made statutes distinctly different from those customary in the French branch. Among others she retained the use of the volume of the Scriptures in the Lodges; also the formula "To the Glory of the Great Architect of the Universe," which had been suppressed by the Grand Orient in 1877 and replaced in French Mixed Masonry by "To the Glory of Humanity." In 1913 a Grand Council was appointed as head of British Co-Masonry, with Mrs. Besant as Grand Master, assisted by Ursula M. Bright, James L. Wedgwood as Grand Secretary, and Francesca Arundale as representative for India. On September 21, 1909, Mrs. Besant installed the Lodge of Chicago. In France the Theosophists apparently soon had an assured preponde once, and hoped in time that London would become the central organism of Co-Masonry Universal. And as we have seen, in 1922 they formed an alliance with the revolutionary Grand Orient of France.

In *Secret Societies and Subversive Movements* Mrs. Nesta Webster writes:

> "That In Co-Masonic lodges we find 'the King' inscribed Over the Grand Master's chair in the east, in the north the empty chair of 'the Master' — to which until recently all members, were expected to bow in passing — and over it a picture, veiled in some lodges, of the same mysterious personage."

The "King" may be Krishnamurti, as representing their so-called

"Lord of Love," and the "Master" is said by some to be Ragocsky-Prince of Transylvania!

Mrs. Besant apparently looks upon Co-Masonry as a powerful organised force, which will bring about the freedom of India from British rule!

The following are the origins of the Theosophical Liberal Catholic Church, another perversion!

The head of the Old Catholic Church in England, Archbishop Mathew, whose real name was Arnold Harris Matthews, was born at Montpelier of Irish parents. A student for Orders in the Scottish Episcopalian Church, he became a Catholic in 1875, and was ordained priest at Glasgow in June 1877. He gave up the priesthood July 1889, and in October 1890 he took the Italian name of Arnoldo Girolamo Povoleri, and married in 1892. He then called himself the Rev. Count Povoleri di Vincenza. About this time he also claimed and took the title of Earl of Llandaff. For a short time he was apparently reconciled with Rome, and in 1908 he was consecrated Bishop by Dr. Gerard Gul, who was head of the Old Catholic Church of Utrecht, Holland. The new bishop in turn consecrated two other unfrocked English priests, Mr. Ignace Beale and Mr. Arthur Howorth, and at the end of less than three years he founded the "Western Orthodox Catholic Church in Great Britain and Ireland," repudiating all subordination to Utrecht or Rome. Soon after this he induced his bishops to elect him archbishop. This Church took, successively, various names, and meanwhile the head tried, at different times, to negotiate for recognition and union with the Holy See, the Established Church, and the Orthodox Eastern Church. In 1911 he was formally excommunicated by the Holy See.

In 1913 he ordained Mr. James Ingall Wedgwood, then General Secretary to the English section of the Theosophical Society; Mr. Rupert Gauntlett, Secretary to an "Order of Healers" attached to the Theosophical Society, and also author of Health and the Soul — "a plea for magnetic-healing"; Mr. Robert King, expert in "psychic consultation based on the horoscope," and Mr. Reginald Farrer. All four had been students for the Anglican ministry, and had later joined the ranks of the Theosophists. Archbishop Mathew, who was completely ignorant about Theosophy, took fright on finding that Mr. Wedgwood and his companions were expecting the coming of a new Messiah, and failing to secure their recantation, he closed the Old Catholic Church and offered his submission to Rome, but withdrew it, and instead founded the "Western Uniate Catholic Church." Mr. Wedgwood, failing to obtain from Mr. Mathew the episcopal consecration he desired, was at length consecrated by Bishop F. S. Willoughby — who had himself been consecrated by Mr. Mathew in 1914, but was expelled the following year from the Old Catholic Church, by Mr. Mathew on account of facts which were then known. Mr. Willoughby consecrated first Mr. King and Mr. Gauntlett, and later, with their assistance, Mr. Wedgwood, February 13, 1916, and then made his submission to the Holy See. Mr. Wedgwood left immediately for Australia, and at Sydney consecrated Mr. C. W. Leadbeater, formerly an Anglican clergyman, as "Bishop for Australasia."

In 1916 an assembly of bishops and clergy of the Old Catholic Church adopted a new constitution, which was published under Mr. Wedgwood's name, in which there was nowhere any mention of Theosophy or a new Messiah. However, in November, 1918, there was another declaration of principles, in which the name of the Old Catholic Church was replaced by that of the *Liberal. Catholic Church*. In the *Vahan.*, June 1, 1918, Mr. Wedgwood writes:

> "... Another part of the work of the Old Catholic Church is the spreading of theosophical teachings in Christian pulpits; and a third and most important side is the preparing of the hearts and minds of men for the coming of a Great Teacher."

In the Theosophist, October. 1916, Mrs. Besant writes:

> "There is slowly growing up in Europe, silently but steadily,

with its strongest centre perhaps in Holland, but with members scattered in other European countries, the little-known movement called the Old Catholic, with the ancient ritual, with unchallenged Orders, yet holding itself aloof from the Papal Obedience. This is a living Christian Church which will grow and multiply as the years go on, and which has a great future before it, small as it yet is. It is likely to become the future Church of Christendom "when He comes.""

What of the "ancient ritual"? for we find in the *Theosophist*, October 1917: "Bishop Leadbeater's great work, which he hopes to carry on uninterruptedly, is the preparation of the liturgy of the Old Catholic Church, in which Bishop Wedgwood, as presiding bishop, collaborates." We are further told: "On Easter Sunday 1917, the revised liturgy was used·at a Mass for the first time." Again the "clairvoyant": "Bishop Leadbeater is investigating the occult side of the Mass, and is preparing a complete book on the "Science of the Sacraments"" (*The Messenger of Krotona*, November 1918).

As Mr. Stanley Morison truly says in his book *Some Fruits of Theosophy,* from which we have drawn the above information: "The so-called High Mass "done" by Mr. Leadbeater has no connection with Christianity." It is merely a method of charging the elements and conregation with the forces of their Christ Maitreya.

In his introduction to *Serpent Power* — translated from the Sanskrit — Arthur Avalon, in criticising Leadbeater's clairvoyant experiences, writes: "This experience appears to consist in the conscious arousing of the "Serpent Fire" (Kundalini or sex-force) with the enhanced 'astral' and mental vision which he believes has shown him what he tells us." It is in fact altogether astral, laying him open to deception and mental suggestion from his so-called Masters.

This Eucharist Service, as described by C. W. Leadbeater (Bishop), in his *Science of the Sacraments*, 1920, is pure paganism, a pantheistic conception evolved out of Illuminism.

Apparently it serves much the same purpose as the rituals and ceremonies of illuminised occult orders, more especially the Corpus Christi ceremony, and those of the vernal and autumnal equinoxes which are held for the purpose of drawing down the astral light into the Order, reaffirming the link with the hidden Centre. The Trinity of the Liberal Catholic Church is that of Paganism and Gnosticism. Their "Kingdom of Heaven" is the "Great White Brotherhood" the so-called "communion of saints": and their so-called Christ is Maitreya, whose power they attract and manifest during the service.

The whole scheme is a perversion of the Roman Catholic liturgy — deleted, added to and altered — using the prayers, etc., as magical invocations or incantations, so as to generate a magnetic force-finer forces of Nature — which in turn attracts the universal life-forces, and through them the influences of their 'World Teacher,' or Maitreya, a method, Leadbeater says, "of spiritual outpouring to help on the evolution of the world!" Always the same old excuse of the Illuminati!

According to Leadbeater, in the "Asperges" the altar and congregation are enclosed in an "etheric astro-mental bubble"— an area cleared for the magical operation! The forces are generated by the fervour, devotion, and enthusiasm of the worshippers, by the ritual, music, and incense, creating vibrations; the Cross is the direction down which the forces descend upon the Host.

At High Mass a Triangle officiate, receiving and distributing the force, very similar, as we shall see, to triangles of power in all occult orders. A deacon and subdeacon, representing positive and negative, gather up the forces generated by the people, which they pass on to the priest, who stands in front of the altar before the Cross, and who, Leadbeater says, with the aid of attending angels and rays (seven aspects of the solar force), builds up an astro-mental-thought-form-eucharistic edifice over the elements, in the form of a Mosque with a square foundation having domes and minarets rising above, enclosing the elements within it. This becomes, he says, a centre of magnetic radiation, condensing and distilling the force, and can be "imagined as a power-house, the etheric eddying round the altar is the dynamo, and the celebrant is the engineer in charge!" The censing, he says, isolates the altar by "a shell of powerf ul magnetism," which later is extended, by a second censing, to enclose the congregation, binding them into a magical whole; they must then think not as individuals but as a body. The incense, more especially sandalwood, recommended by Leadbeater, loosens the astral body, inducing passivity, and prepares the people for the reception of the influences invoked.

The force from the congregation wells up and creates a vortex round the altar, down which rush the forces from above into the edifice and elements. The force radiating from the Host he describes as "a manifestation of the finer forces of matter-a stream of liquefied light, of living gold dust," that is the ether or so-called spirit of illuminism, and the communicant in tum radiates the force upon all around him. He further states: "A bishop lives in a condition of perpetual radiation of force, and any sensitive person who approaches him will at once be aware of this... Whenever he chooses he can gather together this force and project it upon any desired object" This is simply the Astral Light or "Serpent Power" which slays or makes alive, and judging from the past history and present activities of some of these Liberal Catholic Theosophical bishops, can the force radiated and projected by them lead to anything but moral and mental disorder, even when used by them for magnetic healing?

That this is merely llluminism, playing about with Nature's forces, is shown by th following statement made by Leadbeater:

> "The marvellous efflux of the Holy Eucharist is arranged to synchronise with and take advantage of a certain set of conditions in the daily relation of the earth to the sun. There is an outflow and a backflow of magnetic energy between sun and earth — a magnetic tide, as it were, and the hours of noon and midnight mark the change... Therefore the Holy Eucharist should never be celebrated after the hour of noon ... the reserved Host may be administered at any time,"

or used for "Benediction."

What of our Anglican priests who are also Illuminati — is this in part their conception of the meaning of the Eucharist service?

At the beginning of 1927 Mrs. Besant issued an appeal for £40,000 to purchase a Happy Valley in California, "where the seat of a higher-plane civilisation may be prepared for the corning of the Messiah," with Krishnamurti as 'vehicle!' And Krishnamurti himself writes of this valley, December 1926, in the *Herald of the Star*:

> "I have decided to stay at Ojai, California, till April, in order that I may help in building up the Centre there… Ojai will be another World Centre like Ommen (Eerde Castle, Holland). I am very glad indeed that we shall have our own school here in Ojai, and·Mr. N. S. Rama Rao, M. A., of the University of Cambridge in England, and late Vice-Principal of the National University, Madras, India, has kindly consented to act as the Head Master…"

We have seen that Mrs. Besant, the "Protector" of this Messiah, had formed an alliance with the political subversive Grand Orient Freemasonry, who bring about their schemes by means of revolution. Of this higher-plane civilisation, Lady Emily Lutyens, one of Mrs. Besant's most faithful followers, writes in the *Herald of the Star*, March 1927:

> "We are witnessing the birth of a new-world consciousness, of a world civilisation… We are witnessing all around us the destruction of the old world, the old civilisation, with the corresponding suffering which destruction always brings in its train. Old traditions are being broken down, old customs destroyed, old landmarks swept away. The values of life are changing, the emphasis is being laid upon new conditions and point of view. With the sufferring born of destruction goes also the birth pangs of the new world which is coming into being. When the outer form becomes so rigid that the life is in danger of being crushed, when civilisation has become too

material, that form and that civilisation are broken, in order that the life may released... New world conditions demand a new Gospel, and the Teacher is here ... Christianity has also been an intensely individualistic religion, laying emphasis on personal salvation ... but it is a spirit which must give way to the new trend of modern thought and to the world civilisation which is being born. The new Gospel, if it is to meet the needs of the world, must be universal in its application, and the Christ to-day, by the mouth of Krishnaji tells us that He comes to establish the Kingdom of Happiness on earth... There must be anarchy before there can be creation..."

Through such instruments and by such teachings do these subtle masters of subversion and perversion blind te people and pave the way to their long-thought-out 'Universal Republic,' the destruction of Christianity and all old civilisations.

Of this gradual overshadowing or obsession of Krishnamurti, by their master Maitreya, many have written as follows:

In the *Herald of the Star,* January 1927, C. Jinarajadasa writes:

"I knew that, in 1911, the great Teacher was experimenting with the young body of Krishnaji to attune it even then. As Leadbeater told him: Even at that time the great Teacher was using the vehicles of Krishnaji as a pivot from which to discharge forces to movements in the world, of which Krishnaji knew nothing."

Twice he saw the Teacher's face in that of Krishnamurti:

"The second occasion was one evening when I was reading to Krishnaji and his brother... I looked up at him, and there I saw that wonderful Face. Of course not a line of Krishnaji's face was changed... And yet there was such a change as it is utterly impossible to describe. I can only say, it was the face of the Lord."

In all occult societies the chiefs and advanced adepts, at times, look with the face of their Master and speak His words — a partial obsession!

The Rev. Charles Hampton, of New York, writes, *Herald of the Star*, December 1926:

"The Order of the Star in the East, which exists for the sole purpose of preparing the way for the Coming has over 50,000 members throughout the world... The Head of the Order is Krishnamuni, who is now thirty-one years old. The 'Protector' Mrs. Annie Besant, International President of the Theosophical Society... On December 28, 1911. the first overshadowing of the World Teacher took place at Benares, when the Head, then a boy of sixteen, was giving out some certificates of membership. No words were spoken. On that occasion, in the presence of over 400 people, among them many prominent men, the spiritual force was so obviously manifest that almost all of them spontaneously knelt. The overshadowing was unmistakable, but it only lasted a few minutes. It was, however, a most striking scene. Brahmanas and Buddhists, Parsis and Christians, haughty Rajput Princes and gorgeously apparelled merchants, British Army officers, University professors, grey-haired men and young children- all in rapt devotion in the presence of an extraordinary spiritual outpouring flowing from a sixteen-year-old Hindu boy.

"The next public manifestation came when Krishnamurti was thirty years old. On the evening of December 28 of last year he was speaking at the Jubilee Convention of the Theosophical Society at Adyar, in India. This time the World Teacher Himself spoke, although He only said a few sentences. Mr. Krishnamurti was explaining why the Teacher was coming and something of what He would do, when a Voice of penetrating sweetness, speaking in the first person, said these words: 'I come for those who want sympathy, who want happiness; who are longing to be released; who are longing to find happiness in all things; I come to reform not to tear down; not to destroy but to build.'... This same World Teacher will soon come again, speaking through another disciple, as he spoke through Jesus 1926 years ago… In our view we draw a clear distinction between Jesus and Christ… We know that at the Baptism of Jesus, and again at the Transfiguration, *something was added to Jesus* that was not there before. That is perfectly explained by this distinction between the disciple Jesus and the Lord Christ… We look upon Krishnamurti as a disciple, whose body will be used by the World Teacher… At first months will separate the public manifestation of the Lord. Later He will speak more frequently, until we hope it will be possible for Christ to stay with us for many years. When He came before, He was only allowed to stay for three brief years doing public work, when He was murdered. As a result of that effort all He left was a little seed of 120 people… If we make it possible for Him to stay ten times three years, what harvest will not that seed bring forth? When He came before, John the Baptist alone prepared the way for Him. To-day tens of thousands of sincere people are His forerunners… We hope to make it possible for Him to stay many years once the body of His disciple is tempered to stand the strain sufficiently. Will the Christian Churches accept Him? …"

In the Star Camp, Castle Eerde Ommen, July or August 1926 the Teacher again spoke through Krishnamurti to the assembled people, and briefly He told them the "only happiness worth possessing" was to act, think, and feel through the mind and heart of the Teacher! Here are two accounts of this occasion given by Geoffrey West in his Life *of Annie Besant*:

"A retired British officer writes:

'It happened at the evening camp fire… I suddenly felt an overwhelming. impulse to remove my hat reverently… I was conscious that another voice than Krishnamurti's was speaking. The voice used old English (no uncommon habit with these Masters!), which Krishnamurti had never done. This continued for four or five minutes, then Krishnamurti sat down. I was conscious of the utter stillness. Not only the two thousand pilgrims, but the very insects in the trees were quiet, and even the fire-stopped crackling. We felt we had all become parts of one great body.'

"Another witness, a Cambridge physicist … declared he saw a 'huge star over Krishnamurti's head burst into fragments and come raining down. For an instant I thought I was back in France!' This astral light phenomenon is not unheard of in other Illurninised Orders; it is the illuminating 'Serpent Fire' projected by these hidden Masters, and more often it is hypnotic.

Finally, at Ommen 1927, Krishnamurti announced:

> "My Beloved and I are One." The obsession was completed, Krishnamurti's own personality was in absolute abeyance!

In a pamphlet, issued by Mrs. Besant's Theosophical Society, on "The Doctrine of Rebirth Scientifically Examined," W. Y. Evans-Wentz, M. A., D.Litt., D.Sc., appears to attempt to prove the unprovable, and by quoting Celtic beliefs to show the possibility of the reincarnation of the so-called great teachers. As

> "the logical corollary to the rebirth doctrine … the gods are beings which once were men, and the actual race of men will in time become gods … According to the complete Celtic belief, the gods can and do enter the human world for the specific purposes of teaching men how to advance most rapidly towards the higher kingdom. In other words, all the great Teachers — Jesus, Buddha, Zoroaster, and many others … are … divine beings who in inconceivably past ages were men but who are now gods, able at will to incarnate into our world…"

The pamphlet ends:

> "In the same way, what in this generation is heretical alike to the Christian theologian and to the man of science, may in coming generations be accepted as orthodox."

I suggest that this reincarnating Maitreya is neither god nor divine being, but is more likely one of these Cabalistic Jews, still in the body of the flesh, whose aim is perversion of Christian beliefs.

In a speech, given before the Esoteric School of the Theosophical Society, we find Mr. Baillie Weaver propounding the same theories; he said:

"Equally inevitable also is the fact that these superhuman beings take a share in the governments of the world; that they appoint, train, and use pupils and agents, and from time to time come to earth to teach their less advanced brethren, and that this school is one of the agencies, both for training of pupils and the purpose *of transmitting power*."

Again, Mary Gray, of California, writing on the "Path of Probation" in *the Herald of the Star,* December 1926, says:

"As the chela passed successfully the tests, as he proves his capacity to stand alone … he begins to draw closer to the Master and to share in His work. More power is made available for the chela's use, since it has to be proved that he can be trusted to react well to its stimulation. He begins to enter upon his period of service, in which he distributes the Master's force — or, more accurately, *small portion of the force of the White Lodge* — either in active service in the outer world or in intimate contact with those about him. The use of the force expands and develops his vehicles and their powers. His brain increases in power, his devotion in intensity and purity, his actions in accuracy, skill, and power… Moreover, he becomes more radiant, a luminous, serene, and joyous figure in the dark atmosphere of worldly life. At the same time he begins definite training on the inner planes, in which he is taught the use and control of forces there. Little by little he gains knowledge of the control of the various elements there… In all these things he is taught how to command (forces) … in the name, and by the authority of White Lodge, *as an agent of its power…*"

After the consummation of the coming, the "Order of the Star in the East" assumed a new name. They apparently believed that the star of the World Teacher was at last among them and that they no longer required to look for it in the East, and no longer required a herald to announce His coming, so it very simply was reduced to the "Order of the Star," with its national organ the *Star Review* Its organisation was said to be international and national, but nevertheless it was universal. Its objects were said to be (I) To draw together all those who believe in the presence of the World Teacher in the world; (2) to work with Him for the establishment of His ideals. Its international magazine was the *Star*.

In the February issue of this Review, 1928, through his mouthpiece, Krishnamurti, the World Teacher, in the name of Liberation, expounds his doctrine of absolute negation, necessary for the building up of his new Kingdom — the peace, unity and happiness of universality and deindividualisation. Here are a few extracts from teachings given at Ommen, August 1927, and at Paris, September 27, 1927:

> "The purpose the manner of attaining this happiness, of gaining this Liberation, is in your own hand. It does not lie in the hand of some unknown god, or in temples or in churches, but in your own self. For temples, churches, and religions bind, and you must be beyond all dreams of God in order to attain this Liberation. There is no external God as such who urges us to live nobly, or to live basely; there is but the voice of our own intuition... When that voice is sufficiently strong, when that voice — the result of accumulated experience — is obeyed, and you yourself become that voice, then you are God... So the most important thing is to uncover this God within each one of you. That is the purpose of life; to awaken the dormant God (the unused sex-force, the Kundalini within you) to give life to the spark which exists in each one of us, so that we become a flame (illuminised), and join the eternal flame of the world (the universal life-force or ether-as above so below, of Hermes)... In the permanent is established, is seen, the only God in the world — yourself that has been purified."

Here we have the creed of Cabalistic Jews — the "Deified Man." Now Krishnamurti being merely the "vehicle," the flame, the voice and intuition within him, and which he listens to, can only be those of the World Teacher; remembering this, the following extract is interesting:

> "And so it is my desire that you should not be mesmerised by anything I say, because if you are put to sleep by my words or by my thought, by my desire, by my longings, you will be just as much in prison or even more so than you were before you came to this place."

But is this not just what has happened? A negative body prepared for the reception of these hypnotic suggestions; do his followers not all live and move and have their beings, as it were, in Krishnamurti as the 'vehicle' of the World Teacher? By their, Liberal Catholic Church Mass do they not one and all unite in communion with this World Teacher, this so-called Christ?

Further, in a poem in his book *The Search*, an absolute freedom from everything is required — freedom from the narrowness of tradition, custom; habit, feeling, thought, religion, worship, adoration, nation, family possession, love, friendship, even thy God, etc. — then all barriers will have fallen; and what is to take their place? The flame, the voice, the intuition from the World Teacher, the New Kingdom of Happiness — the hypnotic control of Illuminism!

And who is this World Teacher? Mrs. Besant, in *the Herald of the Star*, April 1927, enlightens us Speaking of Krishnamurti's "great initiations," where, in the first, she promised the "Great Ones" to guard him with her *power*, and Leadbeater promised to guide him with his *wisdom* (here we have, with Krishnamurti as the apex, the Triangle necessary for the manifestation of the power of the World Teacher!), she says:

> "And then the day came when our office ended ... we took the child, whom we had received as guardians, as a man no

longer wanting aught of us (the manifestation being accomplished!) ... to the Lord Maitreya ... the then bud had blossomed out into a wonderful flower; and that flower is placed at the feet of its Owner, the Lord Maitreya, the Christ, the Saviour of the World."

Again, in *the Herald of the Star*, March 1927 she said at Ojai, California:

"As much as each can see will be to each of you the manifestation of the Christ. For my own part, who know Him in His far-off Himalayan home (astrally), where I have heard Him speak of His Coming, and being here with our Krishnaji, I need not say how, having loved Him for so long a time, I rejoice to recognise in Him the Presence of our Lord."

Is this not a liberation unto bondage, a body prepared in which to sow the seeds of world disintegration, by the power working behind and through Grand Orient Judaeo-Masonry, to which Mrs. Besant's Co-Masonry is allied?

And what is the outcome of this manifestation? At the 1929 Ommen Camp Krishnamurti announced that the Order of the Star was to be dissolved; all he had desired was to lead people to "freedom," but, he said, they did not want freedom. Mr. Lansbury, for many years a follower of Mrs. Besant and believer in the World Teacher's mission, making the best of the apparent failure, said:

"Krishnamurti has broken the bondage of mere organisation ... with a magnificent gesture he has bid the surrounding young people of all races to develop their own individuality in their own way — responsibility for one's life and character depending on oneself."

A correspondent in the *Patriot*, August 29, 1929, gives some interesting details as to what went on at this Camp Meeting at Ommen which we give verbatim:

"I have studied Theosophy and its kindred movements, such as Co-Masonry, the Liberal Catholic Church, and the Star, for some years, and have formed the definite opinion that behind the mask of the innocent study of symbolism, brotherhood, and comparative religion there lies a deep-seated anti-British organisation. The link between these movements is Dr. Annie Besant…

"Last year the camp at Ommen was a most astounding place. Though the key-note of the Star teaching is "freedom for all," the camp was surrounded by a seven-foot barbed-wire fence; all members had to wear a label which showed clearly their name and number, and without which they were not allowed in or out of the camp; there were endless irritating rules and regulations, all destined to reduce the inmates to the last stage of servility.

"Brotherhood among the different nationalities was supposed to prevail, but it was noticeable that the German contingent, who were frequently in positions of authority, took every opportunity of insulting the English and French members, the Englishmen always allowing themselves and their womenkind to be thus treated.

"The table manners of the campers would have disgraced a farmyard, though, of course, Krishnamurti did not feed with the common herd, but in luxury at Eerde Castle, the residence of Baron von Pallandt, a prominent member of the Theosophical Society, who also holds a very high degree in the Co-Masonic Order.

"The camp was for men and women of any class, creed, or colour, and it was customary to force well-bred Englishwomen at every meal to wait upon Indian and African natives mostly in their native dress. These women were reduced to such a state that they literally fawned upon the coloured men, beseeching them to eat. and often producing special tit-bits for them, while their fellow-countrymen went hungry.

"The clothing worn by many of the members was as scanty as was compatible with the most elementary decency. Photographs brought home prove this, and copies of these photographs are in the possession of the Authorities, and also in my possession. One of these shows a native, in native dress, walking round the camp with an English girl clad in nothing but a flimsy shirt and a pair of shorts, each with an arm around the other.

"Among other details, the smell of ether from one of the tents at night was overpowering; this drug, according to some occultists, being one of the most powerful in 'liberating the spirit from the body'.

"The 1929 camp at Ommen has just ended, and it was apparently there that Krishnamurti publicly announced that the Order of the Star would be dissolved. What is going to happen to his unfortunate dupes who have followed him slavishly, have given up their own religion, and who have worshipped him blindly is impossible to say. His own words and writings urge them to have no other support but themselves, which in plain English means having no other support but him; he is now casting them away with broken beliefs, no ideals, and no leader or Teacher on whom to rely. He has undermined their faith in God and their country, and now leaves them in a state of utter chaos.

"Is it possible that things have been rendered too hot for the Order of the Star to continue? Is it because they have fought among themselves? Or can it be that Dr. Besant and the black Messiah have ceased to see eye to eye in their anti-Empire and occult activities?

"Time will show; at present let us be duly thankful that one group, at any rate, of the subversive societies is as a house divided against itself, and there are still loyal men and women who will risk their time, money, and even more in unrewarded service to their King in order to unmask these subversive and seditious organisations."

Nothing could be more damning than the above, but yet it is only a glimpse of the real diabolical work that is being slowly carried out through secret societies and many other movements, some apparently harmless. It is the work of the same disintegration power as is being carried on in Russia through the "Godless" and similar groups; it means the degradation of humanity, the death of its soul, making it lower even than the brutebeast.

In these secret societies the methods are ever the same; it is gradual obsession by this hidden power through so-called illumination, or the age-old illuminism by means of the perversion of the sex or creative forces in man and in Nature. This is shown in the symbol of the Theosophical Society.

The symbol represents Illumination or Initiation. Most of these esoteric and secret Orders are ruled and directed by the invisible Masters of the Great White Lodge, and under their instructions. illumination is artificially and intensively induced in a comparatively short time. The individual, as directed, works from within, while the master works from without, both using this "Serpent Power" — the dual creative forces of all Nature, the forces of attraction and repulsion. The individual, by means of exercises, meditations, etc., inspired by these masters, awakens within himself this "Serpent Power"—the Kundalini or unused sex-forces—which lies coiled up in the lower part of the body. It is said to be sublimated or purified by fire and water—as indicated by the hexagram or interlaced triangles—the Jewish Star of power-or more correctly perverted; and rising up through the nerve-centres, vivifying them, awaking clairvoyance, clairaudience, and intuition, the head and the tail — the positive and negative forces — unite at the base of the nose, the Pineal Gland. The symbol in the small circle above is the Svastica or electric Hammer of Thor, a whirling, disintegrating electric force breaking down the protective barriers—the will and the reason— creating a vortex down which enters the outside magnetic force of light from the masters. Thus the adept is illuminised, and the Etheric Link is formed by these controlling masters from without just as in the Liberal Catholic Mass.

The Ankh in the centre is the Egyptian symbol of life, it is the creative principle, the lingam. The encircling serpent isolates, conserving the force within, rendering powerful the illuminised tool. This tool is ready for the appointed work; he is free, not to use his freedom for himself, but for these masters. It is a liberation unto bondage. At the top of the symbol is the three, the triangle of power or unity, by means of which the power is manifested in the Order and individual.

Illuminism — can be individual, group, or world, an this can be applied to present world conditions. World revolution — the electric Hammer of Thor. Its consummation — invisible world domination through prepared and illuminised 'vehicles.'

Take the *Protocols of the Learned Elders of Zion,* which have been marvellously correct as prophecy, whatever their first origin, before M. Joly used part of them in1864:

Page 10:

> "To-day I can assure you that we are only within a few strides of our goal. There remains only a short distance, and the Cycle of the Symbolic Serpent — that badge of our people — will be complete. When this circle is locked, all the States of Europe will be closed in it, as it were, by unbreakable chains. The existing constructional scales will soon collapse, because we are continually throwing them out and destroying their efficiency."(The disintegrating Hammer of Thor!)

Epi., page 90:

> "... Constantinople is shown (on the sketch of the course of the Symbolic Serpent) as the last stage of the Serpent's course before it reaches Jerusalem. Only a short distance still remains before the Serpent will be able to complete its course by uniting its head to its tail…"

Page 16:

"Who or what can dethrone an invisible power? Now, this is just what our Government is. The Masonic Lodge (esoteric) throughout the world unconsciously acts as a mask for our purpose. But the use we are going to make of this power in our plan of action, and even our headquarters, remain perpetually unknown to the world at large."

Mr. Philip Graves, in his book, *Palestine, the Land of Three Faiths,* speaking of the Okhrana, or Tzarist Secret Police, said that these police knew the Jewish and non-Jewish revolutionaries so well that it was said no one knew where the Okhrana ended and the revolution began!

After reading *The Tcheka,* by George Popoff, one is inclined to ask, who is the ruling power behind the Tcheka, and who was the power behind the Tzarist Okhrana, many members of which remained in the service of the Tcheka? Was it not Jewish and occult? According to Popoff, whoever took service under the Tcheka immediately changed, and from simple, honest men became crafty, brutalised, and fanatical, and during the examinations of prisoners appeared to use hypnotic force.

Is the same not true of most of those who are entrapped by these secret and subversive societies? They enter with high ideals, seeking spiritual development for themselves and others, the result being often a fanatical obsession, perverting all that is high and sacred; curiously enough, invariably the higher the ideals the greater the blind acceptance of their master's call to take part in their diabolical work of destruction.

Further it is interesting to find that the oath of secrecy and silence demanded from the candidate and adept is always in connection with the astral methods of contacting these masters and the real aims and work of the Order as directed by them in this mysterious secrecy and silence. Of the Theosophical Oath, René Guénon writes:

"One thing with which secret societies, and in particular

Freemasonry, is most often reproached is the obligation under which they compel their members to take an oath the nature of which varies, as also the extent of the obligations which they impose; it is in most cases an oath of silence, to which is added sometimes an oath of obedience to the orders of the chiefs known or unknown. The oath of silence may itself concern either the methods of recognition or the special ceremonial used by the society, or even the existence of the latter, its organisation, or the name of its members; more often it applies in a general way to what is said and done in it, to the power exercised, and to the teachings received in it under one form or another. Sometimes they are pledges of another kind, such as the promise to conform to certain rules of conduct which can, with good reason, appear abusive as soon as they take the form of a solemn oath ... What alone interests us at the present is this, that if it is a valid reproach against Masonry and against some other societies more or less secret ... it is equally, valid against the Theosophical Society. The latter, it is true, is not a secret society in the complete sense of the word, because it has never made a mystery of its existence, and the greater part of the members do not try to conceal their grade... For our present purpose we will here admit as sufficient the opinion according to which a secret society is not necessarily a society which conceals its existence or its members, but is, above all, a society which has secrets, whatever their nature may be. If this is so, the Theosophical Society can be regarded as a secret society, and its very division into 'exoteric' and 'esoteric' sections would be sufficient proof; be it understood, in speaking here of 'secrets' we do not mean by that the signs of recognition, but the teaching strictly reserved to members or certain among them to the exclusion of others, and for which they exact the oath of silence; these teachings in Theosophy appear, above all, to be those relating to 'psychic development,' since such is the essential aim of the 'esoteric' section...

"Let us now return to Mme. Blavatsky's statements, and let us see what concerns the oath of silence: As for the inner section actually known as the 'esoteric' since 1880, the following rule has been determined and adopted: "No member shall use for personal ends anything which has been communicated to him by a member of the higher section. The infraction of this rule will be punished by expulsion." However, now, before receiving any communication of this kind, the postulant must take the solemn oath never to use it for personal ends, and never to reveal anything confided to him, unless he is authorised to do so (Mme. Blavatsky's *Key to Theosophy*, 1889). Elsewhere she refers to these teachings, which must be kept secret: 'Although we reveal all that is possible, we are nevertheless obliged to omit many important details which are only known to those who study the esoteric philosophy, and who, having taken the oath of silence, are consequently *alone authorised to know them' (Key to Theosophy)*. In another passage allusion is made to a mystery relating directly to the power of consciously and voluntarily projecting the 'double' (astral body), which is never revealed to anyone except 'chelas,' who have taken an irrevocable oath, that is, to those who can be trusted" (*The Key to Theosophy*).

"Mme. Blavatsky insists, above all, upon the obligation to observe always this oath of silence, obligatory even for those who, voluntarily or not, should have ceased to take part in the society: she puts this matter in these words: "A man who is asked to leave or forced to resign from the section, is he free to reveal things which he has been taught, or infringe one or other of the clauses of the oath he has taken?" And she replies: "The fact of resigning or being sent away frees him only from the obligation to obey his teacher, and from taking an active part in the work of the society, but does in no way free him from the sacred promise to guard the secrets which have been confided to him... All men and women who possess the slightest sense of honour will understand that an oath of silence taken on a word of honour, still more taken in the name of his "Higher Self," the god hidden in us, must keep it until death, and that although having left the society no man or woman of honour would dream of attacking the society to which they were thus bound" (*The Key to Theosophy*).

"We also see from these quotations that the oath of silence

taken in the 'esoteric' section includes an oath of obedience to the "teachers" of the Theosophical Society. One is forced to believe that this obedience is carried very far, as there have been examples of members who, ordered to sacrifice a great part of their fortune in favour of the society, have done so without hesitation. These pledges, of which we have just spoken. still exist, as also the 'esoteric' section itself … which could not exist under any other conditions… In such a circle all independence is entirely abolished."

Mrs. Besant, on her return from India in 1924, demanded from all members of the "esoteric", section an oath of implicit belief in and obedience to her as the mouthpiece of the hidden Masters. However, the London Lodge, numbering about sixty members, refused to comply or recognise Mrs. Besant's autocratic rule and political aims. They therefore formed a small group outside her jurisdiction for the study of comparative religion. The "esoteric" section of the Theosophical Society is said to consist of three inner circles — Learners, Accepted or Initiates, and Masters of the Great White Lodge. Very similar to the "Temple of the Desert" in the Near East, to which some of these hidden masters belong, as will be seen when speaking of the "Stella Matutina."

As we have shown, Mrs. Besant's political aims are largely connected with disrupting India under the mistaken idea of forming India's heterogeneous peoples and religions into a "self-governing community."

In 1907 from social work she turned to politics, although not until 1913 did she definitely declare for Home Rule. Lord Sydenham, speaking in the House of Lords, October 24, 1917, said of Mrs. Besant and her aims:

> "She wrote a book, which contains more reckless defiance of facts than I have ever see comprecced into the same small space, and in her paper *New India* … she said that "India was a perfect Paradise for 5,000 years before our advent, that it had become "a perfect Hell" owing to the "brutal British Bureaucracy."… The Government of Madras decided to

enforce the provisions of the Press Act, and Mrs. Besant was ordered to give security for the good conduct of her paper. As the violence of New India continued quite unabated, the security was sequestrated. That gave her a right to appeal to the High Court of Madras. The case was heard by three judges, of whom two were Indians, and the action of the Madras Government was confirmed… Well might one of these·judges point out that "this pernicious writing must tend to encourage assassination by removing public detestation of such a crime."

In his book, *India as I knew it*, Sir Michael O'Dwyer writes: "Mrs. Besant's Home Rule Movement in India, which was afterwards adopted and amplified by the Indian extremists, was started in 1916 soon after the Easter Monday rebellion in Ireland." It was introduced as a private bill in 1925 and again in 1927, but it aroused little or no interest except among the Labourites who sponsored it.

Mrs. Besant was one of the original promoters and shareholders in the Socialist Publication Company, registered April 12, 1918, under the title of Victoria House Printing Co, Ltd., in which Mr. Lansbury and other Theosophists were the moving spirits. This company produced the *Herald*, which became the *Daily Herald* in March 1919.

Further, Sir Michael O'Dwyer writes in the same book of an interview given by Mrs. Besant at Bombay, August 28, 1924, in which she said:

> "I may say … that I have worked for the Labour Party for these fifty years of my public life, and also that I have been a member of the Fabian Society, to which several of the Ministers belonged, since 1884… I think we may fairly say we have made India a burning question in the political life of England. We found the Labour Party entirely with us, and as Mr. Smillie publicly said, the majority of the Cabinet (Labour) are with us."

The *Patriot*, April I, 1926, speaking of the 'Labour Research Department,' originally the 'Fabian Research Department,' remarks: 'Most of these names show plainly how Red these pink Fabians have become in pouring over the iniquities of the existing capitalist systems.'

George Lansbury's political outlook is well known — he joined the Theosophical Society in 1914, and was a follower of and believer in Krishnamurti — and his seditious utterances are many. In connection with the railway strike in 1919 there was one inciting class hatred as follows:

> "A General Staff for London is needed to avert the bloody revolution desired by the master class, which only the statesmanship, the courage, and the solidarity of the working-class can prevent. We know well that there is to-day a large element in the master class which deliberately desires and intends to provoke a bloody revolution in order that the workers may be shot down like dogs, and forced back into slavery by bayonets and machine guns."

This from the follower of the so-called 'Prince of Peace and Love!'

In *New India*, January 26, 1928, Mrs. Besant's voice was heard once more stirring up the people of India to revolution!

> 'Awake! Arise! men and women of every caste, class, and community. Your Mother's voice calls you, to make Her Mistress of Her Household. Do not desert Her in Her Hour of need. Boycott the Simon Commission — *ANNIE BESANT*.'

And as President of the Indian Journalistic Association she urged the editors of the Nationalist papers to boycott all reports of the proceedings of the Simon Commission.

In *Freemasonry Universal.*, Mrs. Besant's official organ of Universal Co-Masonry, Spring Equinox, 1929, there is an article reproduced from *New India,* which says:

> "In the midst of a crisis such as the present, every effort must be made by those who have the inner knowledge to carry through one of the greatest triumphs the world shall ever know... Try to perceive the Great Plan as a whole... It is all one plan, and each part is but a part, however much it may seem to be a whole, all by itself... India is the keynote, India is the centre of that great storm which shall usher in *a splendid Peace...* No true Theosophist, and certainly no one who is working for the *Inner Government of the World,* will be careless of India's welfare... Masonry offers a very special opportunity for the practice of Brotherhood... There must be most careful selection in the beginning as regards admission, and insistence on the most scrupulous observance of the Obligations.·Co-Masonry has been given to India that it may be a powerful, organised force for India's service."

Apparently India too is to be broken asunder, if necessary, by the 'giant harrow' of revolution, so that she may share in this same 'splendid Peace,' under whose yoke the true Russia now groans and suffers — a peace which is to usher in the Universal Brotherhood and World Domination of the Invisible Centre of the revolutionary Grand Orient Judaeo-Freemasonry, to which Mrs. Besant's Co-Masonry is allied.

She follows this up in the U.S.A., August 24, 1929, as reported by the *Chicago Tribune,* with false statements against the British Empire, spread over the four quarters of the globe.

At the world congress of Theosophists in Stevens Hotel, Mrs. Besant said that recently she had been trying to help India obtain political measures by which the country may throw off the 'yoke of England.' 'It is etimated that 70,000,000 of India's 300,000,000 population are actually starving.'... 'England's rule has throttled the education of India and the fine civilisation she had before England came... The trouble started when the village system under which India prospered was destroyed.' And she stated that 'Taxes' was the cause of the widespread starvation

(Patriot, September 19, 1929).

> "... I have been trying to help obtain the dominion system of government for India — her only salvation. I hope revolution will not come... If a revolt were to flare up, the English, with their bombs from the air and their land and water machines of war, would simply cut them down like grain before a scythe."

She had previously announced that she was going back to India to increase the movement for Indian Freedom, which might mean a war of colour. And what is at the back of this evil work of Mrs. Besant? In *The Theosophist,* October 1928, it is said: "The Masters have assured her that Dominion Status for India is part of the Great Plan, and she knows that she will not pass away until that freedom is accomplished!" And she has said: "If you see any one of us working for any particular movement in the world, you may know it is part of the World Plan." And the Great Plan is, "A New Heaven and a New Earth, built upon the ruins of all old-established systems and civilisations."

CHAPTER III

THE ANTHROPOSOPHICAL SOCIETY

R udolph Steiner's early history is somewhat of a mystery, but it is said by some that he was born in 1861, at Krakjevic in Hungary, by others that he was an Austrian. In 1902 he became a member of the Theosophical Society under Mrs. Besant, and was Secretary-General of the German section until 1913, "when he broke away from Mrs. Besant, nominally because of the Krishnamurti affair and the Madras Lawsuit; fifty-five of the German Lodges seceded with him — about 2,500 members in all. He then formed a new group, under the name, 'Anthroposophical Society,' a name doubtless derived from a work, *Anthroposophia Magica*, dated 1650, by the well-known alchemist and occultist Thomas Vaughan.

His centres were Munich and Stuttgart, but being unable to obtain the required ground in Munich for his proposed Temple, he finally built it at Dornach in Switzerland. The 'Johanneum,' later changed to 'Goethenum,' was finished in 1920, and to help to meet the enormous expenses he formed an association called the 'Society of St. John,' alluding, it is said, to the ancient brotherhood of operative Masons. In this Goetheanum he professed to give a new architecture, a new painting, and a new sculpture. It was in fact a symbol of his teaching, wholly pantheistic and entirely unbeautiful in form and design. This was mysteriously burnt down one night at the end of 1922, but was later rebuilt on a smaller and less expensive scale. Steiner apparently never got over the loss of his Temple, and died in Dornach, March 30, 1925, to the last an instrument in the hands of his masters, recording their teachings and instructions.

In an article in *the Patriot,* October 1922, a soun authority has given some interesting information concerning Dr. Steiner and his past history. It says:

"At this stage of my inquiry I may refer briefly to the existence of an offshoot of the Theosophical Society, known as the Anthroposophical Society. This was formed as the result of a schism in the ranks of the Theosophists, by a man of Jewish birth, who was connected with one of the modern branches of the Carbonari. Not only so, but in association with another Theosophist he is engaged in organising certain singular commercial undertakings not unconnected with Communist propaganda; almost precisely in the manner in·which 'Count St. Germain' organised his dyeworks and other commercial ventures with a like purpose. And this queer business group has its connections with the Irish Republican movement, with the German groups already mentioned, and also with another mysterious group which was founded by Jewish 'intellectuals' in France about four years ago, and which includes in its membership many well-known politicians, scientists, university professors, and literary men in France, Germany, America, and England. It is a secret society, but some idea of its real aims may be gathered from the fact that it sponsored the 'Ligue des Anciens Combattants,' whose aim appears to be to undermine the discipline of the Armies in the Allied countries. Although nominally a 'Right Wing' society, it is in direct touch with members of the Soviet Government of Russia; in Britain it is also connected with certain Fabians and with the Union of Democratic Control, which opposes 'secret diplomacy.'... The third (force) is the pan-Jewish organisation, which is probably the fountain head of all internationalism, yet is strictly national in its ultimate aim—World Domination... Lastly, there is the vast underground network of Arcane Sects and Occult Societies which in Europe and America are represented by the various Continental Rosicrucian and Templar Orders, the Theosophists and higher degrees of Orient Freemasonry, whose real aim is the overthrow of Western ideals, Western civilisation, and the Christian religion. Of this system of intricate secret societies the various Socialist, Communist, Syndicalist, and Anarchist organisations are the political mole-hills that indicate the nature of the underground burrowings, which are sapping the foundations of our Western civilisation... It has been suggested, and there may be a measure of truth in the idea, that behind all subversive movements there is yet another nameless Force, deeper in the shadows of the underworld of international secret intrigue — something greater than all, and directing all..."

According to a leader in the *Morning Post*, May 15, 1925, Dr. Steiner 'made a link between the Bolshevists and pan-German and Monarchist societies as well as with the higher grades of Grand Orient Masonry,' and was also associated with the Bolshevist Tomsky.

As stated by the late Dr. Carl Unger, one of Steiner's most devoted followers, Dr. Steiner, when asked to define 'Anthroposophy' for the *Oxford Dictionary*, wrote: 'Anthroposophy is a knowledge produced by the Higher Self in man'; that is the man whose 'inner senses' have been awakened by certain processes, etc., taught by Dr. Steiner in his so-called Spiritual Science. It is the building up of a medium. To his disciples his definition was: 'Anthroposophy is a path of knowledge to guide the Spiritual in the human being to the Spiritual in the Universe.' Here we have the Hermetic axiom, 'As above so below'; the union of the life-force or Kundalini within man with the universal life-force without, forming the 'deified man,' knowing all that was, is, and shall be, reading the records imprinted on the astral light, under control of these so-called spirit beings or masters. It is initiation.

Speaking of this initiation in his lecture, 'Christ and the Twentieth Century' (see *Anthroposophy*, Xmas 1926), Steiner says:

"The processes to which the soul of man was subjected in the ancient Mysteries were such that through the influence of other, more highly advanced, personalities (who themselves had passed through this 'Mystery Initiation'), a kind of sleeping state (trance) was induced … the body was left behind … but the soul (astral body) was able for a certain period to gaze into the spiritual (astral) world *consciously.*"

Having been led back to the body, 'this soul, having participated in spiritual life (astral), could then come forth as a prophet before the peoples…' According to this Spiritual Science, the ancient Wisdom-teachings "emanate from the 'Initiates'." He continues: "At the time of the beginning of Christendom the soul of man had become ripe for 'Self-Initiation,' under the guidance of those who knew the experiences which it was necessary to undergo, but without the active cooperation of the leaders of the Temples or Mysteries." But we have good reason to know that the leaders of Mysteries still co-operate on the astral plane, shaping, hewing, and initiating their future instruments or 'prophets.'

He further tells us that the Mysteries,

"stepped forth upon the great stage of world history through the founding of Christianity… Jesus of Nazareth reached the point where… He could unite Himself with a Being who hitherto had not been united with any human individual — with the Christ-Being… The Christ permeated the being of Jesus of Nazareth" for three years. and "mighty forces stream out from this event as an impulse for all later human development… And the fact that it was possible for the Christ impulse to enter humanity was brought about by the ancient Initiation principle becoming *historical fact.*"

After initiation 'through my own ego, God speaks to me.' That is, He becomes clairvoyant, clairaudient, and intuitional, as in all illuminised groups. All this means that the Christ impulse is merely the initiating force of the Serpent or Logos of the Gnostics! We are elsewhere told that the Christ, was sent forth by the Gods of the Sun, Moon, and Saturn—the Serpent Power!

Dr. F. W. Zeylmans van Emmichoven writes, *in Anthroposophy*, Easter 1929: "At the Goetheanum in Dornach stands a great group sculptured by Dr. Rudolph Steiner. It represents the Christ as the Representative of Humanity, placed between Lucifer and Ahriman." Of this Christ he says: "In the face all the forces seem to be concentrated at one point on the forehead, where divine wisdom seems to shine." This is the Pineal Gland, where the Serpent Power within unites with that which is without. producing illuminism and control. In his Stuttgart lectures, 1919, Steiner said that for the rescuing of the world from materialism the Orient is too Luciferian and the Occident (Anglo-American) is too Ahrimanic — materialistic knowledge. It is the German mission to steer a right course between the two extremes and save the world! In other words, Germany was to act as the Christ Impulse to the world!

According to Mrs. Besant, Krishnamurti, in trance, was initiated by the 'Great Ones,' and thus became the 'vehicle' of the Master "Maitreya, the Christ, the Saviour of the World." As such he taught the world in his book, *Life in Freedom*: "As every human being is divine, so every individual in the world should be his own master, his own absolute ruler and guide... There is no God except the man who has purified himself (by initiation) and so attained the Truth." Yet as we have seen, Krishnamurti's individuality is in abeyance, he is but the "prophet" of his "owner" and bondmaster "Maitreya."

In his lecture on "Exoteric and Esoteric Christianity," given at Dornach, April 1922, Dr. Steiner expounds his cult of Christian Illuminism. Speaking of the early Christian traditions, he says:

> "The most that can be said is that they·exist in the form of historical notes in the archives of certain secret societies, where they are not understood. Anything that goes beyond the fragmentary indications relating to the Christ after the Mystery of Golgotha must to-day be rediscovered by Anthroposophical Spiritual Science... It is possible for humanity to have Divine teachers ... beings who descended to Earth from the realm of the Hierarchies, and who ... actually gave spiritual teaching. The men who received such teaching... were able to induce in themselves a condition of

consciousness in which their souls (astral body) withdrew from their physical bodies..."

This is Yoga, such as is taught in all illuminised groups. The nature of the so-called "Divine Teachers" is thus explained: "The Beings of the Higher Hierarchies are endowed with forces whereby they created Saturn, Sun, Moon, and (from these) finally the Earth." Then for the evolution of man they decreed that the development of intellect was necessary, and this these Gods themselves were incapable of doing, so "the Gods were forced ... to enter into a pact with Ahriman (the "black god of the Manicheans, the Ahriman of old idolaters," according to Eliphas Levi)... They realised that if Ahriman were once admitted as Lord of Death, and in consequence Lord of Intellect, the earth would no longer remain in their keeping..." To prevent this the Gods themselves must gain knowledge of Death. It was only possible for them to learn of death as it takes place on earth by sending one of themselves — the Christ Being — down to earth. It was necessary for a God to die upon earth..."

> "The Beings of the Hierarchies, belonging to Saturn, Sun, Moon, and Earth, allowed Ahriman to play a part in earthly evolution, but succeeded in restricting his dominion, in that they used him for the purposes of earthly evolution. Without Ahriman the Gods could never have made man into a being of intellect; were it not for the fact that the edge of his power was broken at the time of the Christ event, Ahriman would have succeeded in intellectualising the earth completely, in reducing it to a state of utter materialism."

One cannot fail to see at a glance that this is but another pantheistic, illuminised cult of the I.A.O. — the Sun, Moon, and destroying Fire, the Serpent Power or life-force of all Nature, interwoven with the earth." That is the "fixation of the astral light in a material basis," forming illuminised tools. It is the God Pan once more arisen, playing upon his old mysterious pipe, showing forth the mysteries of the interlaced triangles-generation, creation. By this force the world, was to be initiated or illuminised, but first Saturn had to disintegrate and destroy all old-established systems and religions, and from the ashes, like the Phoenix of old, was to rise up the new kingdom of Lucifer — the Great Perversion! Not by intellect and reason, but by negation and blind faith was this to be accomplished.

After studying Steiner's "Knowledge of the Higher Worlds," or "Way of Initiation," it becomes increasingly clear that it means in reality a preparation for obsession by these hidden beings, so much spoken of by Steiner, who, working on the astral plane, are everywhere seeking for dupes and tools through whom they can carry out World Revolution leading to World Domination. By this means these beings instruct and orient, building up a "Spiritual Science," through an illuminised adept and teacher such as Steiner was, whereby many more are trained, instructed, and gathered into their fold of devilish usefulness, largely under the mistaken belief that the scheme is divinely inspired for the "higher evolution of the world."

Although, as we shall see, Anthroposophy has been declared by Steiner to be entirely a public society, still he writes: "Only so much will here be explained as can be publicly imparted." His science is still "occult," and in all that matters remains secret and hidden. There are three stages in his Initiation scheme:

> (I) *Probation.* — The awakening of the inner senses by meditation. For this, devotion, reverence, humility, the muting of all criticism or adverse judgment is required; the personal must be subdued, the universal outlook must be awakened for the service of "humanity." Calmness, leading to complete passivity, must be cultivated, and all impressions of the outer world shut out; then comes the "inner silence." in which "hidden beings" speak to him. For the awakening of these senses he must if possible live near Nature, among the pine-perfumed forests and the woodlands, or gaze upon the snowy peaks. In these meditations his thoughts must be oriented by the thoughts of advanced men who, according to Steiner, throughout the ages have been thus inspired by similar beings — "Bhagavad Gita, St. John's Gospel, Thomas à Kempis, and Spiritual Science!" Here we have Johannism

and one of Weishaupt's wellknown methods more or less universally employed in illuminism. The Kundalini must be awakened by concentration on the *feeling* produced by growth and decay in nature, one akin to a "sun-rising," the active life-force, and the other to the "moon-rising," the passive life-force; and this opens up the "astral plane." He must never *intellectualise,* only *feel.* This leads to orientation: he begins to hear. The passivity must extend "to listening without criticism, even when a completely contradictory opinion is advanced, when the most hopeless mistake is committed before him; then he learns, little by little, to blend himself with the being of another and become identified with it." This would train him to let go his own personality and opinions, laying himself open to obsession by another, or even by these hidden beings," on the astral plane, who only under such conditions can communicate with him, implanting their ideas in an "empty vessel."

(2) *Enlightenment.* — Again. by further awakening these positive and negative forces of the Kundalini — the united force which must eventually attract the controlling forces from the masters — he becomes clairvoyant, and sees the colours of these forces: they are red-yellow and blue, the positive and negative poles of the OD of the Jews, the astral light. Finally, he awakens the central and uniting force, then he meets these beings. Further, all fear must be conquered, for, as the Stella Matutina ritual says, "fear is failure," for without the fearless faith of the hypnotised subject, on the part of the adept, these beings cannot safely attempt the final stage of this diabolical obsession.

(3) *Initiation.* — He must pass through "trials," to test his endurance and faith. In these all his doubts are removed, he acts instantly as inspired by these beings, he ceases to act and think for himself, he is controlled — "as above so below." He now becomes a vessel of light, and is taught by these masters how to apply the knowledge given and use it for "humanity," or more correctly, against humanity. He is told that "he must only lend his hand to destruction, when he is also able, through and by means of destruction, to promote new life" —

the ancient creed of Illuminism, "the evil helps forward the good!" It is perversion, and the way to World Revolution, not to the "salvation and higher evolution of man," but leading to his collective retrogression, and to death of all Christian civilisation as seen in the Russia of to-day.

The following, taken from M. Robert Kuentz' article, "Le Dr. Rudolph Steiner et la Théosophie actuelle," in *Le Feu*, December 1913, is interesting as being apparently written from inside knowledge.

He gives verbatim twenty-four questions which he put to Steiner's representative in France, concerning Steiner's society and its connection with Grand Orient Masonry and Rosicrucianism, a questionnaire which was evaded and never answered. Here are some of the questions:

> I. Is there, or is there not, similarity between Steiner's occult ceremonies and those of the Grand Orient? Are the formulae the same? Do you find in them the history of Hiram and the three circumambulations in the darkness, with the eyes blindfolded (the latter must be familiar to members of the Stella Matutina!)?
>
> 4. The exercises given by Steiner, incompletely, in his book *Initiation* — exercises the details and occult developments of which I have seen given by Steiner himself — do they not very surely lead to that masonic state of mind, so well known to me?
>
> 5. The exercises, for example, called 'Faith,' and that which develops 'Passivity,' do they not orient the pupil in such a manner, towards *credulity* on one side and terror of all critical spirit on the other, that the mind thus worked upon is ready to digest everything offered to it and to find it good and beautiful even when it is ugly and evil?
>
> 6. Are there, in truth, a large number of fools or unbalanced minds in Dr. Steiner's masonry and few really intelligent?

8. Does not Dr. Steiner say in his books that Theosophy, which has no creed, rises above religions which have creeds and dominates them?

9. Does not Steiner, however, officiate before the altar in his Temple of the Rose-Croix?

10. Is he not the High-Priest of this Order?

11. Has he not the sacerdotal vestments, even as the Catholic priests?

12. Does he not marry the Theosophical Masons?

14. Do you wish to construct the "Temple," named "Vault," at Munich, because, moreover, it will represent the symbol which that word expresses?

16. Why in Steiner's writings is there no trace of all that, of this "Holy of Holies," of this Masonic school, where only the "elect" penetrate, that is to say, those who have consciously studied Steiner's books and who have done the exercises indicated in the book *Initiation?*

17. Do they themselves swear (under the penalty "of wandering through space for all eternity without a guide") to keep secret what they are going to see in the Temple, before they know anything whatsoever of what they are promising by this oath, which assuredly must terrorise the visionary and the feeble-minded (similar to the taking of the oath in the Stella Matutina!)?

24. Is not the title 'Lucifer Gnosis,' of the old Steiner review, unfortunate and needlessly troubling, if it does not really mean a true Luciferian (satanic) and Gnostic initiation?

M. Robert Kuentz continues giving the equivocation he got in place of answer to his questionnaire:

"Behold the command of masonry. To reply in a straight-forward manner to these direct questions would have simply conferred upon me the initiation itself, then and there, without the ordinary rites and required conditions. The initiation is nothing more than the answer to these questions, after promising on oath on the part of the candidate not to betray this secret, and when the disciple has been sufficiently alienated from his own free judgment to stand and to accept this 'truth' without horror, or no longer understanding the nature of it or to what it is leading. This pulverisation of the mental faculties, this treatment of the mind by the process of 'occult exercises' to which the disciple is subjected, and who will without doubt soon become the "patient," explains in Steinerism these adepts of good faith of incontestable morality who are victims following an end and masters of whom they are ignorant, under the illusion of idealism. (This applies to all such Orders.)

"The answer of Steiner's representative was "to confess that it is such doubts which formed a sieve around the teachings of Steiner, which scatters all feeble minds from his esoterism."… Also he would give no further information than that contained in the documents I already possessed, so that 'my belief in his explanations should not take the place my own free and absolute judgment alone ought to inspire!'"

Speaking of his own questionnaire, M. Kuentz remarks:

"Was it not a chivalrous gesture of confidence and trust to ask, not for proofs, but a word of honour denying the incriminating facts. *We are therefore obliged to accept the facts!*"

Describing these mind-pulverising exercises of Steiner's Initiation, M. Kuentz writes:

Without going further, however, one can easily guess that has to do not with "Faith" but with "Credulity," and a rare and devastating "passivity," if one is to be able to accept with calmness the religious and historical monstrosities embodied in the first part of this study. Nevertheless, Steiner calls this "passivity, equilibrium" and I willingly yield to him the originality of his expression. In describing a quality allowing one to accept with trust that the 'Clock of the neighbouring church has, during the night, suddenly placed itself in a horizontal position.' The disciple, says Steiner, in the fifth exercise ought not to reject the bizarre as absurd. All astounding things presented to you should be put to one side without rejection. In order to arrive thus far there must be a complete training, a depressing regimen to be submitted to, varying according to the candidate; these are the stages of the prostitution of the mind.

"From the first exercise which consists in 'concentrating on a thought' (trivial to begin with), the pupil is habituated to lose touch with the sense of what is practical and real; the second inculcates in him a mad routine, indispensable to the perfecting of his inner derangement. Exercise third is in truth "passivity." … It is that which blunts the power of feeling and suffering, which mechanically extinguishes enthusiasm, horror, and all strong and sane sensation, which blows on the mind in the name of "equitable temper" like a sirocco of indifference. Then one is ready for "positivity" — exercise four-veritable erosion of the critical faculty… It is said that the esoteric pupil knows well that if he still retains the critical mind, he must give up all hope of occult development, rather must he help to cure himself of such! Only then is he capable of the fifth exercise: "in order to develop a certain feeling of faith, he must no longer reject straight away anything, whatsoever it may be, that is presented to his mind."

"This is the terrible noviciate that must for long be submitted to in order to become an apt initiate! One sees here the systematic formation of the masonic mind; as also the insinuating and subtly deceptive inspiration of a kind of hallucination (or hypnosis) which assures his docility. These exercises occupy all the faculties and have curious precisions.

Read this!

"The inner exercises are done evening and morning in bed. You must imagine yourself to be in seas of light from which the waves of fire enter into the body. Then the head, the middle of the body, and the whole body ought successively to live separately: through the forehead (pineal gland) the light enters, and you hear a voice at the root of your nose say: "The pure rays of the divine are in you." The heart in its turn hears something similar, only the rays pass through it. Then the abdomen speaks (don't laugh!), so that the world force can come out through the navel"

Now we know that Steiner's movement is not only allied to, if not actually Grand Orient Freemasonry, but is also Rosicrucian; concerning the latter they have perforce to be silent as, like Weishaupt's Illuminati, no Rosicrucian may admit that he is so. M. Robert Kuentz thus describes Steiner's "Initiation to the Grade of Rosicruacian Apprentice":

"On the evening they begin by gathering together all new adherents, and after a little sermon from Steiner, vague and fraternal, you are told to sign a paper by which you acknowledge that Steiner is *the Grand Master of the Order of the Rose-Croix*; it is added that you must subscribe to the expenses of the Order, that you must consider your inferiors as your equals, and it ends with the formula of the oath indicated in my questionnaire... You are told beforehand to dress preferably in white. You enter, you recognise the Theosophists; there is an air of mystery; all speak low... You are blindfolded, and all metal taken away from you — chains, rings, etc. An officer behind you places his hands on your shoulders, then the procession begins.

The first dialogue takes place before the Temple door... The Temple door opens, and you pass in, and circumambulate the room three times, sitting down three times, during which the "Master of the Ceremonies" declaims in a religious voice, mysterious and sphinx-like, the well-known formulae of the rite used by the Grand Orient... Then at last you sit down still blindfolded, and you feel something happening at your waist and neck. Suddenly the bandage is raised by the guide, and you see in front of you a skull which Steiner holds under your nose. Steiner has a sever, one on each side — a deacon and vice-deacon (as in the Liberal Catholic Mass!) — bearers of wax-candles: the whole in dense obscurity. The bandage falls again: after a time it is taken away altogether, you are... *Initiated*: you begin to see light. This light comes from wax-candles placed on three altars; black draperies hang everywhere, symbolising the darkness which is always near... Steiner, the High Priest, is completely clothed in red, with a long Mephistophelian tail and red cap; he is before an altar, in the form of a cube, on which are a crucifix, a cup, and a candle; the two servers, wearing masonic aprons, are before another cube holding candles; the Grand Master of the Ceremonies is near to Steiner (a woman of high Bavarian nobility, well-known to the Theosophists, at times took this office; she had a kind of alb and chasuble). You glance at yourself and see the masonic apron in front with triangle and trowel. You place your hand on the Gospel of St. John (Johannism); then you are told the password, the apprentice sign, and the sacred name which you can only stammer; it is YAKIM. Then with two extended swords curious signs are made in front of you. Then a sermon from Steiner on the legend of Hiram and Solomon... Then the Repast, during which they look for the underground Temple, the Vault, then being built in Munich (no doubt the pantheistic repast of illuminism). Second address from Steiner, he has taken off the red robe and now wears an alb of lace; he speaks on the Triangle and the eye of God (?), which is in the centre of the Triangle and of man's being. (This is the Triangle of manifestation, and the eye is the power manifested — the Universal Creative Principle, the astral light of Illuminism, for such is Steinerism). Close of ceremony, which has lasted four hours: ritualistic knocks with mallets on the three cubes; candles extinguished and again lighted, the black draperies of burial are removed; you are surrounded with red of bullock's blood (ruby the colour of unity); it is the light at last! ... Ite missa est! ... You are *Initiated!*

"I know no form more precise and insidious than the occultism of Steiner (of this Satanism of the twentieth century).

"This is the conclusion to which my inquiry has led me ... Steiner first attacks the individual whose faculties he deranges; then he ruins society by drawing his adepts from among it; and lastly and above all in making man God (the 'Deified Man') his laical ritual defies and scorches religion with the anarchy of Lucifer. To justify and conclude this study, we cannot do better than quote M. Ferrand: "To know Theosophists is a social duty, to unmask them a political duty, and to fight them a religious duty!"

"Let us add that the Apprentice-Rosicrucian is only just the fringe of the Rosicrucian Order. There follow minor Orders and sacred Orders in which initiation goes farther — very much farther!"

Robert Kuentz speaks of the 'underground Temple,' the "Holy of Holies" which Steiner was then building in Munich. This I presume contained the "Vault" or Tomb of the Adepts, which figures in all higher Rosicrucian grades and ceremonies.

Notwithstanding the secret and "occult" nature of Steiner's teachings, leading to final initiation and loss of personality under the control of these so-called spirit beings or masters on the astral, and notwithstanding his secret masonic and Rosicrucian grades, Steiner, in his *News Sheet*, Xmas 1923, wrote:

"The Anthroposophical Society is an entirely public organisation: politics it does not consider to be among its tasks. (Yet consider Steiner's political and subversive activities!) All publications of the society will be open to the public, as are those of other public societies. The same will apply to the publications of the School of Spiritual Science; but in regard to these works, those responsible for the school reserve the right from the outset to deny the validity of opinions unsupported by the proper qualifications, namely, by the training of which the works themselves are the outcome. In this sense, and as is customary in the recognised scientific world, they will admit the validity of no judgment which is not based on the requisite preliminary studies. The publications of the School of Spiritual Science will therefore contain the following notice:

"Printed in manuscript for the members of the School of Spiritual Science, "Goetheanum" class ... no person is held qualified to form a judgment on the contents of these works who has not acquired through the school itself or in an equivalent manner recognised by the school — the requisite preliminary knowledge; other opinions will be disregarded: the authors decline to take them as a basis for discussion."

The investigator into this reliable (?) Spiritual Science thus gains his knowledge:

"He, by the faculties that are in him (his awakened inner senses!), enters consciously the worlds where spiritual beings dwell and spiritual processes take place. He sees spiritual beings and spiritual processes, and he sees too how the beings and the processes of the physical world arise out of the spiritual. It is then his further task to express certain domains of what is revealed to his spiritual sight in the form of ideas... The school will lead its members on into the regions of the spiritual world which cannot be revealed in ideas — where it becomes necessary to find the means to express imagination, inspiration, and intuition. Here too the various departments of life-artistic, educational, ethical, etc. — will be pursued into those regions where they receive the esoteric light and impulse to creative work."

If we substitute 'astral' for 'spiritual' and flesh and blood men working on the astral plane 'for·spiritual beings,' we again arrive at the age-long game of these Cabalistic Jews, seeking World Domination through credulous dupes and illuminised tools-permeating, in this way, all departments of national, social, and religious life with their disintegration ideas and systems of perversion.

Another method evolved by Dr. Steiner for bringing about this mind-destroying illuminism is "Eurhythmy," built up, as in other occult Orders, from mystic and magical inspiration. Here we are playing with the hidden forces of Nature, and it becomes magic, black or white, according to the inspirational source. There are to-day many simple forms of Eurhythmic, Swedish, and folk dances quite harmless and even health-giving. Most of these Orders have been built up through communications from hidden masters largely or altogether for subversive purposes; therefore eurhythmy inspired by them would be a danger not only to the individual but to the country in which it is taught, for we are told by Eliphas Levi: "Black magic is a contagion of vertigo and an epidemic of unreason"; even such as our country is suffering from to-day.

We must first understand that man himself is a little universe — the *Microcosm* — within the Great Universe — the *Macrocosm* — bound by the same laws and built up of the same forces. Ether permeates all, and links all together — "as above so below." In his "Eurhythmy" Steiner uses the vowels as representing planetary activities, and consonants those of the Zodiac. In the sixteenth century Cornelius Agrippa ascribed the five vowels and j and v consonants to the seven planets; the consonants *b, c, d, f, g, l, m, n, p, r, s, t,* to the twelve signs of the Zodiac; *k, q, x, z,* to the four elements, and h, the aspiration, to the spirit of the world — ether.

Further, Arthur Avalon, in his translation from the Sanskrit *of Tantra of the Great Liberation,* says:

> "A Mantra is composed of certain letters arranged in definite sequence of sounds, of which the letters are the representative signs. To produce the designed effect, Mantra must be intoned in the proper way, according to rhythm and sound ... a Mantra is *a potent compelling force,* a word of power."

In one of the Tantras it is said: "I fear, O Lord! that even that which Thou hast ordained for the good of men, will through them turn out for evil." Is, then, Dr. Steiner's eurhythmy for the "great good or for the great evil"?

His eurhythmy appears to be magical, awakening and reawakening corresponding forces in man and in the universe, even as we know takes place in all ceremonies in these occult orders. The vibrations are set in motion by sound, rhythm, colour, and movement, attracting by polarity Nature's finer magnetic forces, creating links not only with like universal forces, but with other minds working with the same set of vibrations, having the same keynote, no doubt, with those who inspired the eurhythmy! In *Anthroposophy* it is said: "Eurythmy indeed is an expression of the Song of the Stars, of the speech of the gods to man." This is the pipe of the pagan god Pan, the vibrations of the seven-voiced harmony of the planets. The gods being Nature's forces, so with the ancient Egyptians Osiris represented the Sun, Isis the Moon, Apophis the destroying fire-sun, moon, and fire of the Serpent Power, the astral light which Eliphas Levi tells us is in itself a blind force, but under the impetus of powerful wills is the basis of all magic, both black and white. Again *Anthroposophy* says: "The movement in eurhythmy passes in plastic visible form into the *light,* and is seen by the eye." These movements therefore attract and bring down this same astral light, and these forces are drawn into the individual who "becomes the bearer of the spirit self," or is it not the spirit of another obsessing mind!

We would therefore ask: Did Steiner, by clairvoyance, clairaudience, and impressional teachings, inspired by the masters or "spiritual beings," evolve and build up his eurhythmy? Were not these masters the same Invisible Power which directs and instructs all these occult groups for the accomplishment of their world schemes? If so, is this eurhythmy not simply a means of creating "vessels of light," receivers and transmitters of these forces, hypnotically controlled by these masters, blindly obedient to all their subtle and secret suggestions? Are they not just eurhythmic mantras, potent compelling forces, awakening the Kundalini, creating illuminism, brought about by the will-power of these masters from without?

In The *Socialist Network*, quoting Walter Pahl's account of the religion of the "Youth Movement of Germany," Mrs. Webster writes:

> "They were Christians no longer, so they released the body, and set themselves to *"the dance of the earth and the stars within us,"* in order to restore the great harmony and holiness into our lives. *'Dancing, in fact, offers the greatest religious emotion to a great part of our German youth.'* It is here we can trace the inspiration of the eurhythmic dancing practised by the Steinerites of Germany, etc."

In *Anthroposophy*, the first number of that Steinerite quarterly, we find an article on 'Eurhythmy,' in which it is said: "Eurhythmy has grown out of the essence of Anthroposophical Spiritual Science, and is based on an understanding *of the true nature of man and his relation to the Earth, as well as to the Planetary and Zodiacal Mysteries of the Cosmos.*" Is this not "the earth and stars within us" of the "Youth Movement"?

Again, to quote the Steinerites:

> "The etheric body derives its inner mobility from Planetary and Zodiacal (starry worlds!), hence from Cosmic forces... In Eurhythmy the mobility is carried over by the ego consciously into the physical body (earth) ... (the ego can draw these forces into the various bodies). Life spirit is coming into expression."

This is fixation of the astral light in a material body; it is the illumination or illuminism as depicted in the drawing "Anthropos," — as above so below — at the beginning of the second number of their quarterly. Does not this emotional dancing of the "Youth Movement" in Germany awaken the Kundalini in the same way and for the same purpose? And in fact both movements are wholly pantheistic!

In trying to explain the *raison d'être* of the Steiner cult and its eurhythmy, which is even now penetrating education and schools

— as the "Protocols" say: 'Reeducation of youth by new temporary religions' — it might serve a useful purpose to compare it with the rhythmic dances and cult of the primitive Russian Sect, the "Khlysty," or "People of God," to which Rasputin, that licentious and evil genius of Russia, belonged.

Dr. Rudolph Steiner's cult is, as we have seen, largely Gnostic, and is Manicheanism, which supposes dualism in Deity, inequality in the Absolute, inferiority in Supreme Power. It is Luciferian. It has for goal the Pantheistic deification of man.

The Khlysty — a sect directed by Christs or deified men — is generally dated back to the middle of the seventeenth century. The founder was said to be a fugitive soldier, Danila Philippovitch, who threw his many books of piety into the Volga, declaring that he was a reincarnation of "God the Father," and that there was no God but himself, that the one and only 'Golden Book' of inspiration was within each one of us; is this not just 'intuition,' the god of Krishnamurti, the "Higher Genius" of the Rosicrucians, the "God within" of Mme Blavatsky? Along with Ivan Timothéiévitch Souslov, his "Christ," he wandered over Russia, spreading his cult, and this cult was said to be a form of Gnosticism, in particular Manicheanism and Montanism. Montanus was given over to boundless licentiousness of frenzy and ecstasy, such as is apparent among the Khlysty; they pretend to spiritualise matter, but actually they materialise spirit, and the cult of the Khlysty shows a Pantheistic conception of Deity. The sect was more or less secret, and the newly affiliated was sworn to keep secret all he saw and heard during the ceremonies; to suffer fire, the knout, torture, and death, rather than deny his faith. He was further bound to celibacy — apart from his cult!

In their cult the Father, Mother, Prophets, and Prophetesses officiated, and its principal and most popular form was the "fervour." The fervour consisted of numerous rhythmic figures of circular dances always moving with the sun, always quickening, and accompanied by chants and exclamations, sometimes "Eva Evo!" — the cry of the Bacchantes of the god

Dionysus, the I.A.O. of the Rosicrucians — the chants marking the rhythm the fervour. It produced the illusion of moving as on wings, and usually continued many hours — it ended sometimes with the utterance of the "word" or prophecies, or the light would be extinguished, followed by a sexual orgy. Before long they found that they could not live without this fervour; they would sooner give up a point of dogma or a moral rule. The aim of the fervour was the descent of the "Spirit" or astral light, deifying and creating "Christs" — Illuminism!

In his book, *The Russian Sect, the People of God*, or the Khlysty, M. J. B. Severac quotes the following as explanatory of this fervour:

> "History at all times, writes M. Ribot, abounds in physiological processes, employed to produce artificial ecstasy … so to say, having divinity within oneself. There are inferior forms, mechanical intoxication produced by the dance, rhythmic music of the primitives, which excites them and puts them into a condition ripe for inspiration; the soma, the wine, the Dionysia, the orgies of Ménades, the shedding of blood so widespread in the cults of Asia Minor, the Goddess Atys, the Corybants, the Gauls, mutilating and cutting themselves with swords; in the Middle Ages the Flagellants, and in our day the fakirs and dervishes, etc."

M. Séverac says:

> "The fervour of the people of God has its place alongside these examples of physiological processes of inferior form destined to attain this divinity."

This Eurhythmy of Dr. Steiner, which is also accompanied with rhythmic music, however learnedly, scientifically, and occultly thought out and applied, attains to no more and no less than the fervour of these primitive Gnostics, the Khlysty. Their god is no less and no more than the god of all Illuminism, the creative principle of all Nature, and in both groups they seek to awaken the Kundalini, the serpent within, that they may be, according to both beliefs, "penetrated" by the universal "spirit" of Nature from without, in order to bring about the condition known as "deification," an Illuminism which may unite them, unknown to themselves, with their "masters," the Cabalistic Jew, the originator of Gnostic mysticism. Thus they became but an oracle or instrument.

Dmitry Merejkovsky, the Russian historical writer, makes one of his characters in "Pierre le Grand" thus describe the creed of the Khlysty, a creed applicable to many more or less degrading and unbalanced movements of to-day:

> "I will explain a great mystery: if thou desirest to live, mortify, for the glory of God, not only thy body but thy soul, thy reason, and even thy conscience. *Free thyself from all rules and all laws, all virtues of fasting, of abstinence, and of virginity.* Free thyself from holiness. Descend into thyself as into a tomb. Then mysteriously dead thou shalt rise again, and in thee will dwell the Holy Spirit, and thou shalt never lose it, no matter what thou mayest do." "He believed he was flying without knowing where he was flying to, whether it was towards Heaven or towards the abyss, towards God or the Devil!"

This is the way of the cross of Illuminism, and leads without doubt to the abyss and moral degradation.

In Steiner's lectures, given at Stuttgart in 1918, we get a very clear idea of his political outlook at that time, and we are forced to conclude thaht it was not that of a high spiritual teacher. Here is an authentic résumé:

> "He speaks of the War throughout as a German, and gives the impression that Germany ought to have won, and it would have pleased him. He speaks at length of the violation of Belgium, but says not a word of condemnation. He explains the Bolshevist system; he apparently approves of it, as he gives as his own opinion that only the workers ought to have rights, capital is wrong and ought to disappear; means of

living must not depend on work, etc. When you buy, say a coat, with your money you are buying men's work, and he condemns it! Money should be allowed to buy only goods. (He does not explain contradictions.)

"A work of art is, say, in Rome; a 'bourgeois' (capitalist) can go there to see it; his money will command the work of many railway men, etc... to enable him to enjoy the sight of that work of art. Why should a poor worker, to whom it belongs as well as to the bourgeois, not see it? The works of art should be brought to the workers everywhere. Money left with compound interest in a bank will double itself in fourteen years, and yet the capitalist will have remained idle. Money is the power of commandeering other men's work!

"There are in England occult societies which inspire English politics. They know the course of evolution for the next few decades, and are using their knowledge for the material advantage of England. The English will try and keep the people east of the Rhine (Middle Europe and Russia) in a weak state by keeping up socialistic institutions amongst them; in order to exploit their work as slaves, for the benefit of the British Empire as Masters.

"It is the English occultists who have caused the Tzar to be overthrown and Bolshevism to gain power. They are making socialistic experiments at the expense of Russia and Middle Europe. But as the English-speaking people (England and America) will only be able to evolve materialistic occultism which ultimately would destroy their evolution, they will make use for their advantage of the other kinds of occultism which their victims will evolve — the hygienic occultism of the German and the eugenic occultism of the Russian and the Asiatics.

"The English occultists are already in possession of knowledge which will soon enable employers to work their machines by some force which will do away with most workmen. The masses of idle workmen will revolt in anger, but the English occultists know of the means which will

subdue them. (Steiner does not explain the means!). The
cause of the present unrest in Europe is the kind of stuff a
'lazy' clergy has been preaching in the churches for a long
time, because its preaching has no connection with men and
lives. Steiner explains at length what the Bolshies want and
what they have done. While he never misses a chance of
insulting the churches he is very polite about the Bolshies and
is careful even to say that he is not criticising them. When
explaining what they have done with their opponents he does
not use the word 'murder' or even 'execution'; he says they
have 'chased them away' or got rid of them.

'About British politics he says they are very powerful, and
will succeed in ruling the world because they are essentially
selfish; he says that selfishness must not be criticised, as it is
part of the evolution, the development of self-consciousness.
The French are finished, because their qualities of logic,
intellect, reason, etc.. are merely the perfecting of the Roman
civilisation. The only nation in the world that knows right
from wrong is the German nation (1918)! Steiner is
apparently so anxious to show that he means what he says,
that he adds: "The other nations·do not understand anything
about it at all." German politics are always idealistic!

"The telephone, wireless, express trains, and other modern
conveniences have been placed at our service at the cost of
misery to millions of workers. It was very easy for the early
English Theosophists in the second half of the nineteenth
century to take kindly to the new teaching in their
comfortable rooms well-heated with coal extracted in the
terrible conditions to which they never gave a thought.
Humanity as a collective whole is on the verge of going over
the threshold more or less consciously, and this momentous
step will be done by the proletariat. If proletariat thinking is
still chaotic and wrong, it is because it is still imitating
bourgeois mentality.

"As far back as 1880 the Anglo-American occult leaders,
directing the political leaders, knew about the coming World
War and prepared for it. The German leaders knew nothing,

and would not take warning, that is why they lost! The physical war was easily won by England, but it will be followed by a spiritual war between East and West (East-India, Russia, and Germany; West-Anglo-America), which will be much more dangerous for the West. For instance. India, which is half starving (according to Mrs. Besant!), will rebel and be helped by powerful spiritual forces out of her past. Germany must fulfil her mission, otherwise the European civilisation will be ruined.'

Remarks. — From beginning to end, in that course of about eight lectures Steiner is almost continually abusing everybody and everything except himself and his teachings. He is repeatedly drawing general and even cosmic conclusions from purely local German conditions (for instance, the autocratic hold of the Government on education, religion, and the Press), and threatening the whole world with awful catastrophes if those conditions are not altered. His state of mind is obviously that in the whole Cosmic evolution Germany is IT and the rest nowhere.

On being asked what will become of money and capital in his "Threefold" scheme, he said he need not worry about such details, because his scheme being so clearly founded on a practical basis, every detail would work out of itself in the right direction!

In this mad, communistic scheme of a "Threefold State," again evolved out of this dangerous "Spiritual Science," under the direction of unknown beings on the astral, Steiner advocated that all nations, peoples, and races should be divided up into *three international*, independent, autonomous Corporations (headless as someone remarked!) — spiritual (religion and education), political, and economic. And to cover the enormous expenses of this disintegrating scheme he formed a public limited company called "Der Kommende Tag Act"—"The Coming Day, Ltd.," or as known in England, "Futurum, Ltd.," but it was soon found to be too communistic for English ideas and was closed down. Among its supporters were the late Dr. Carl Unger and Dr. Arensohn.

Another of Steiner's experimentations, based on this "Spiritual Science," is his "New Therapy," and to dispense the results of this so-called "Anthroposophical Medical Research," the British Weleda Co., Ltd., was incorporated January 19, 1925, with a capital of £2,000 in £1 shares. The first directors were Daniel Nicol Dunlop, Heinrich Dank, an Austrian, and Josef Emanuel Van Leer, Dutch. The International Laboratorien of Arlesheim, Switzerland, held 1,050 shares on March 5,1925, received for rights sold in the British Empire (except Canada) for certain medicinal remedies. The business is described as that of Chemists and Druggists; office, 21 Bloomsbury Square.

In his laboratories he carried out his "researches for future medicine — the art of healing through spiritual knowledge." He had no medical degree, but apparently based his "New Therapy" on psychical investigations, whereby he claimed to see the processes without in Nature, and their relations to the processes within the human body, claiming by special processes to be able to arrest the required plant activity and free it within the human organism as kinetic energy, entrapping cosmic energy! We would leave those who are still free from this mind-destroying "Spiritual Science" to realise the possible danger of subjecting their minds and bodies to this new and psychic therapy.

Further, as Dr. Steiner himself has declared that "all publications of the Society will be open to the public as are those of other public societies," we would strongly advise all members of the Anthroposophical Society and those interested in Dr. Steiner's teachings to obtain not only these eight or so Stuttgart Lectures, but also Steiner's *Apologia Germanica,* written at the end of the War, and whether they have received the training considered essential by Dr. Steiner for the true understanding of such teachings or not, judge for themselves whether, as Mr. Dunlop would have us believe, these are the teachings of a spiritual leader whose object is "to turn the life and mind of man to the true things of the spirit," or an Illuminatus, subversive and revolutionary, aiming at the destruction of all national life, of old-established systems, and of Christianity itself.

CHAPTER IV

THE STELLA MATUTINA AND THE ROSAE-RUBEAE ET AUREAE CRUCIS

We have in our possession one of the original copies of a short history of the Stella Matutina, drawn up by Dr. Felkin in 1912, before going out to New Zealand for the first time. He went there in order to found a Temple in Havelock North, largely at the suggestion of a London member, a father of the Community of the Resurrection and of Mirfield, a training college for young clergy, who had been doing mission work in New Zealand, and at the same time a little propaganda for the Stella Matutina. In 1921, when two of the London Chiefs, who had reason to suspect that the Order was subversive, stood out against Dr. Felkin, demanding more definite information and investigations into the true nature of the S.M. and his more recent German connection, this history, at their request, was gone over and annotated by one of the original Chiefs, Dr. Wynn Westcott, who wrote at the end: "I give a general assent to all that I have not marked—*(Signed)* Sapere Aude 5–6; Non Omnis Moriar 7-4," these being his Outer and Inner mottoes. He further advised the two Chiefs against handing over any Order documents, then in their possession, either to Dr. Felkin or his delegates until definite and satisfactory information could be obtained. Nothing satisfactory was ever vouchsafed, and from 1919, when suspicion was first definitely aroused, up to the present moment, investigations have been carried out by a small group, and gradually the suspicion has become a certainty.

The Order of the "Stella Matutina," or as it is called in the original MSS., *"The Order" of the Companions of the Rising*

Light of the Morning — the Golden Dawn in the Outer;" was built up from certain cypher MSS., found by a clergyman, the Rev. A. F. A. Woodford, in 1884, on an old bookstall in Farringdon Street. These he took to Dr. Woodman and Dr. Wynn Westcott, both well-known and high Masons, and learned in the Kabalah; the MSS. consisted of notes and rough diagrams for the five rituals of the Outer Order-O-O to 4-7—along with certain lectures in elementary occult and cabalistic knowledge. Accompanying these MSS. was, it was said, a letter in German, saying that if anyone cared to decipher these MSS. and would communicate with "Sapiens Dominabitur Astris," c/o Fräulein Anna Sprengel, living in Hanover, they would receive interesting information. Having deciphered the MSS., they were then told by S.D.A. to elaborate the rituals, which was done by a Mason, MacGregor Mathers, assisted by Dr. Wynn Westcott. They were then told that if diligent they would be permitted to form an elementary branch of the Rosicrucian Order in England, and finally S.D.A. wrote to Wynn Westcott and authorised him to sign his (or her) name to any warrant or document necessary for the constitution of an Order, and promising later on further rituals and advanced teachings if the preliminary Order was successful. On March 1, 1888, a Warrant was drawn up according to a design given in the MSS., and was signed by Dr. Woodman, MacGregor Mathers, and, for S.D.A., by Wynn Westcott, all three of whom received the honorary grade of 7-4 from S.D.A., so as to enable them to act as chiefs in the new Temple.

Several letters passed between these men and S.D.A., c/o Fräulein Anna Sprengel, but none of them ever actually met her, and nothing was ever known save that Anna Sprengel died in an obscure German village in 1893. There is no date on these MSS., no address, nor are they signed by any adept except in the accompanying letter. When deciphered they were found to be drawn up in English, although the letters received were in German. Therefore we are led to believe that these MSS. were not the work of S.D.A., and were undoubtedly intended for the use of English-speaking people, possibly with the idea of penetrating England and English Masonry, and were purposely deposited on the bookstall by some member visiting England.

Among other instructions given in the MSS. we find, "Avoid Roman Catholics, but with pity"; and the obligation to be taken in the Initiation was, "The candidate asking for Light is taken to the altar and forced to take an obligation to secrecy under penalty of expulsion and death or palsy from hostile current of will." In the elaborated version this became: "In addition (to expulsion) under the awful penalty of voluntarily submitting myself to a deadly and hostile current of will set in motion by the Chiefs of the Order, by which I fall slain or paralysed without, visible weapon, as if blasted by a lightning flash."

A.E. Waite, in his *Brotherhood of the Rosy Cross*, 1924, quoting from the *Transactions and History* of the "Societas Rosicruciana in Anglia," recapitulates much of the above information about "the Isis Urania Temple of the Hermetic students of the Golden Dawn," the Hebrew name being "Chabreth Zerech Aur Bokher." Waite concludes that these cypher MSS. were post 1880 (but possibly they were part of the reorganisation of Weishaupt's Illuminati in 1880). "The grades, besides a *Neophyte*, were four (the four elements or the Tetragrammaton)—*Zelator, Theoricus, Practicus, and Philosophus*; also a sub-grade, the Portal, leading from the Golden Dawn" to the *Rosoe Rubeae* et *Aureae Crucis*, the Inner Order. Apart from the cypher MSS. and MSS, found in libraries by MacGregor Mathers, most of the early teaching-still used in the Stella Matutina — was received clairvoyantly by Mrs. Mathers, a sister of M. Henri Bergson, the Jewish-French writer, from the 'Hidden and Secret Chiefs of the Third Order'; against her wish she was induced to take an oath of secrecy before the teaching was given, and it was later said by these unknown Chiefs: 'In the case of Mathers, the former Chief, there was a human adept (as intermediary or etheric link), and also communication was given to him by clairvoyance, clairaudience, and impressional teaching, whereby the true interpretation of existing MSS. was given to him.' Mathers was, we also find, doing political work under these Secret Chiefs, and was mixed up with war and military matters.

In 1897 Dr. Wynn Westcott resigned from the Order, and from

then ceased to take active or official part in the work. His own account of the reason was, that the Chairman of the Coroners' Society in London heard that he was teaching magic and got him to resign from the Order.

René Guénon, in *Le Théosophisme*, 1921, says: "The English secret society of 'The Order of the Golden Dawn in the Outer' is a society of occultists studying the highest practical magic, somewhat akin to Rosicrucianism. Men and women are admitted on equal terms. There are three principal officers. *Imperator, Praemonstrator,* and *Cancellarius.*" He further says, MacGregor Mathers writes in a letter, *Lucifer* July 1889: "This society studies Western traditions … The Theosophical Society is in friendly relation with them." The letter bears the following mottoes "Sapiens dominabitur astris (the continental adept), Deo duce comite ferro (Mathers), Non omnis moriar (Westcott), Vincit omnia veritas (Woodman)." It ends with these words: "Published by order of the Superior, ' Sapere Aude ' (Westcott), Cancellarius in London." René Guénon further continues, that much stir was created in Paris in 1899 and 1903 over an attempt made by Mr. and Mrs. MacGregor (Mathers) to restore the cult of Isis. Mr. MacGregor Mathers represented the G.D. in Paris, and was a member of the Theosophical Society.

An account of this attempt was given in *the Chronicle*, March 19, 1899, which said:

> "M. Jules Bois, the littérateur … recently discovered here a High-Priest and High-Priestess of Isis … and induced them to go through their 'devotions' in public, at the Bodinière Theatre… This couple of devotees to ancient deities profess to have been converted to the strange and passionate mysticism of worship of Isis during their travels in Egypt. They pretend that they constituted the rites and ceremonies of the religion, and for some time past they have been carrying on their devotions in an underground chapel which they established at their residence … After preliminary prayers, the High-Priestess performed the ceremony of "unveiling the gods," and then she invoked Isis with such passion and

force … that she quite saved the situation … which otherwise might have turned into the ridiculous … in conclusion … the men (in the audience) were supplied with a few grains of corn, which, deposited upon the 'altar,' would bring success in the enterprise they had in hand, even if of a political and worldly character."

A. E. Waite was an early member of the 'Golden Dawn,' but at a meeting held at Dr. Felkin's residence in 1903, according to Dr. Felkin's history, 'a split occurred, as Waite and his followers denied the existence of the Third Order, refused to have examinations in the inner, objected to all occult work, and said they must work upon purely mystic lines.' A Concordat was drawn up between the two Temples, but in 1912 it came to an end, as it was proved unworkable by both sides. When Waite and those who seceded with him left, they took with them certain properties and retained the name 'Golden Dawn,' and Dr. Felkin and his supporters eventually became the politico-pseudo-religious 'Stella Matutina,' a Temple of mediumship. Waite still used the same magical rituals, somewhat modified, to suit his mystical ideas. He ceased to be Chief of the 'Golden Dawn' about 1915, and soon afterwards it went into abeyance. He, however, formed a new Temple, calling it the 'Rosy Cross,' and still, we have reason to believe, using the old Cypher MSS. rituals, and thus retaining the link with these unknown continental Rosicrucians and Illuminati.

Since early in the nineties the 'Stella Matutina' (then known as the 'Golden Dawn') has been directed and instructed by unknown chiefs, acting under various pseudonyms. Curiously enough, it was at one time suggested that Dr. Falk, the cabalistic Jew who came to London in 1742, was the author of the original cypher MSS., but that cannot be vouched for. In this Order we first hear of them as 'The Hidden and Secret Chiefs of the Third Order,' under whom Mathers and his wife worked. In 1900 the London Temple revolted against Mathers, who had "issued a manifesto to the T.A.M. (inner) members, demanding personal allegiance to him … and this manifesto was greatly resented by the senior members in London." A meeting was held, and he was deposed. In an interesting document, printed in London during this revolt, Mathers is described as 'the Earl of Glenstrae, otherwise Count MacGregor,' and his emissary, who was sent from Paris to take possession, in Mathers' name, of the London Temple and property, variously known as "E. A. Crowley, Aleister MacGregor, Count Svareff ... arrived in Highland dress, a black mask over his face, and a plaid thrown over his head and shoulders, an enormous gold or gilt cross upon his breast, and a dagger at his side!" Needless to say, the bluff was called, and after some trouble Crowley was removed and expelled. During this revolt we find Mathers writing to the "rebels," April 2, 1900:

> "I therefore know ... when the Great Adepts of this Planet, still in the body of the flesh, the Secret Chiefs of our Order are with me ... and I tell you plainly that were it *possible* to remove me from my place as Visible Head of our Order—the which cannot be without my consent, because of certain magical links—you would find nothing but disruption and trouble fall upon you all until you had expiated so severe a Karma as that of opposing a current sent at the end of a century to regenerate a Planet. And for the first time since I have been connected with the Order I shall formulate my request to the Highest Chiefs for *the Punitive current* to be prepared to be directed against those who rebel, should they consider it advisable."

Again, in 1902 Dr. Felkin and the chief of the Edinburgh Temple "Amen Ra," were contacting this Third Order through the "Sun Masters." Now these were the hidden masters of a Sun Order, still, we are told, in existence, and to which these chiefs belonged, closely connected with and influencing the "Golden Dawn," and which was started in Edinburgh some time in the early nineties. We are told in the history that after the revolt of 1900, "it was then decided that the Order should be ruled by a committee of ten. This went on for a year, but was not very satisfactory, and then it was decided to revert to the rule of three chiefs, and Fratres L.O., F.R. (Dr. Felkin), and S.S. (Edinburgh), were appointed chiefs (May 3, 1902)." On May 28, 1902, we find Dr. Felkin saying:

"We beg to assure you that we are in entire sympathy with the view that if in fact the Order is without the guidance and inspiration of higher intelligences its rationale is gone. It occurred, however, to certain members that it might be possible, by reverting to the original constitution, to re-establish a link with the Third Order. There are now tangible grounds for believing that this step has not been taken in vain, and while we, as nominal chiefs, will not lightly yield allegiance to any force, power or being purporting to act as the Third Order, the prospects seem to us sufficiently encouraging to warrant our own continued activity in the Order, and also we suggest your co-operation."

These masters controlled and directed both Outer and Inner Order in this way until at least 1911-13—this included instructions concerning rituals and Temple regulations, and even their attitude to Waite, who bad seceded from them.

In 1909 a pledge was demanded, and was to be signed before these masters would give the chiefs further and higher teachings; it pledged them to absolute belief in messages, teachings, and rituals given by these unknown beings, and said:

"Frater F.R. (Dr. Felkin) — Thy communication has been submitted to the inner and secret Chiefs who rule the Order of the R.R. et A.C., and in reply they say — the communications with the Third Order (secret) are resumed, but only through the present means, and you are to take a pledge by all that you hold most awful and sacred never to betray that means to mortal man... There has always been some connecting link between the Second and Third Orders in every Temple receiving teaching, through which such teaching is given... One member of our Council, being also an adept of the Third Order of the RR et A.C., believing that in the Temple of Amoun there were serious students, full of faith and anxious for progress, was willing to act as intermediary, and to allow communications and teachings to pass. Thou must understand that this is the way permitted, and that there is no other... A small and faithful band is far more powerful than a large body divided against itself.

Therefore be of good courage ... if the following pledge ... be written out and signed by each member of the Order entitled and desirous to receive further teachings in the R.R. et A.C., the Adept I have mentioned will crave leave to reopen communications: 'I declare, in the presence and in the name of all I hold most awful and sacred, that I fully believe in the genuineness of the messages and communications, the teachings and the rituals of the Order of the ... That I know not, neither will I seek to know, how the same are transmitted or received, but I will receive them without question from their appointed medium, and that if hereafter I am assailed by doubt, I will reveal such doubt only to the Masters. I will in no case ever attempt, directly or indirectly, to destroy or weaken the faith of any other, but on the contrary will attempt to remove doubts and confirm faith. I will neither bring, nor will. I listen to any accusations or any imputations of bad faith, against any one of my brothers or sisters of the Order, but I will reprove any who shall attempt to do so in my hearing and recall to them their pledge of brotherhood. And if in the past I have ever transgressed against the pledge, I promise that to the best of my ability. I will make reparation... And this shall apply also to all communications from the Third Order of the R.R. et A.C. which may be vouched by the Masters of the (Sun) Order through their appointed medium. Finally, should I at any time find myself unable any longer to keep this pledge, I will say nothing to my brothers and sisters of the Order to weaken their faith, but I will quietly pass into abeyance'."

That this was taken and signed we have reason to believe, for the above Chief writes, April II, 1911:

"So far I have kept perfect faith with the Masters and acted on their advice."

Here is another curious and interesting communication received from this Third Order by Dr. Felkin:

Ordo R.R. et A.C.

"The Inner and Secret Chiefs of the Third Order, unto the V. H. Frater F. R. Imperator of Amoun Temple, greeting.

"Hereby by the hand of Q.M. our scribe, we sanction and approve for general use the 5–6 ritual sent for approval, and which we herewith return. Delay in sanctioning this was unavoidable, as no word or letter or symbol of any ritual may lawfully by the constitution of the Order be altered after being once sanctioned, save by the consent of a council of the Third Order, which only meets occasionally, or under powers conferred by them on certain adepets. Yet shall ye not discard altogether the ritual preyiously in use, but shall retain the same and the copies thereof which ye have, for reference and for use on special occasions if so ordered, but ye need make no new copies.

"The password for the ensuing six months shall be Osiris Onophris-Osiris the Justified one, signifying that your zeal and the progress of your Temple have found favour with the Inner Chiefs of the Third Order, and that hereby ye are justified and signifying also that your hopes and trust must be in him whom the Lord of the Universe (I.A.O. — the Creative Principle) hath justified by whatsoever name men call him. Fare thee well."

Further, the following shows how unsuspecting adepts are controlled and used by these Masters, May 19, 1902:

"In coming to thee he came not of his own initiative, but in obedience to an impulse from the Chiefs of the Third Order, who desired to use his aura as a vehicle for testing and examining thee. But this was wholly unknown to him who was used unconsciously."

About 1908 suddenly another astral teacher appeared, an Arab-Ara Ben Shemesh; he said, on January 26, 1909, that he came

"from "The Temple in the Desert," and those who live there are the "Sons of Fire." There are three ranks — *Neophytes or*

Catechumens; the Accepted and *Proven*; and the *Indwellers.*
The last are those we call Masters. They live in personal
communion with the Divine (deified), and being no longer
bound in the flesh (liberated) their material life is entirely a
matter of will. So long as they are required as teachers, so
long may they continue to inhabit the earthly tabernacle.
When they have completed their task they have only to cease
to will and they will dematerialise. Christian Rosenkreutz
came to us and learnt much. From us he took the letters C.R.,
the true interpretation is one of the great mysteries of the
Universe."

The Temple he said was in the Near East—Mesopotamia!—and
he professed to be a personal teacher of the Felkins, but gradually
and insidiously he dominated and controlled the Order, and not
only in England but in New Zealand prepared the Order and
members for the part they were expected to play in the drama of
this Great World Movement, which he said was to bring about
the "Union of the East and the West." Towards the end of 1918
this work was accomplished to his satisfaction in New Zealand,
but new teaching, he said, would be given to the London Temple,
Amoun, which they would find difficult to assimilate. Then in
1917-19 the Lord of Light — the cabalistic "Prince of
Countenances," the transmitter of light — and his Twelve
Brethren made their attempt to take possession and control this
Temple through a Triangle of adepts as will be explained later.

Further, Christian Rosenkreutz, the mystical and perhaps wholly
mythical Head of the Rosicrucians, was said to be contacted in
the Vault of the R.R. et A.C., and it was also said that he was to
reincarnate about 1926-33 by possessing himself of some adult
body-suspiciously like obsession; lastly, we find these masters
impersonating a Christ (solar) with Cross of Light and Red Roses
— a symbol of what is expected of all adepts thus controlled —
crucifixion through suffering and absolute sacrifice of their own
individuality, upon the Cross of Illuminism — a veritable
Christian Rosenkreutz!

To return to Dr. Felkin and the history of his chiefship. Later he became dissatisfied with the status of the Order, and he tells us in his history that in his travels in Germany he made many efforts to contact Rosicrucians, and

> "... finally met a professor, his adopted daughter, and another gentleman near Hanover, who he believed were undoubtedly Rosicrucians. They were, however, very secretive, and averse to giving much information, because they said that although they knew him as a scientific man, he was not a Mason, nor did he belong to any occult society that they had knowledge of. Owing to his, Frater F.R. immediately applied to his old friend ... of Edinburgh, and was initiated as a Freemason in Mary's Chapel, Edinburgh Lodge, No. I., on January 8, 1907.

> "In 1908 Frater F.R. with Soror Q.L (his wife) at last got into touch ... with several members of the Third Order in Germany."

Yet as we have seen previously, Dr. Felkin apparently signed a pledge in 1909, given to the mysterious astral Third Order! Again:

> "In June and July 1912 Frater F. R. and Soror Q. L. were able to go to Germany, and altogether visited five Rosicrucian Temples in different parts of the Continent, and were initiated themselves, Soror Q. L. obtaining grades equivalent to our 7-4 and Frater F. R. 8-3... The rituals not being in MS. form, they are memorised."

They brought back notes of these ceremonies 6-5 to 8-3, and elaborated them, using for this purpose the Egyptian "Book of the Dead," some extracts from Mabel Collins's writings, also the "Hymn of Hermes," and a mantra — a compelling force — given to them by the Arab of "The Temple in the Desert," and these became the Higher Grades of the R.R. et A.C.! These, as they advanced in grade, are more and more given on the astral plane by the hidden chiefs, while the adept is in a trance or semi-trance condition, brought on by the preparation and opening ceremony, or by these hidden chiefs themselves. The last grade, 10-1, is never given on the material plane, but wholly on the astral; the adept is in trance and completely under hypnotic control, and from then onwards is merely the oracle and vehicle of these Masters! It is Illuminism!

The history continues:

> "But an arrangement has been come to whereby anyone conversant with German, French, Italian or Dutch, who is full 5–6, may be sent abroad with an introduction signed by F.R., and should it be considered that a candidate is sufficiently developed, one or more grades may be given him. This is not essential, as, if the new methods are carefully introduced into our curriculum (psychic processes leading to Illuminism), the candidates will progress just as well without the necessity of going abroad."

It is known that some members of the R.R. et A.C. have had training and grades under Steiner, and some Steinerites have been members of the R.R. et A.C. Again, the history says: 'F.R. was given the commission to represent the Order (Continental) in Great Britain and Ireland, and also in the Southern Hemisphere.'

Dr. Steiner was questioned, March 1921, and report said:

> "Dr. Felkin was anxious to get a charter from Dr. Steiner, and made many attempts to gain this and be appointed his sole representative in England. Dr. Steiner, in a letter to Dr. Felkin, of which I (our informant) was the bearer and which I read, said he was unable to grant his request, for though ready to admit that Dr. Felkin's Order was beneficial and useful, his way of working was quite different... Dr. Felkin was a spectator at one of Dr. Steiner's ceremonies in Munich. No grades were given him by Dr. Steiner, no grades given him in Munich, but Dr. Steiner gave Dr. Felkin a great deal of instruction, such as he gives to other pupils who desire it."

Further, his Arab teacher said to Dr. Felkin:

> "Go on with Steiner, which is not the ultimate end of search,

and we will come in contact with many serious students who will lead us to the real Master of the Order, who will be so overpoweringly impressive as to leave no room for doubt."

In 1914 Dr. and Mrs. Felkin got as far as Pyrmont in Hanover, meaning again to get in touch and receive further grades and instructions, but the War intervened, and they were forced to return to England about the end of August. It was mainly due, we believe, to the help given to him by the Masons in Hanover and Amsterdam that he and Q.L. at last got out of Germany. When they questioned their astral teacher, the Arab, August 9, he "repeated our work is not yet over, and until it is we are safe… Sorry this has happened now, it *was not expected till some months later*." The scheme did not apparently work out to date!

June 9, 1918, F.R. writes:

> "From what I was told abroad I was under the impression … that a few, I was told TWELVE, were to be picked out of all the Temples to be trained to be ready to help C.R.C. when he again manifested in about 1926-33 or 35. The whole of that was to have been told me face to face in 1914 when we went to Germany. We had the tickets then which took us to a place S.S.E. of Austria, where we were to have been met and taken to the Old Vault, and also to have met several Hidden Chiefs. Why we were not told to go earlier in the year is a mystery, as we could have done so had we been told. They knew when we proposed to go."

The War "was not expected" so soon! In his "Suggestions" for the future working of the Order, Dr. Felkin said in 1916:

> "In addition to C.R.C. (Christian Rosenkreutz), there are certain members who still function on the material plane; most of them live very secluded lives (all of the grade equal to 9-2 are said to retire from the world!), and can only be met with after much difficulty has been overcome… Q.L. and myself have also met them at various times, and received instructions and help"

In reading the above we must realise that Dr. Felkin was a mere tool in the hands of some subversive men, who would inform him as they saw fit for their game.

What then is the truth about this mysterious Third Order, and Dr. Felkin's claim to "sole German authority?"

There is ample evidence to show that the Stella Matutina and the R.R. et A.C. are, constitutionally, in no way akin to British Masonry, but are linked up with Continental Masons and Rosicrucians — subtly and secretly subversive and controlled by these "Unknown Chiefs," *all still* "functioning on the material plane."

To continue Dr. Felkin's history:

> "... The methods which (S.D.A ., c/o) Fräulein Anna Sprengel, sanctioned were (said by these Germans to be) totally against the methods which were and always had been in vogue in Germany, and it may be mentioned now that the first three grades were very much like the first three grades in ordinary Masonry (yet Steiner approved of them as useful!), and, as a matter of fact, up to a date which cannot be given accurately, Masonry and Rosicrucianism went hand in hand. It was about 1597 that the Masons separated themselves entirely from the Rosicrucians, and decided to modify their procedure, and they refused in future to admit women to their ceremonies. This was partly due to political circumstances, as both Masons and Rosicrucians tried to influence the political development of the nations amongst whom they lived and worked... Practically the Masonic Lodges became very active political agencies, whereas the Rosicrucian branches were more secret in their operations, and it was, and is, an absolute rule that no one should confess to being a Rosicrucian. So strict was this that Rosicrucians who even knew one another were not allowed to speak or discuss matters connected with their society within the confines of a city or town. There were definite rules as to when a member of the Fraternity went to a new place and met a Frater or Soror.

They appointed a time to meet outside the town or city with reference to certain points of the compass. It is quite true that on several occasions leakages of MSS. did occur. One was due to the action of a certain number of Roman Catholic priests who belonged to the Order; and again in 1777 a leakage of rituals took place in Paris, and this made our Continental Fratres and Sorores still more strict in their methods... F.R. had received the promise that the Council would investigate the condition of the Branch of the Order in London with which he was connected, and would if possible enter into definite relations with him... A definite arrangement was then come to between E.O.L. (of whom more later) on behalf of F.R., and the heads of the Rosicrucian Society in Germany, that he should bring over the necessary 'processes,' for psychic development to F.R., who is alone permitted to transmit them (to his members for the purpose of arousing the Kundalini and bringing about Illuminism)."

In 1916 we find the Chief of Amen Ra, Edinburgh, writing to Dr. Felkin of this claimed German connection:

"Whatever was the origin of the rituals and the teachings (Stella Matutina and R.R. et A.C.), they indubitably came to us from Mathers, he being, as I know for certain, the intermediary of Higher Authorities (Hidden Chiefs)... Your Temple pursues, and still pursues, this up to a certain point — when you come in contact with the Germans. Then came the pledge (demanded by these Germans, not to work with Mathers!), the effect of which was, to use all Mathers' work and to repudiate him, also to assert that further teaching and help were to be had on other lines ... given to members picked out seemingly, as a reward for accepting the German position, all the time, as I say, using and basing on Mathers' work. This again could emanate from nothing but German sources ... the honest course would be to leave behind all the rituals and teachings, and begin de *novo* on the superior system."

Again, another member writes to Dr. Felkin with regard to the above:

"You cannot, of course, accept his proposition, because you have accepted *sole authority* from Germany, but this he does not know!"

Notwithstanding this claim of "sole authority" from Germany, Dr. Felkin became sadly in need of further advanced teaching for his adepts, who were clamouring for it; and having apparently received little or none from his German connection, he wrote in 1913 to the Chief of Amen Ra in Edinburgh, seeking to draw from his well of hidden knowledge. In reply this Chief wrote:

> "To me it matters little personally: I have stacks of MSS. and teachings going to far further lengths than I used to think possible... All the teaching I have got I will gladly pass on to you on the same conditions as I have received it ... I received the MSS. as Deputy Archon Basileus in this country. (August 5, 1913). My commission as such comes from the Third Order—or not to make any ambiguity of these words from those Higher Adepts whom I so term—and I can pass them on to such as acknowledge my authority and position. This of course involves also recognition of Mathers, who has committed his authority to me."

In spite of the above pledge not to work with Mathers or any of his followers, certain of these MSS. became the 6-5 teaching under Dr. Felkin.

The following letter, written to a German member by the above adept E.O.L., who was for a time trained by the German connection, is interesting, in that it shows the proposed method for the penetration of England and British Freemasonry by Continental and Grand Orient Illuminism, 1912.

> "DEAR SIR AND BROTHER (Baron C.A.W.),—
>
> "I have heard from Dr. F—of the proposed International Bund, which seems in many ways an excellent scheme to which I wish every success. As. Dr. S-'s name is so potent on the Continent, it is bound to prosper there. In England he has

a band of admirers, but his name is not so generally known. The conditions in England are also peculiar. Dr. S. himself said to me that he recognised the difference. Therefore, I write to you, for we have a double tie — the Rosicrucian Fraternity both of the Continent and in England, we can speak freely. What I say now I wish to be laid before Dr. S. by you, and the risk is mine. For if do not speak without fear or favour, no one else can.

"Dr. S. is a statesman in his schemes (?). But a statesman, when inquiring into the conditions of a country unknown to him, does not go only to the members of one party of it. For Austrian politics one would not consult only Magyars, nor for German, members only of the Catholic Block. In England the few members of the Continental Order are all Theosophists, i.e. members of the T.S. They are none of them members of the English Freemasons. They see things from the T.S. point of view, and they have to use their spectacles. I am the only member of the Continental Order who is not and never has been a T.S. member; I owe no allegiance to Mrs. Besant. I am, as the Doctor knows, entirely with him in the policy of abandoning Oriental and Indian for European or Kabalistic training; I am also an English Freemason, so that I can give him the point of view of the other parties.

"English occultism is roughly divided into (I) members of the T.S., i.e. Mrs. Besant's followers headed by the co-Masons in one sense; (2) members of the Hermetic Orders and Freemasons; (3) Independents, whether in small groups or individuals.

"The first class is the only one really known to the Doctor. Of the second Dr. F. is very representative. Of the third, Mr. T. P.... Now when the Doctor comes to establish his BUND, there are certain considerations of great importance. With regard to Group I, the T.S. and its branches, I cannot pretend to say what will happen. Mr. S. and Mr. C. both know the T.S. people and its style of work — by lecture, etc. The risk, however, is with regard to Groups 2 and 3. The BUND will, unless carefully managed, be regarded merely as a schism of the T.S. It will command as much attention as the Quest Society of G. R S. Mead, and it may arouse great prejudice, for many will take it exactly in the spirit in which England took the German telegram to President Krüger. I am quite serious when I say that to many the BUND will be thus considered — 'We don't care for Mrs. Besant any more than we cared for Jamieson and his raid, but after all, Mrs. Besant is English; who are these Germans to interfere?' It may sound ridiculous, but I know my country.

"The next point, a very serious one indeed, is the attitude of the Freemasons. This must be taken into consideration. Here for a moment I must apparently digress. I wish to contrast the working of Groups I, 2, and 3. Group I works on the familiar lines of lectures, magazine publications, etc. Dr. S. does much the same. Group I attracts a large number of idle women who have the leisure to take a little occultism with their afternoon tea, practically all the members are people with time and money. It attracts numbers, but each lecturer is apt to get a personal following, hence schisms, i.e. the Quest.

"Group 2 is small in numbers. It works by Lodges and circulates manuscripts. Its teaching is done by correspondence, by individual officers, etc. It seldom has lectures. It taps a wholly different class, gets at more varied social strata, has a far larger proportion of men. Being highly organised it has more coherence; at the same time each Temple is apt to be jealous of outside interferences. Most of its men are Freemasons. Some entire Temples are·Freemasonic, e.g. the Societas Rosicruciana in Anglia. Now these people are busy, there are singularly few idle, moneyed or leisured women and men among them, they are very proud and independent. In course of time, if they can get teaching in their own manner, by MSS. in circulation, by visits of members from Lodge to Lodge, by or through their own Chiefs, I am certain they will all, given time, join your BUND. But they will not accept any T.S. dictation, they will not tolerate Chiefs whom they do not know, they will not care for attending cycles or lectures for which they have no time or inclination These bodies are older than the T.S.and they do not forget it. Humoured they will help you. If they are not considered, they will neither oppose nor regard you. They will simply leave the BUND alone exactly as they leave the T.S. alone, the co-Masons alone, etc. *They must be got at from within, not from without.*

"The third group I can assist with in course of time. But how they will act now I do not pretend to know. Most of them will accept no authority over them. Now I come to the Freemasonic point.

"Here I tread on very delicate ground. But I feel that I must state the case, as I said, without fear or favour. The Doctor is too great a man to be vexed with me. After all, all I wish to do is to secure that the best teaching reaches those most fit for it in the easiest way.

"At present to establish a definite branch of the Continental Order giving grades, etc, in England will be a very difficult matter. You are not yourself a Freemason. We sometimes call our Order, the Continental Order, *Esoteric Masonry*. The grades are closely akin to Freemasonry. Dr. S indeed has some link with certain English or Scotch Masons—he gave me the name—from whom he derives a certain authority, a link in the physical (not etheric!).

Now English Freemasonry is not occult, though it has occult Lodges, and most English occultists not T.S. are Freemasons, if men. English Masonry boasts the Grand Lodge of 1717, the Mother Lodge of the world. They are a proud, jealous, autocratic body. Co-Masonry derives from the Grand Orient of France, an illegitimate body according to English ruling. No English Mason can work with co-Masons. Now the Masons who gave Dr. S. his link are regarded — you had better get Dr. F. to verify me here — as eccentrics who invent spurious grades. If the English Grand Lodge hears of anything called 'Esoteric Masonry,' derived from such sources, under Chiefs once T.S. members, under a head in Berlin, it will not inquire who Dr. S. is or what is the nature of his work; it will simply say 'no English Masons of the Free and Accepted Masons may join any society working pseudo-Masonic Rites,' i.e. no one of ordinary accepted Freemasonry can attend any meetings or take any grades in this illegitimate body! Finis!

"Then we who are members of Dr. S.'s Lodge and who are Freemasons will be in a sad plight At present this would affect only myself, well, and Dr. F. too. But if esoteric Masonry is breathed of in England, and the fiat goes against it, no English Mason will wish to join the BUND. [*Note by Dr. Felkin:* 'This is what has already happened with the "Ancient Masons" (mixed), to whom many regular Masons would be perfectly friendly personally but are precluded by their oath.']

"After all this cold water, you will ask what useful suggestion do I imagine I have to make. Well, perhaps nothing very useful. Still, this is my practical suggestion. Let the Bund be started. Let Messrs. S. and C. get all the MSS. they can, and let them establish relations with the bodies in Group 2. Either let them supply such written teaching as can be given to the heads of the Lodges that will come in, and seek no interference with the Lodges, or let them form a definite committee under Dr. S. with representative people in it. All this must be done slowly.

"The system of having people in the Lodges like Dr. F. to teach 'processes' (see above in Dr. Felkin's History) within Group 2 is the most practical, and to have BUND officials like Messrs. S. and C., one of whom should join an English Lodge, to go between England and the Continent, and to get the written teaching will probably work well enough.

"But if a Lodge of the Continental Order is to be established in England, Dr. S. will be faced with the Masonic difficulty. This is really serious, and no one of the T.S. will understand it, nor even any Continental Freemasons. Look at my position and again at Dr. F.'s-if we were banned from all association with Freemasons, i.e. from practically all Lodges in Group 2, or else from association with the BUND. Either we must be cut off again, or our usefulness for general purposes is gone.

If Dr. S. would summon one or two non-Theosophical persons to discuss with him, he would see this at once. The practical solution will be found in a compromise. If he avoids the name 'Esoteric Masonry' and allows perhaps a ritual like those used in the Societas Rosicruciana or in the S.M., and has for officers in England a mixed group, including the Heads of the chief Hermetic Lodges, etc. — as well as T.S. people, who will join anything of Dr. S.'s — it will succeed. Otherwise, I fear much that only a few T.S. people and a few whom Dr. F. and myself … can influence directly, will be all that will join at the outset. As a Theosophist schism, and a foreign intrusive Masonic schism, the BUND will arouse every possible English prejudice against it. Devoted to the Doctor as we are, we should both regret it.

'Yours fraternally."

Mrs. Nesta Webster, in her *Secret Societies* and *Subversive Movements*, writes of a Masonic Congress held in Geneva in September 1902, at which a proposal was unanimously adopted, "tending towards the creation of an International Bureau of Masonic Affairs"; and Brother Desmons, of the Grand Orient of France declared that the "dream of his life" had always been that "all democracies should meet and understand one another in such a way as one day to form the Universal Republic."

Again she quotes Lord Ampthill as pro-Grand Master of the British Freemasons, March 2, 1921 in answer to an invitation to British Masons to attend an International Masonic Congress in Geneva; he said:

"A further consequence of certain happenings of the War is to make more firm our resolve to keep, as far as in us lies, Freemasonry strictly away from participation in politics, either national or international… For these reasons, the invitation to participate in the proposed International Conference of Freemasons at Geneva cannot be accepted … we cannot detract from full recognition of the Great Architect of the Universe, and we shall continue to forbid the introduction of political discussion into our Lodges."

Under this new Continental authority Dr. Felkin, in 1916, before finally going out to New Zealand, drew up a "New Constitution," duly and astrally approved of by thee hidden chiefs, and under this Constitution attempted—to establish three daughter temples in England, hoping in this way to link Yarious outside esoteric Masonic groups under the shadow of the Srella Matutina, thus helping forward the "International Bund."

In this New Constitution Dr. Felkin says:

"As you are aware, I can personally permit any branch Rosicrucian Societies to be started. But as I am leaving England, I naturally feel that such branches should be in close relationship with the Stella Matutina and the R.R et A.C. I propose, before leaving England, to form three such branches, and it will rest with you to make any arrangements which you may wish with regard to their utilising your rooms, etc., or not... The two I propose to form in London could either pay you a yearly sum for the use of the Temple and Vault, on a definite day to be settled by you, or you might arrange for them to pay half their initiation fees to you, which should be, I think, the Mother Temple. With regard to a Branch in Bristol, which I am going to form, they can at present work their Outer entirely there, and make arrangements with you when they have any candidates for the Inner.

"The conditions under wich I should found these three branches are as follows:

"I. Each Branch must be absolutely autonomous and ruled by three Chiefs who are at the present time full 5–6 in the R.R. et A.C., and they must follow exactly the traditions of our Order.

"2. The first three Chiefs I should appoint myself; if any one of them should relinquish office, the Ruling Chiefs and Three Adepti of the Mother Temple (Amoun) should confer with the remaining two Chiefs as to the appointment of a successor.

"3. The Daughter Temples must finance their own Temples, and the Mother Temple is not responsible for their finance in any way, except in so far as above stated; they should pay dues in some form if they make use of the Mother Temple's rooms.

"4. The Members of the Daughter Temples who are full 5–6 will belong to the College of Adepti of the R.R. et A.C. in Anglia…

"5. With regard to the Bristol Branch (Hermes), the first Three Chiefs will be: V. H. Sorores Lux Orta est, Magna est Veritas, Benedicamus Deo, the latter only acting until a Frater in that district is qualified.

"6. The first London Daughter Temple will be confined to members of the Societas Rosicruciana in Anglia, who have taken at least Grade 4. I may mention here that the reason why I am obliged to form it is as follows: When E.O.L. and I made our arrangements for recognition by our Continental Fratres, they stipulated, and he agreed, that the Masonic Rosicrucians, of whom there are large numbers, should be given the opportunity of being linked up with us. The first Three Chiefs of this Temple will be: V. H. Fratres Pro Rege et Patria, Fortes Fortuna Juvat, Faire sans dire.

"With regard to the third Daughter Temple (Merlin), there are some fifty or sixty members of the Temple (Golden Dawn) which used to be ruled by S.R. (Waite) and a number of the members of the Anthroposophical Society who are seeking admission. It has been pointed out to me, that as these people have worked on different lines from us, it would not be well to admit them to the S.M., as they would undoubtedly cause confusion in the S.M. Temple. I therefore propose that they should form a Temple of their own, and that the first Three Chiefs should be:V.H. Fratres Cephas, Benedic Animo mea Domino, and Non Sine Numine. This Frater you do not know, but he has been a member of the Society for twenty-five years, is full T.A.M., and was for many years one of S.R.'s three Ruling Chieis.

"7. The first three ruling chiefs of the Daughter Temples would become the first three adepti in their respective Vaults should they have them.

"I take full responsibility for the formation of these three Daughter Temples, and it rests with you to do all in your power to help them to be an added power to the Rosicrucian Movement.

"Our password for the present six months is ACHAD, signifying 'Unity,' and it is my great desire that all the scattered Rosicrucian Forces within our reach should be gathered together into a harmonious whole instead of drifting off into comparative uselessness, or into undesirable channels.

"(*Signed*) FINEM RESPICE CHIEF, June 18, 1916."

Having therefore formed and launched his Master's subversive petard, Dr. Felkin, in the middle of the War, took his departure to the comparatively calm atmosphere of New Zealand, and left his more or less untried trio of Ruling Chiefs to handle these fiery elements and face as best they could the inevitable explosions. As might be looked for, it has left its trail of tragedies and suffering. Of these Three Daughter Temples, the only one to survive is the Hermes Temple of Bristol, which was, and no doubt is, much under the influence of Dr. Rudolph Steiner's subversive and pantheistic teaching.

That the Steinerites still dream of some such "International Bund" is quite apparent from their *Anthroposophy·*, Easter 1929, in which it is said: "This leads to all manner of 'movements' beneath which the real longings are concealed. Yet will men enter more and more into the goals which Rudolph Steiner revealed, and they will thus become his followers." And this dream — spiritual, political, and economic — is the dream of the Grand Orient Judaeo Masonry.

Further, Dr. Felkin's Arab teacher, January 9, 1915, gives the following interesting instruction:

> "The alternative training for those whom we were speaking of should be definitely fixed now and put on the same footing as the Daughter Temples, as a special group for healing. It should be called the Healers or Therapeuts, and Father F. should be made specially and definitely the head of it, and those who wish to follow that training should be taken from all the different Temples and kept in touch with one another."

Has this not eventuated in the Stella Matutina Healing Guild of St. Raphael, which is therefore Continental and International Masonry?

After the London Chiefs had closed down the Temple in 1919, Dr. Felkin wrote: "I have time and time again written that A.B.S., the Arab, has nothing to do with the Order." Yet as far back as June 9, 1912, we find this Arab instructing Dr. Felkin, Q. L. and Q.A. in the London Vault:

> "*Re* New Zealand, we will have an opportunity such as has not occurred in thousands of years in going to an entirely new and clear atmosphere which will leave us free to form fresh symbols unprejudiced by any previous tradition. It is most important that everything should be new and clean and fresh; as far as possible we must try to discard recent errors and get the more accurate symbolism.

> "Select a few people to devote themselves entirely to occult work, including healing, and others to see to the material needs of the few, to live together equal numbers in a divided sort of monastery; others can go and stay for periods. Must always have a guest-chamber and a sort of special healing wing.

> "Everything we take must be carefully purified, consecrated, and wrapped in white. Will have to look after it for a considerable time. It will develop along independent lines to

a great extent. Name of Temple: "Emerald of the Sea No. 49-Smaragdine Thalasses."

"The new venture is much more important (than London)... He is greatly impressed with the importance of virgin soil, no occult order has been there before, Theosophists only breaking the soil."

Again, July 15, 1919, one of the New Zealand Chiefs wrote "to the Ruling Chiefs in Anglia":

"For nearly six years A. B. S. taught us regularly, meeting us every week. His teaching we found most helpful and his advice sound... You can understand that we had a difficult time after the Order was first founded in New Zealand. I consider that the help of A.B.S. and the fact that we had a balanced and united group at the centre, enabled us to keep going..."

As the "Hidden and Secret Chiefs" said to Dr. Felkin in 1909:

"A small and faithful band is far more powerful than a large body divided against itself!"

The following instructions, received in 1914 by Dr. Felkin from this Arab, are significant of the work required of the Order:

"Our function is to direct the new life which will spring up when present disturbances have cleared the ground; it is as if a giant harrow were passing over the face of the world, and when that is done those like us (Illuminati) must be ready to *sow the seed*. This war was an inevitable means of destroying the old order of things to make room for the new; that already the ideas of peace and unity (pacifism or apathy and Universal Brotherhood) have been implanted, but they could not spread freely until the old had been broken asunder. It is the 'Tower struck by Lightning' — the 'Rending Asunder of the Veil.' "

This, according to Papus and other Cabalists, means fixation of the astral light in a material basis-individual and universal Illuminism.

The instructions continue:

> "Vitality is being forced into action just now, and the reaction will be complete depletion unless those who are not actually taking part in the conflict *store up a power to be set free as soon as the conflict ceases.* Not only our own group, but all those we know of should be instructed to devote themselves to this aim. The means towards this end are found in meditation and prayer… In meditation, contemplation, and ecstasy the human spirit seeks to free itself from earth and rise to the greatest heights of which it is capable (As in Steiner's *Way of Initiation!*) … but the human brain is like the transmitter of a wireless station, its machinery is limited, yet it can send out a vibration which continues to echo through space until it finds its corresponding receiver, and for every aspiration there is a reply… And prayer is also an invocation; it not only brings you into communion with that which you pray to, it also awakens and formulates forces which were previously latent (as in the Liberal Catholic Mass). A man praying to the devil enters into the communion of evil, but he also formulates the evil forces which react upon all those who are not positively in search of the good. For you must never forget that any force which can be contacted through such prayer is not only a negative receiver but also a positive transmitter which sends out its currents and vibrations to all those who are capable of receiving them. (In tune with them)."

It goes on to say that by forming a circle seeking this *peace and light*, they contact not only these nvisible supreme controlling beings who govern the world, but also open up very powerful channels through which these beings can pour down their influences and suggestions — beneficent they are called!

The above is apparently an example of "Reciprocal Influences between the Visible and Invisible Worlds" the Unknown

Supreme Committee spoken of by Wronski in his *Mysticism and Magic*. The R.R. et A.C. is Illuminism and Rosicrucian, linked to the Grand Orient Freemasonry, and the wonderful work of the Rosicrucians was to begin in Russia, but where is the "Peace and Light"?

The above savours much of Weishaupt's methods of camouflage!

> "... The greatest caution must be exercised not to reveal to the novice doctrines that might be likely to revolt him. For this purpose the initiators must acquire the habit of 'talking backwards and forwards' so as not to commit themselves. 'One must speak,' Weishaupt explained to the superiors of the Order. 'sometimes in one way, sometimes in another, so that our real purpose should remain impenetrable to our inferiors.'"

There are three forms of initiation — individual, group, or universal — all three leading to conscious or unconscious control by a central power, who in some mysterious way makes its influence felt; often clairvoyantly and clairaudiently seen and heard, but *never* physically present or visible. The system in all three is the same — cabalistic. Secretly here and there individuals are prepared; these again form groups or centres from which influences spread until they form a veritable magnetic network covering the entire world. Like rays from a hidden sun these groups are apparently divergent and detached, but in reality all issue from the same central body. Studying all these different groups and movements the system is seen to be an insidious and secret dissemination of ideas, orienting and creating the required outlook on life, etc., eventually breaking down all barriers of family, religion, morality, nationality, and all self-initiative thought, always under the cloak of a new and more modern religion, new thought; new morality, a new heaven and a new earth; until it evolves a gigantic robot merely answering to the will and commands of a secret Master Mind. They dream they are free, original, self-determining individuals; they are but the negative moon reflecting and reproducing the light from the same hidden and cabalistic Sun. It is called *regeneration* by the Illuminati; it is in truth individual death and disintegration, followed by a resurrection as negative "light-bearers" of this cabalistic Sun. As is said "in the 6-5 grade of the R.R. et A.C.: "Arise, shine, for thy light hath come and the glory of thy Lord is upon thee." The light and glory of the cabalistic Sun! Illuminism!

In the July occult issue 1929 of the *Revue Internationale des Sociétés Secrètes*, there is an interesting and rare design called, 'The Dragon and the Woman,' which depicts apparently the Pentagram of illuminised and revolutionary Masonry, a symbol of the magical and potent powers by which the mysterious centre would hope to obtain empire over the universe and thus govern men. The lower part is the Dragon of the Apocalypse with the seven heads; written across its body is the word 'Kabalah,' as also in Hebrew, "Schem Hamphoras" and "Yod, He, Vau, He"—the Tetragrammaton. The Schem Hamphoras, the cabalistic Keys of Solomon, the keys of universal science, by whose combinations all secrets of Nature are said to be revealed. The four letters, the material basis as it were, are the four beasts of Ezekiel's vision; they are the Sphinx with the head of a man, the body of a bull, the wings of an eagle, and the claws of a lion. Also the four properties of the astral light or Serpent Fire-dissolving, coagulating, heating, and cooling — which, directed by the will, are said to modify all nature, producing life or death, health or disease, etc., in accordance with the given impulsion. Further, it is the cross of life or generation—the Kundalini.

Death and disintegration must precede so-called regeneration; therefore the tail of the Dragon ends with the head of the vulture of Saturn, the destroyer, who holds in his beak the magical sword of the adept with the dual crescents of unity on the hilt; this is thrust into the body of the Dragon, for the blood must be poured out. Beneath the Dragon the fire burns, it must be immolated, as the Phoenix of old, so that from the ashes it may rise renewed and regenerated. As Rabaud Saint-Etienne has said: "Everything, yes everything must be destroyed, since everything must be remade"—it is revolution. The number of the beast is 666, which cabalistically is 9, the number of generation. The seven heads represent the seven planets or powers of the Sun or colours of the prism; cabalistically they are placed on the Interlaced Triangle, the dual creative forces, each angle having a planet with the Sun in their midst. Together they represent complete magical power—the Hebrew Talisman, the Shield of David!

Above this basis rises the woman BABALON, the mother of all pantheistic and abominable cults. She stands in the hermetic attitude, "as above so below," her left hand raised above holds a lighted torch shaped as the Hebrew letter Shin; this letter, together with the Tetragrammaton below, forms the Pentagram-the "Christ" or instrument of illuminised revolutionary Masonry. On the torch is this curious inscription, as deciphered by M. Henri Guillebert: "As for the children, kill them in great numbers. Holy, holy, holy is the act of immolating them, as also of exterminating them." Is this not Saturn again, who ever devours his own children — revolution and anarchy? Across her breast is written "Democracy," the negative and inspired instrument of all revolutions. The inspiration is shown by the letter "M" Over the pineal gland, ,where the head and tail of the serpent unite, producing illuminism. She is the intermediary, receiving and transmitting the influence from above. From a cup in her right hand she pours upon the fire below all abominations and impurities, thus inciting the holocaust, preparing for the domination of the unseen Powers. Old civilisations must be disintegrated and established systems destroyed.

Now in 1914 in the instructions received from the Arab teacher of the R.R. et A.C. it was said: "Before any ceremony, either in temple or private, *fire* must be banished (energy) and *earth* invoked, and the invoking ritual of *Saturn* performed 'to bring peace and calmness!'" Pearce tells us, in his *Text-book of Astrology*: "The influence of Saturn is the most lasting and malignant of all planets," it brings upon the world not peace but disintegration, suffering, disgrace, class war, and anarchy. "Saturn resembles a consumption, which, though hardly perceptible in its progress, is hard to be averted by any effort of human skill." Is this not true of the cancerous growth of the influences of these secret subversive societies and of Bolshevik propaganda?

It is curious to note with all these illuminised instruments of the "Hidden Hand" how magnetic-healing and magically inspired politics went hand in hand. One has only to consider the present Illuminati in England to see that this is the case. In the Stella Matutina, from the late Dr. Felkin, their former High Chief, to their St. Raphael Guild of Healing, run by a certain influential group of clerical members, you find magnetic-healing joined to a subtle form of invoked political influence often ending in Communism, Socialism, and Pacifism, weakly inculcating the doctrine of peace and love your enemies at any price, all inspired by their "hidden masters."

Ceremonies as arranged by the Arab teacher were carried out in the R.R. et A.C. during the War to establish the power of the Pentagram, with special concentration upon Russia and other countries, preparing centres of force for the diabolical work of this "Hidden Hand"; magnetically linking up the group in New Zealand with the groups in England, forming a band round the world controlled by the Invisible Power carrying out the 'Protocol' idea of the unbreakable magnetic chain of the Symbolic Serpent.

In his *Transcendental Magic* Eliphas Levi thus explains this "Magic Chain":

> "To make the Magic Chain is to establish a magnetic current which becomes stronger in proportion to the extent of the chain... Herein is the secret of their force, which they (the clerics) attribute solely to the grace or will of God! ... Concentration is by isolation, and distribution by the magnetic chain."

That is those "set apart" as receivers of the forces from the masters and the transmitters of the same.

> "This force is of itself blind, but it can be directed by the will of man, and is influenced by prevailing opinions. The Universal Fluid (life force) … being the common medium of all nervous organisms and the vehicle of all sensitive vibrations, establishes an actual physical solidarity between impressionable persons, and transmits from one to another the impressions of imagination and thought."

In all illuminised groups the ceremonies, exercises, teachings, and messages from the masters set in motion a magnetic current, and as Elipbas Levi explains:

> "The action of the current is to transport, and often exalt beyond measure, persons who are impressionable and weak, nervous organisations, temperaments inclined to hysteria and hallucination. Such people soon become powerful vehicles of magical force and project efficiently the astral light *in the direction of the current itself.*"

As seen in the meteoric figures of all revolutions! To fight successfully against such a current steady concentrated will and initiative are required. Together these many groups form the magnetic chain transmitting the forces of the Cabalistic Jews into social, religious, political, economic, art, healing, and educational life. As the late Dr. Felkin wrote in 1917: "We are the little leaven that leaveneth the lump." According to Weishaupt, artists are among the most desirable instruments!

It should, I think, be clearly understood that the object of this book is not to show that the Great Hermetic Arcanum is in itself evil, but rather its perversion, and that the knowledge of, and power of applying these hidden laws of nature can become, in the hands of evil and ambitious adepts, more especially "unknown chiefs," a tremendous danger to unwary and unsuspecting "Humanity." The power used in Illuminism is largely based on a deep understanding of the science of light, form (geometric symbols), movement (rhythm), numbers, sound, colour (Minutum Mundum), scents, etc. All these, in the form of correspondences, are used in occult societies, to awaken forces-vibrations which act upon the mind and nervous systems of men and women. As it is said, the 5–6 ritual of the R.R. et A.C.: "Colours are forces and the signatures of forces, and Child of the Children of the forces art thou."

For example, take a square with a symbol in the centre, coloured a brilliant red, and place around that symbol and in juxtaposition to it the correct complementary or negative colour of that red; at once the whole square will flash and will become alive with vibrations.

As illustrating sound-vibrations, the late Max Heindel, of the "Rosicrucian Fellowship," California, wrote in his *Rosicrucian Cosmo-Conception:*

> "These invisible sound-vibrations have great power over concrete matter. They can both build and destroy. If a small quantity of very fine powder is placed upon a brass or glass plate, and a violin bow drawn across the edge, the vibrations will cause the powder to assume beautiful geometrical figures. The human voice is also capable of producing these figures; always the same figure for the same tone. If one note or chord after another be sounded upon — a violin — a tone will finally be reached which will cause the hearer to feel a distinct vibration in the back of the lower part of the head ... that note is the 'keynote' of the person whom it so affects. If it is struck slowly and soothingly it will tone the nerves and restore the health. If it be sounded in a dominant way, loud and long enough, it will kill as sure as a bullet from a pistol."

De Quincey has said:

> "This Temple (Solomon's) is to be built of men, of living stones, and the true method and art of building with men it is the province of (Rosicrucian) magic to teach."

These then are some of the forces used in building this Temple of living stones.

Now it is interesting to find Dr. Felkin's Arab teacher was also a builder using living stones, for we find him saying:

> "The stones must all be there before the circle can be of use. Each stone must first be hewn into proper shape. Each must be able to stand upright hand in hand with the others. The Light within each must become strong so as to radiate far enough, and blending with the others a rainbow will be formed (uniting and forming the so-called 'Divine White Light or Brilliance,' the I.A.O. or Serpent Power). There must be harmony among the members and self-reliance. Each stone will intuitively perceive within itself a symbol which will at once denote the function of the individual stone and its fitness to fulfil it. This symbol must be watched for and developed from within; for though the symbol is in the mind of the Arab and is therefore suggested to each from without, it must be developed from within, gradually meeting the impression from without. The force necessary to develop these symbols from without would be so great it would involve a waste of force, and it is not the right way to be done."

The stones were to be seven Planets for the inner circle, and the twelve signs of the Zodiac for the outer.

As an example of these methods, the following is enlightening: One of the members of the Arab's group was greatly depleted after a sitting, and the reason for this was thus explained by the Arab:

> "She must be more positive getting herself resolutely *to stop formulating thoughts at certain times,* thus rendering the pool of her aura smooth. She should before meeting with strong vibrations make an equal armed cross on the inside of her aura; this will meet with one that I am making on the outside of it also. This done, it will form a door for the vibrations to enter by, and they will then come in an equilibrated way."

Therefore, if these instructions were followed, having induced a state of passivity and having opened a door, thus breaking down all opposition, the Arab would be free to pour in whatever vibrations and suggestions were required in order to shape this stone for the niche she was appointed to occupy in this temple of living stones.

Again, the following shows how a more advanced adept is used, even at a great distance, to act upon another adept for the furtherance of these schemes. Dr. Felkin in New Zealand wrote, February 4, 1918, to the Ruling Chief in England:

> "I suddenly felt a presence there (in his study), and it was a tall man, not unlike Tagore (Eastern), dressed in a brownish sort of dress with brown shoes with longish turn-up toes. Long, beautiful, white hands and no head-dress. He said, 'The time of a great crisis is now coming, send all the help you can to Het-ta (the ruling Chief), who needs help.' The vibrations were so strong my mind went numb. I tried for more, but the words seemed quite incomprehensible. As he gave a sign … a cloud enveloped him and he vanished. He came twice last week."

The so-called help was to break down possible opposition on the part of the London Ruling Chief to their devilish schemes. Their efforts were successful, but for a short time only. Who can say who these invisible magic-workers are, who would build this Temple of living stones-of men and women, whose lives they would "eat up"? They alone hold the real secrets, and thus ever remain the Masters.

In four articles in the *Morning Post*, October 25– 29, 1927, Sir Oliver Lodge discusses. "Physics and Psychics" — the mystery of the ether, his object being to advocate scientific investigations of all psychic phenomena, etc., apart from the use of mediums or photography, both of which methods he very rightly considers unreliable as proof of the reality of communications with the dead. He writes that students of metapsychics,

> "know by actual experience and experiment that there is a telepathic method of communication between mind and mind

which does not utilise the organs of sense and is conducted in what is at present a quite unknown way … the safest plan is to assume that some physical vehicle is concerned even in telepathy and clairvoyance… Those who study metapsychics are aware of facts which have suggested the existence of an *etheric* body — that is, of some physical instrument which can transgress the limitations of space and perform feats impossible to a more material organism. *Travelling clairvoyance* (or astral projection) is one of them, apparition is another… The ether is abundantly substantial, and can transmit every known kind of force."

Ether, he says, has three properties—"dielectric coefficient, magnetic permeability, and velocity of light." These three, according to Clerk Maxwell, are connected, and together can form "definitely and absolutely unity"—electro-magnetic force, the Serpent Power, the all-pervading ether!

In occult societies much psychic work and magic is done for the purpose of loosening the astral body from the material — always retaining a connecting link — so that it may at will be projected through the ether to any distance and at incredible speed. More often it is the will and magic of the Master, that, unbeknown to the adept, withdraw and sends the adept's astral body hither and thither — somewhat after the method of a medium under hypnotic control — creating etheric links, and otherwise doing the work of helping forward the schemes of these Illuminati. He is their instrument. As illustrating this, Mrs. Felkin writes, in a short History of the Order, 1919:

> "The Hidden Order is therefore International, belonging to no one race or nation. Although it is always secret and hidden, the Masters from time to time select one or two to send out as teachers when the world is ready for them… Such teachers gather round the inner secret Orders, and to members of these who are found worthy messengers from the hidden masters are sent to give them teaching, not materially but on the astral plane.

"If the pupils have the courage, patience, perseverance, and loyalty to follow this teaching, and to practise the methods, the time will come when they will receive direct instructions from the hidden masters, either singly or in groups; and it may be that the pupils will eventually be led to one of the great secret hidden temples that there are here and there in the world. We, your chiefs, can say that we know this to our knowledge, because we have thus received and visited. It is in your power to do as we have done, but it requires patience, faith, self-sacrifice, and the ordering of the outer life before the inner teaching can be received. There must be sacrifice, and you must be ready to give up even your own will at times and eliminate much work and pleasure which others may seem to enjoy."

The above is undoubtedly inspired by these masters themselves in order to deceive and obtain the tools necessary to their Great Work. The way to such teaching is "initiation," and that we have seen leads to loss of personality and possible obsession.

The Temple spoken of above visited by the Chiefs was a Sun Temple, to which they were taken astrally by the Arab. It had many little chapels, each representing one of the twelve signs of the Zodiac and the planets, etc., and having as heads a Triangle of Masters—the Master of Light, the Master of Peace, and the Rose Master. They took part in many ceremonies and received much teaching. Of this Temple the Arab said, November II, 1911:

"Each chapel foreshadows a life-force which we are now to begin to experience. We have been putting together as it were the ingredients, and now the FIRE has to be lit, and the ingredients are to be boiled down. Till this has happened he cannot complete our instructions, because we cannot penetrate the veil which always hangs over the East...

Again he explained:

'We are not to put ourselves out or force it, but if any opening comes we are to be quick and·ready to take it, because it would help towards linking up the (magnetic) chain that he has been gradually forming psychically. All these ceremonies and people we have seen when with A.B.S. have been with a definite purpose which he is slowly carrying out, but when we can pick up a link here and there on the material plane it greatly strengthens the effect of the other.'

Again we get a further message from the supposed Christian Rosenkreutz which says, June 15, 1919:

'We are coming to a crisis, and those who have been admitted to the Inner have a right to a clear statement of what we ourselves believe concerning the Order. If we will go forward without fear, trusting to what we have received, he (C.R.C.) will stand even as he has hitherto stood, behind us, using us as instruments in the work which he has undertaken. If we are to be *instruments,* we must put aside the thought of self and think only of the message.'

To show in what way Mrs. Felkin is used as the mouthpiece of these dangerous and insidious powers, the following statement, made by Dr. Felkin, is more than significant (June 1919):

'Yesterday we had a splendid Corpus Christi Day (ceremony for bringing down the light into the Inner Vault and Temple and reaffirming the link with these masters) ... as we passed through the Vault it seemed like passing through liquid fire. Later, when the 'Divine White Brilliance' (astral light) was brought down, the electric light looked really dim it was so strong. Everyone was greatly impressed; when Q.L. (Mrs. Felkin) spoke, her voice seemed quite changed, and she said afterwards she said things she had not been at all prepared to say, but words came to her.'

This is very similar to Krishnamurti's overshadowing by Maitreya; it was a partial obsession by these masters, C.R.C. or the Arab! It is the result of blind and credulous faith!

To allay any doubts or suspicions about the messages the Arab said:

> "Angelic visitors are constantly passing, they bring their messages swiftly, they may touch you with their wings, they may but sweep past you, clothing you with their atmosphere for a moment, but in these mysterious and wonderful moments they leave within thy being a message from the divine, and thou wouldst be missing an opportunity if thou didst not accept this message and meditate thereon; it might be long ere they come again, and when they did come, it might be too late for the same message ... Let thine ears be alert and thine eyes ever open, and fear not to accept such messages. The using of them cannot harm thee as long as thou remainest in the protection of the Order. So long as thou dost dwell in the Sacred Heart and kneel in humility at the foot of the Cross whereon thy Master died for thee."

Not the Christ of the Christians, but the Master of Grand Orient Judaeo-Masonry. And according to the Arab their true symbol of eternal life is the *Ellipse*—the pathway of Light which all Nature follows: it is shown in the egg, from which issues life — containing all things. Their wisdom is therefore the wisdom of Nature, and not of the Omnipotent Divine Creator.

Thus they deceive and enslave those they would use as instruments. How, therefore, are these scientific investigators going to satisfy themselves and others that these spiritual apparitions and their accompanying phenomena are not these hidden masters masquerading as spiritual teachers and spirits of the dead seeking whom they may devour? To occultists, as well as spiritualists, this is an all-important question; both look for a New Heaven and a New Earth, a New Race and a New Age — the age-old dream of Israel!

It is curious to note the following instructions, sent from New Zealand by Dr. Felkin and given by the supposed Christian Rosenkreutz in the Vault of the Inner Temple; it is apparently a subtle method of reciprocal vibrations to be set up between the New Zealand and London Temples, binding them together by means of the Serpent Power or finer forces of Nature, inaugurating a powerful instrument, a magnetic chain controlled by this mysterious Centre, which is ever seeking thus to dominate humanity. Here are the instructions and explanations:

> "The Ruling Chief in London is to do as we are doing here take each of the 5–6 members in turn to the Vault and introduce these personally to C.R.C., receiving for each of them a special card of the TAROT pack. When each is introduced C.R.C. gives them·a card, and this card is a key to the development of the individual (his symbol)… If they can, and we can get the complete Temple of 78 (number of the. Tarot pack!), our Temples will be capable of functioning to the full, and if each one can discover the true spiritual (astral) significance of their own card, each Temple will then, as a whole (be complete). When these two Temples are complete in their Inner members they will become polarised, and the reciprocal currents will be awakened, and those who get the similar cards (in the two Temples) will make pairs and should be in touch with each other, for each card has a positive and negative aspect… When the time comes the two Temples should be ready to act in concert."

Here we have again the "unbreakable chain" of the "Protocols," and for what purpose? "The existing constructional scales will soon collapse, because we are continually throwing them out of balance in order the more quickly to wear them out and destroy their efficiency" World Revolution and the destruction of the hated British Empire!

In *the Great Known*, a book written by the head of the "Sadol Movement," an illuminised masonic group of California under control of the Great School (or Great White Lodge), we find a method whereby they are taught to contact these unknown masters, who are spoken of as "the very wise and powerful Luminous Ones." It teaches that "the material body as it evolves upon the spiritual planes of life becomes a dynamo of everincreasing power and LIGHT." In speaking of this condition, Eliphas Levi, in his *History of Magic*, writes: 'This may take place when, through a series of almost impossible exercises ... our nervous system, having been habituated to all tensions and fatigues, has become a kind of living galvanic pile, capable of condensing and projecting powerfully that Light (astral) which intoxicates and destroys.' It attempts to show that it leads to mastership and self-control, but on careful consideration it proves to be merely conscious mediumship inspired by crafty and wilful deception, giving the adept a false confidence, inducing him to let go his physical senses and work upon the astral, where, enclosed by formulae given by these masters themselves, he is comlpetely at their mercy.

The method is common to other illuminised groups—the R.R. et A.C. as well as the Sun Order of Edinburgh—and may be used by one or a group of adepts. A regular hour must be fixed, and kept to — Sun hours are best, as sunlight apparently assists communication — the room prepared by formulae which, being secret, are not given, but they serve to enclose and isolate the workers and to awaken certain forces and set up vibrations which are necessary in order to bring about the contact. The adept must sit in front of a black curtain, consciously concentrating and endeavouring to "bridge the chasm of sense perception," which must be crossed if the contact is to be made. This may be realised in the form of suggestion, words, symbol, picture, by the coming of the Master himself in his astral body, or even by the projection of the adept's own astral body to a Temple or any other desired place, always under control of the Master! There is no way of testing these masters; they must be taken on trust, a matter of blind faith, the abrogation of all reason, which inevitably leads to Mediumship not Mastership. Such was the method used by the worshippers at the Arab's shrine; they were to form a dynamo of power and Light, to be used for the coming world *regeneration* by the Illuminati!

Of a truth there is apparently much method in all this madness! The only possible name for it is Black Magic, and can one be surprised at the blasphemous and seditious outpourings of our "red, clergy, some of whom at least are members of the Stella

Matutina and the R.R. et A.C., the main object of which was, and is, to get hold of as many clergy as possible so as to bore from within, disrupt the Church, and hold it up to public ridicule, even as is done by the Soviet! Now, who are these masters and what is the Great White Lodge"?

In the publications and proceedings of Theosophists and some other secret societies, the Great White Lodge, is frequently referred to as an outside Superior Power directing the affairs of these earthly societies. In many references it would appear that the Lodge is composed of superhuman or even celestial beings, and in others that they are merely human. Our own belief is that they are a group of flesh-and-blood men, who can form *etheric links*, from any distance, with the leaders of these societies, and who secretly work by means of that Light which can "slay or make alive," intoxicating, blinding, and, if need be, destroying unwary men and women, using them as instruments or 'Light-bearers' to bring to pass this mad and evil scheme of World Domination by the God-People-the Cabalistic Jew.

According to the late Max Heindel, a disciple of Steiner and late head of the 'Rosicrucian Fellowship,' California:

> "There are in different places of the earth a number of these schools of the lesser mysteries, each of them composed of TWELVE Brethren, and also a *Thirteenth* member. The latter is the link between the different schools, and all these heads or thirteenth members compose what is ordinarily known as the White Lodge — namely, a supreme conclave of the Eldest among our Brothers, who are now in full charge of human evolution, and plan the steps we are to follow in order to advance."

For some years Dr. Felkin and a group of R.R. et A.C. members met on Sundays to contact and do astral work with the Arab teacher, whose mission was, as we have seen, to bring about the union of "the East and West," by forming a magnetic chain of adepts round the world as a means of control by these masters. The following is one of the most significant of these astral experiences. As it took place it was recorded word for word by the scribe, and the "channel" — who, with two others, saw it — was our informant:

"*April* 16, 1916.

"A dark room with dark polished floor and dark walls. People sitting round a long polished table. An old man sitting at the head in a carved arm-chair. There are lights in sconces round the walls reflected on the polished floor. All are in dark robes; the old man has a curious cap, not unlike that of the Jewish High-Priest, curved up at the sides like horns. It is red, embroidered with gold and jewels. A brazier is in the centre of the table; every now and then somebody casts a little incense on it. Each has a dish of incense before him, each of a different kind, and they all sprinkle in turn. The seat at the foot of the table, similar to that at the head, is vacant, so *thirteen* in all; there are six people on either side of the table. The old man is speaking. He has bright dark eyes with rather drooping lids. He seems to say: 'The time is approaching, and we are not yet fully prepared. I must remain here to keep the fire burning, but you must return each to his own country, and when we gather here again the vacant chair will be filled.' They all make a sign with the left hand, as if they quickly draw a line with it on the right hand which was held with the fingers stiffly together, the right elbow resting on the table. They have deeply engraved seal rings on the first finger, large dark stones. We may meet the one that is to come back to this country. It is difficult to see the faces, as they wear dominoes with hoods pulled over their heads. Now all are standing up and repeating a Latin verse. First something in unison—I John IV.7–12 (Johannism!). Then each says a word in turn from one of the texts. The man that is to come here says "Amor." Then together they say, 'Nobis hoc signum'. The old man looks Italian or Jewish… It is very mountainous outside… He is standing now, and has stepped to the side of his chair, which seems to be on two steps, so that he is level with the table. The people file past him, and each gives a grip and a password. This password seems to be the word from each that was said in the sentence. They line up at a curtained door and face him. He has a heavy gold cross round his neck with which he blesses them. They make a gesture like a salaam and disappear behind the curtain. On the table before the old man's seat is a black ebony lotus-wand. The lotus is closed to form a cone; it has a light round it. The old man is left alone; he goes round the table and puts the remains of the incense from each dish on to the brazier. Now he takes off his curious cap and sets it on the table beside the wand. He takes off his domino, he is looking very thoughtful. He is not more than fifty-five or sixty, has a silky dark beard, dark moustache, dark hair parted in the middle, curling and just showing thin on the top. He has got on a cassock. Now he is picking up his wand; he presses a little knob in the handle of it and the flower falls open. The flower is of mother-of-pearl with a shining crystal centre. It is flat, but sparkles in the light. He is saying something in a foreign language about the Law: 'The Law shall be fulfilled'!"·

The reason for showing the above was: "The Arab wants us to realise that all over the world those who are the Light-bearers to the future are bestirring themselves to be in readiness." There are, then, mysterious men still in the body of the flesh — who appear astrally, and do establish etheric links, and build up channels through which they can prepare the world for the so-called "Pentecostal Flame" or World Illuminism, which is to bring about the Grand Orient Judaeo "Universal Republic."

Now, the Stella Matutina and the R.R et A.C. have for hidden masters a head and Twelve Brethren, as we shall see later, working under him.

In Jane Lead's Prophecies, 1681–1704, which are Rosicrucian and Illuminism, and closely correspond to the S.M. teaching, and are, with their seven successive Prophets the inspiration of the present Panacea Society, we find: "He (the Master) will now also elect and assign TWELVE principal persons as the foundation builders ... as directed from their principal Head: and so to go on, to multiply the number of disciples, till they are numberless." The Prophecies concern a Second Advent.

With regard to the use of I John, Mrs. Nesta Webster, in her *Secret Societies and Subversive Movements, writes:*

> "Thus Dr. Ranking, who has devoted many years of study to the question … in a very interesting paper published in the masonic journal, "Ars Quatuor Coronatorum," observes: "That from the very commencement of Christianity there has been transmitted through the centuries a body of doctrine incompatible with Christianity in the various official Churches. That the bodies teaching these doctrines profess to do so on the authority of St. John, to whom, as they claimed, the true secrets had been committed by the Founder of Christianity, that during the Middle Ages, the main support of the Gnostic bodies and the main repository of this knowledge (Johannism) was the Society of the Templars." And he further said, "The record of the Templars in Palestine is one long tale of intrigue and treachery on the part of the Order." "

Many of the groups of to-day believe themselves to be in direct communication with Christ!

Again she quotes Lecouteulx de Canteleu:

> "In France the Knights (Templars) who left the Order, henceforth hidden, and so to speak unknown, formed the Order of the Flaming Star and of the Rose-Croix, which in the fifteenth century spread itself to Bohemia and Silesia."

Curiously enough the symbol of the Stella Matutina is the Five-pointed Star, and that of the R.R. et A.C. the six-pointed Star and the Rose-Cross.

Further, she tells us that in the "Melchisedeck Lodges," the Rose-Croix degree occupies the most important place. That the Order was usually described as the 'Asiatic Brethren,' of which the centre was in Vienna, though its real origins are obscure.

> "Their further title of 'Knights and Brethren of St. John the Evangelist' suggests Johannite inspiration … de Luchet, who

as a contemporary was in a position to acquire first-hand information, thus describes the organisation of the Order which, it will be seen, was entirely Judaic. 'The superior direction is called the small and constant Sanhedrim of Europe ... the Order has the true secrets and the explanations, moral and physical, of the hieroglyphics of the very venerable Order of Freemasonry.' The initiate has to swear absolute submission and unswerving obedience to the Laws of the Order... 'Who,' asks de Luchet, 'gave to the Order these so-called secrets? That is the great and insidious question for the secret societies. But the initiate who remains, and must remain eternally in the Order, never finds this out; he dare not even ask it. He must promise never to ask it. In this way, those who participate in the secrets of the Order remain the masters.'" (See Dr. Felkin's pledge to the Third Order in 1909.)

This is profoundly true of present-day secret societies. In Jane Lead's Prophecies, they speak of the "Upper Court and Council," and we read: "In order unto the rising-up to the successive degrees of the Melchisedeck Order, the whole burnt-offering is required." In the S.M. we find a special ritual for the invocation of Melchisedeck, and also a higher Grade in the R.R. et A.C. As the Count de Saint-Germain said of his Melchisedeck Priesthood: "You shall guide the course of stars, and those who rule empires shall be governed by you." Is this not equally true of these secret societies to-day, or at least the power that is working through them?

Further, Mrs. Nesta Webster writes with reference to "the Master" of Mrs. Besant's Co-Masonry:

> "But in the third degree the astonishing information is confided with an appearance of great secrecy, that he is no other than the famous Comte de Saint-Germain, who did not really die in 1784, but is still alive to-day in Hungary under the name of Ragocsky ... the Master is in reality an Austrian of royal birth."

In Eliphas Levi's *History of Magic* a note says: "Saint-Germain testified on his part … that he was the son of Prince Ragocsky of Transylvania."

Now it is interesting to note among the Orders of to-day how closely the dates of their various consummations correspond:

Theosophists and Order of the Star·in the East — 1926. The Coming World Teacher supported by twelve Apostles. He has come and gone and failed to captivate or convince the World!

S.M. and the R.R. et A.C. — 1926 to 1933-5. Reincarnation of Christian Rosenkreutz, with a probable support of twelve priests.

Panacea Society — 1923-7. Second Advent supported by twelve women Apostles.

Spiritualists — 1925-8. A catastrophe leading to a purged and purified world and Church! A new Heaven and a new Earth!

Must we not therefore conclude that all these Movements are but "channels" used by the "Great White Lodge" — or is it "the small and constant Sanhedrim" of the Learned Elders of Zion? — to bring about World Domination by the Jews — for they decree, "The Law must be fulfilled!"

Here is another piece of significant pictorial teaching given to Dr. Felkin in 1916 by his Arab Master. It depicts the great World Work by these hidden masters, as accomplished in Russia to-day, and now being attempted among all other races and nations—it is World Revolutionary Initiation; it is the *solve* and *coagula* — the destruction and reconstruction — of Illuminised Grand Orient Judaeo-Masonry; for "everything, yes, everything must be destroyed, since everything must be remade." It is the establishment of the Kingdom of Adonai, the Jewish Lord of the Universe, built upon the ruins of all old civilisations.

"It is the picture of a woman, weeping and seated — she is

the Spirit of Earth. Behind her is another figure in flowing robes; he is Adonai, the Lord of the Universe. His arms are stretched out, and a crown is on his head; in his left hand is a sword pointing upwards with drops of blood running down the blade to the hilt. In his right hand is a cup, and from the cup blood is spilling, falling on to the woman's green robe. The figure behind holds the cup to the woman's lips; she drinks and her tears fall into the cup; he turns the sword and drives it through her side so that it transfixes her. As he does this, still holding the cup to her lips, his arms embrace her, and one, or both is saying: 'I am thou, and wheresoever thou seekest thou shalt find me.' And the two figures seem to dissolve into LIGHT and one tremendous and glorious figure emerges."

This initiation can be individual as well as universal, and we have seen how such initiation means untold suffering and sacrifice and loss of one's personality; out of it emerges a mere lifeless illuminised automaton.

The following somewhat recondite cabalistic teaching was given to Mathers, one of the early Chiefs, by the "Hidden and Secret Chiefs," and was passed on to Dr. Felkin by the then Chief of Amen Ra Temple, Edinburgh. It is a curious description of how a Triad or Triangle of adepts, forming an etheric link, bringing into action "reciprocal vibrations" with the hidden masters, were to transmit their influences and control the Order. It is given here for the benefit of the few who may be able to follow it, as it explains what happened later when the masters attempted to establish such a Triangle of Power in the R.R. et A.C. in 1917-19. For those who cannot, or do not care to, follow, it may be passed over.

THE LAW OF THE CONVOLUTED REVOLUTION OF THE FORCES SYMBOLISED BY THE FOUR ACES AROUND THE NORTHERN POLE

"... In the book T. (the Tarot) it is written, 'Also the Dragon (i.e. Draco the constellation of the Northern Pole of the

Heavens) surroundeth the pole of KETHER of the celestial Heavens.' It is furthermore laid down that the four Forces symbolised by the four Princesses or Amazons rule the celestial heavens from the North Pole of the Zodiac unto 45·degrees of Lat. North of the ecliptic, and from the Throne of the four Aces which rule in KETHER. And again it is stated that the Throne of the

Ace of Cups = Head of Draco.

Ace of Swords = Fore part of the body.

Ace of Pentacles = Hind part of the body.

Ace of Wands = Tail of Draco.

"Regard thou therefore the form of this Constellation of Draco. It is convoluted in four places answering to the rule of the Aces. For in the four Forces of Yod, He, Vau, He, fire and water be contrary and also earth and air be contrary. And the Throne of the elements will attract and seize, as it were, the force of the element, so that herein be the forces of antipathy and sympathy, or what are known chemically as repulsion and attraction...

"It is said KETHER is in MALKUTH and again that MALKUTH is in KETBER, but after another manner. For downwards through the four worlds the MALKUTH of the less material will be linked into the KETHER of the more material. From the synthesis of the ten corruscations of the Aur proceedeth the influence into ... the KETHER of ATZILUTH, and the connecting link or thread of the AIN SOPH is extended through the worlds, through all the ten sephiroth and in every direction... Now the symbol of the connection between the MALKUTH of YETZIRAH (mental) and the KETHER of ASSIAH (material) will be of a form somewhat resembling an hour-glass, the thread of the AIN SOPH, before alluded to, traversing the centre thereof and forming the connection between the worlds. So that the symbol of the connection between the planes is this, and also the *modus operandi* of the translation of the force from one plane to another is this. And hence does the title of the sphere of KETHER of ASSIAH signify commencement of the whirling motion.

From the diagram of the hour-glass symbol it will be manifest that the MALKUTH of YETZIRAH will be the transmitter of the Yetziratic forces unto KETHER of ASSIAH, that the latter will be the recipient thereof, and that the hour-glass symbol or double cone will be the translator from the one plane unto the other. Hence therefore let us consider the nomenclature of the tenth path (answering unto MALKUTH) and of the first path (answering unto KETHER).

"The tenth path answering unto MALKUTH:

"It is called the Resplendent Intelligence, and it is so called because it is exalted above every head and sitteth on the Throne of BINAH, and it illumineth the splendour of all the Lights and causeth the current of the influence to flow from the Prince of Countenances" (i.e. Mettatron or the Lord of Light).

"The first path answering unto KETHER:

"It is called the wonderful or hidden intelligence (the highest Crown). For it is the Light to cause to understand the Primordial without commencement, and it is the Primal Glory — for nothing created is worthy to follow out its essence."

"Whence it is plain that MALKUTH is as it were the collector and synthesis of all the forces in its place or world: while KETHER, being superior to all, also in its place and world, will be the recipient and arranger of the forces from the plane beyond, so as to distribute them into its subordinate sephiroth in a duly ordered manner.

"And therefore any force of the multitudinous and

innumerable forces in MALKUTH may act through the upper cone of the hour-glass symbol, and by means of the lower cone translate its operation into the KETHER below, but its mode of transmission will be through its cones by the thread of the AIN SOPH or of the unformulated. So that in the transmission between the two worlds the formulate must first become unformulate ere it can reformulate in new conditions (death and disintegration!). For it must be plain that a force formulated in our world if translated into another will be unformulated according to the laws of a place different in nature, even as water in its fluid state will be subject to different laws to those governing it when in the conditions either of ice or steam.

"And as before said, there being a chief elemental division of the sephira MALKUTH in the MINUTUM MUNDUM diagram, each of these will have its co-relative formula of transmission unto the succeeding KETHER. Hence is there the dominion of the four knaves or Princesses of the Tarot around the North Pole in the book T. attributed unto the Heavens—(The triangle and Unity).

"Now as KETHER has to receive from MALKUTH, it is necessary that in and about KETHER *there should be a force which partaketh of the nature of MALKUTH, though more subtle and refined in nature,* and therefore is it that the final "He" or Princess forces have their dominion placed above KETHER, that so they may attract from the MALKUTH of the higher and form the basis of action for the Aces. So that a refined matter may attract its like, and that the spiritual forces may not lose themselves in the void and so produce but a mistaken and whirling destruction for want of a settled basis. And herein is the mutual formula in all things, of a spirit and of a body, seeing that each supplieth unto each that wherein the other is lacking. Yet herein also must there be a certain condition, otherwise the harmony will not be perfect, for unless the body be refined in nature it will hinder the action of the spirits cognate unto it; and unless the spirit be willing to ally itself to the body the latter will be injured thereby, and each will naturally react on the other... But it is as necessary to govern the spirit as to refine the body, and of what use is it to weaken the body by abstinence if at the same time uncharitableness and spiritual pride are encouraged. It is simply translating one sin into another, and therefore are the final "He" forces necessary in KETHER as it is said in the tenth path of YETZIRAH, "It is so called because it is exalted above every head and sitteth on the Throne of BINAH." Now, in the Tree the sephiroth CHOKMAH and BINAH are referred unto the BRIATIC world, which is called the Throne of the Atziluthic world, unto which KETHER is referred in the Tree, and referring unto the dominions of the four Princesses, thou shalt find that in the sphere they include CHOKMAH and BINAH as well as KETHER.

"Now there will be not one but four formulae of the application of the four forces of MALKUTH into the revolution of the ACE in KETHER, and these acting not singly but simultaneously and with a different degree of force. And seeing that while (were MALKUTH and KETHER in the same plane or world) the transmission of these forces from the one unto the other would proceed more or less in direct lines, in this case (seeing that MALKUTH and KETHER be in different planes and worlds) the lines of transmission of these forces are caught up and whirled about by the upper cone of the hour-glass symbol into the vortex, where and through passeth the thread of the unformulate — i.e. AIN SOPH (etheric link). Thence they are projected in a whirling convolution (yet according unto their nature) through the lower cone of the hour-glass symbol unto KETHER. Hence it resulteth that these formulae are of the nature of the Dragon or *Serpent*; that is to say, moving in convolutions, and hence are they called the Dragon or Serpent formulae (winged, air; finned, water; or footed, earth).

"Another action of the forces of MALKUTH of YETZIRAH transmitting into KETHER of ASSIAH will be that of continued *vibratory rays* acting from the centre of the circumference, and that bringing into action the forces from the Thread of the unformulate (AIN SOPH).

"Recall that which is written in the chapter of the Chariots, Ezekiel Iv. 5–6: 'And I beheld, and lo! a tempestuous whirlwind came out from the north, and a mighty cloud and a fire violently whirling upon itself and from the midmost as an eye of brightness from the midst of the fire, and from the midmost forms of four chariots.' "

This then is the method whereby these devilish Masters of the Cabala work on the mental or astral plane, forming etheric links through which they can act upon an Order and again through it directly upon the world. An example of how this was attempted in the R.R. et A.C. will be given shortly, showing how these masters sought to form a Triangle of adepts "KETHER, CHOKMAH, and BINAH, through which their EYE of Power was to manifest. But first the Triangle was to become, as it were, an 'empty vessel,' which was to be filled with astral light — illuminised — a dynamo, condensing and projecting the Masters' forces, receiving their instructions, and like automata passing them on to those around them. In this way, like an epidemic or like wild fire, these teachings and forces spread along the magnetic chain, orienting an Order, group, nation, and the world. It is a devilish scheme which could only be evolved out of a cabalistic mind.

But first let us attempt the difficult task of explaining this universal ether or life-force which is the basis of their power.

A candidate when desiring to enter the Stella Matutina must sign a form of personal consent and secrecy, in which the aim of the Order is stated to be 'spiritual development'—that is, awakening the inner senses. And they are further told that the reason for this secrecy is that the teaching can be used either for black or white magic, and would therefore become a danger if made generally known. The great aim, however, of all these secret societies is to train the member to let go his hold on material things, and function consciously on the astral plane; for only on that plane can these diabolical masters, without betraying themselves, contact, influence, link together, and use adepts in their secret universal plans. In the early grades of the S.M. neophytes are given meditations, breathing exercises, and processes brought over from Germany by E.O.L., the adept who had been trained there to act as etheric link between the German body and the Order in England. These arouse and raise the unused sex-forces, the Kundalini or "serpent within" the adept, and awaken the inner senses.

Some little time before entering the Inner Order, the adept is taken a stage farther in this astral development; he is initiated into the mysteries of Tatwic vision, a form of Yoga. Briefly, according to the yogis, there is in the Universe a Great Breath or *Swara*-evolution and involution; it is the universal creative principle or life-force. It is *Pingala*, the positive or Sun breath, *Ida*, the negative or Moon breath, and *Susumna*, the uniting or destoying fire. It is the Serpent Power or Triangle of manifestation in all creation. Within the adept it is the Kundalini, and the merging of this with the universal life-force without, Nirvana, is the end of all yoga. Further, there are five modifications of this Great Breath, called *Tatwas*, ethers, or refined matter, each having distinct vibrations, different functions, a different form and sense; each of these is again charged in turn with all five. They are akin to ether and the four elements—the Pentagram.

They are: (I) *Akasa* — ether (called spirit), dark, egg-shaped: sound. (2) *Vayu* — gaseous, air, blue sphere: touch. (3) *Tegas* — igneous, fire, red triangle: sight. (4*) Apas* — liquid, water, silver crescent: taste. (5) *Prithivi* — solid, earth, yellow square: smell. All four states of terrestrial matter exist in our sphere — and each is constantly invading the domain of the other, and thus we get what is called the mixed or intercharged Tatwas. These Tatwas or breaths flow in regular rotation throughout the nervous system of the human body exactly as in the universe without — as above so below.

Ráma Prasád, in a book, *Nature's Finer Forces*, written for the Theosophists in 1889, tells us that the whole process of creation, on whatever plane of life, is performed by these Tatwas in their aspects of negative and positive, and that everything in every aspect that has been or is in being on our planet has a legible record on the ether. He further says that at will "the practised yogi can bring any picture of any part of the world, past or present, before his eyes," and "a yogi in contemplation might have before his mind's eye any man at any distance whatsoever, and might hear his voice also"; that it only requires sympathetic minds — that is, tuned to the same key. He calls it "the phenomena of mental telegraphy, psychometry, clairvoyance, and clairaudience, etc." Also reciprocal vibrations. Again, we are told in a S.M. MS.: "The student will by degrees become able to look into futurity at will, and have all the visible world before his eyes, and he will be able to command Nature; this power also lays bare the secret workings of the world." By the power of this life-force, willed and directed and controlled by an adept, "an enemy may be destroyed, power, wealth, pleasure, etc., obtained." Also it can cause or heal disease, and by it hypnotic control can be exercised. And by this power apathy can be engendered in any body or group, a form of mass hypnotism! In these orders the use of this power is always controlled by the masters!

These, then, are the forces used in all illuminised groups to bring about so-called spiritual development and attainment, and by these forces and its profound knowledge of their potentialities, this mysterious centre seeks to influence the mind and actions of the adept, not for the good of humanity, but for its enslavement. Always in the Stella Matutina the adept is assured that as long as he remains within the Order, using Order methods, no evil can befall him! In this Order these coloured Tatwa symbols, with their corresponding formulae and cabalistic divine names, which are potent astral forces, are used to obtain astral vision according to the nature of the Tatwa, always using incense to help to loosen the astral from the material body. At first these visions are vague and slight, but grow in clarity and seeming reality as the adept develops, until suddenly one day, from apparently nowhere, a mysterious brown-habited monk or brother, a guardian of the Order, a master, or even a false Christ, appears and takes charge of the astral expedition, carrying the adept away perhaps to some isolated monastery, rocky stronghold, temple, gloomy cavern, or even to the North Pole! where some sinister and magical rite is generally performed and instructions given symbolically or in words. These astral adventures continue and grow in intensity until gradually the adept's outlook on life is oriented towards these masters' world schemes, and the niche he himself is to occupy.

The dangers to the adept's individuality and mentality are indeed great and very real. For instance, two inner adepts, who knew nothing of Dr. Felkin's Atarab Master, by means of these Tatwas found their way, time and again, to an isolated monastery perched high up on a rocky precipice overlooking a somewhat turbid stream, and before entering the monastery they had to give a sign of recognition which later proved to be that of the Arab Master! Within the monastery an attempt was made to obsess one or both of these adepts, and who is to say that they were not eventually controlled by that master? They both continued for long these astral visits, and remained faithful instruments when others doubted and departed! Other adepts using the same Tatwa arrived apparently at the same monastery, where they were shown the pastos, or tomb, in which lay, they were told, the Master who had been slain! No doubt Adoniram or Hiram, the Master of the Templars whose death was always celebrated by the Templars, as a pledge of vengeance! Dr. Felkin wrote that he had also astrally visited this same monastery!

In time this work becomes as the intoxication of hashish, inciting an eternal craving for more and ever more astral dreams and gymnastics, and gradually the adept's own personality becomes withdrawn, life becomes shadowy, the masters dominate his every thought and act, he becomes their instrument, carrying out their sinister, deceptive, and often little understood commands. This is "liberation" or freedom within these Orders, and, like the Russian Khlysty with their "fervour," life to the adept soon becomes dead without astral excitement. It becomes his life-work and even his religion!

Throughout the whole history of the R.R. et A.C. we find controlled "channels," forming etheric links with these hidden masters, who are almost invariably, mentally and physically worn down, by way of trials and tests, until absolutely exhausted they clutch at the "peace and rest" — self-immolation and enslavement — offered by their ambitious, fanatical, and devilish torturers.

Dr. Felkin, in his already quoted history, writes:

> "Frater F. R. (Dr. Felkin), 1910, was able to introduce E.O.L. (who was abroad seeking health) to the members of the Third Order (in Germany). These Fratres then said that in order to form a definite etheric link between themselves and Great Britain it was necessary for a Frater from Great Britain to be under their instructions for a year... Frater E. O. L. decided that he would place himself under the instruction of the Third Order. He commenced his teaching at once, and after residing for some time in North Germany and Austria, he was sent for a time to Cyprus. He was then sent to Egypt, then to Mount Carmel, and should have gone to Damascus, but did not. He was then sent to Constantinople (where he was in close touch with the 'Young Turk Party!'), and finally returned to Germany, where, having passed his tests, he was initiated by special dispensation into the first few grades of the Rosicrucian Society, corresponding to our 6-5."

Although the German Third Order was supposed to be training E.O.L., we find the ubiquitous Arab teacher saying, January 29, 1911: "E.O.L. will get all he can from Steiner, and we will find someone else in process of time." And again, July 5, 1911:

> "He is following after his own desires instead of the quest which was set before him. He ought to have gone to Damascus, but he cannot be driven; he received the messages which were given him, and he has not accepted them. The Arab will make one more effort and try to bring him in contact with someone in Constantinople, but it will be more difficult, and the result will be more than doubtful."

November 26, 1911, we find the Arab forming a group of the R.R.

et A.C. members to attract and bring down the forces, and so fix the Light in the Order as a material basis for his world work:

It is similar to the Druidic circles:

> "... around the symbol (in the centre) was gathered the Inner group (seven planets or aspects of solar force) from which arises the LIGHT or flame, but that light will only burn steadily if each member contributes his own share of the necessary energy or fuel.

> ... Each has his own element to give, and without each the fire cannot burn. But the outer group (Zodiac signs) is in part a shelter to the inner, and a source of energy to the inner members and to fan the flame. Inner members are to draw from them..."

E.O.L. was given the symbol of Luna — the waxing and waning moon of Baphomet of the Templars. Apparently he was to be the negative vessel which was to receive the LIGHT from the masters and transmit it to the Order — the etheric link. He had evidently been brought to such a condition of depletion and depression that the Arab warned him:

> "E.O.L. is consuming his forces by misdirected energies (asserting his own individuality!); his time has not yet come, but he is attracting the destructive forces instead of repelling them, and unless he ceases to do this he will die before his time, thereby missing the fulfilment of his destiny and vocation ... Forcibly ejecting the demon of melancholy which is attracting the outward form of death ... he must substitute a centre of Light in its place, and then he will attract the forces of life and get well."

What of the malignant and negative forces of his symbol Luna? And further, there were to be pairs of adepts and E.O.L's opposite "should be someone of very intense vitality from whom E.O.L. can draw force when necessary." In other words, E.O.L. was to obey his bondmaster and become his "vessel of Light," and thus this master builder sought to build his "Temple of Living Stones!"

On the eve of Dr. Felkin's first visit to New Zealand in the autumn of 1912, E.O.L., who, though still in ill-health, was to take over charge of the Order during Dr. Felkin's absence, suddenly and unexpectedly died. The Arab was greatly upset, for his devilish game had gone awry; and he said there was no reason for his death, he simply let go and slipped out! Was that all? The Arab, however, declared that E.O.L.'s work was not yet finished; like Christian Rosenkreutz, he would in time find and take possession of an adult body, ousting the rightful owner, and in it he would fulfil his interrupted destiny! Later, Dr. Felkin was told that he must find someone else to take E.O.L.'s place as etheric link!

In reading these authentic accounts of the inner workings of these illuminised orders it is well to bear in mind — as one explanation of the mystery of the directing power — what Hoëné Wronski wrote in 1823-5, as shown in *Mysticism and Magic* at the beginning of this book: "Secret societies which have existed and still exist on our globe ... which, controlled from this mysterious source, have dominated and notwithstanding Governments continue to dominate the world ... all parties, political, religious, economic, and literary." This centre, as many writers, and even Jews, point out, is "the supreme and Invisible Hierarchy of Cabalistic Jews." The Orders controlled all claim to be working to the end of leading the world into "Peace and Light"; but they all gamble with the lives and souls of their members, while never admitting them into the inner circle.

It is a queer and almost incredible story, and can only be sketched here, how another adept of the R.R. et A.C. was chosen, and though rebellious was "shaped and hewn," battered and bruised, in an attempt by these masters to fill E.O.L.'s place as etheric link in the Order. Dr. Felkin, before finally returning to New Zealand in 1916, as we have seen, under these masters' directions drew up a New Constitution, and he attempted to include in it a "Delphic Oracle," adepts who were to be the vehicle through which these masters were to work upon the Order and issue commands. But this was vetoed by the committee. Three Ruling Chiefs were appointed, one of whom only had been trained in magic, the other two were clergymen (one of whom resigned about 1919), who were to carry Order teachings into healing, religious, social, and ethical problems. Dr. Felkin made the War the excuse for not entering into details concerning his claimed German authority, but he retained nevertheless his office as High Chief in London.

The legacy left to the Ruling Chiefs by Dr. Felkin's rule, which was no rule, was far from enviable, and Dr. Felkin was aware of this himself. What followed was an illustration of the methods described by the Protocolists: "It is imperative in all countries to disturb continually the relationship which exists between people and Governments." And so with Orders! —The Arab Master, speaking to Dr. Felkin of the dissensions in the London Temple said, December 1918: "They must pass through a time of conflict before they enter the House of Peace," the "giant harrow" again preparing the ground! Before Dr. Felkin had left England, and up to the closing of the Temple in 1919, the Order was rent by dissensions, jealousies, underground whisperings, and open strife and rebellion, which apparently was to lead to that peace which meant unconditional and willing surrender to the masters and their work.

The masters were, however, determined to have their oracle, and this was to be a Triangle of Adepts, as the Serpent Power, manifesting their forces and teachings in the Order. This was to be brought about by means of psychic fluidic exchanges, as spoken of in M. Henri de Guillebert's *Studies in Occultism*. According to him the Master and adept or adepts would be in the position of hypnotist and subject under hypnosis, and the completion of that state would be for the adept, "the final annihilation of his personality, the destruction of his chief attribute."

To bring about this polarity and consummation the mind of the adepts had first to be oriented. For this purpose in the R.R. et A.C. early in 1917 messages from these hidden masters suddenly poured forth almost daily; the language was cabalistic, dignified, and beautiful, though at times arrogant and dominant. They created an atmosphere, they awakened an expectation, and in 1919 the consummation was definitely said to be a Great Initiation. As a preparation for this Initiation, three adepts were formed into a Triad or Triangle, and symbolically placed upon the cabalistic Tree of Life, as KETHER, CHOKMAH, and BINAH, as in that curious teaching previously given, "the Law of the Convoluted Revolution of the Forces," so that the forces from the Masters should be attracted from above by a refined material basis, and flow down through it into the Order, forming an etheric link with these Hidden Powers.

The refining process brought many unexpected troubles said by the masters to be naught but tests in preparation for some wonderful consummation. As these Powers said: "Learn that which thou hast to learn and all will be well!" which meant absolute obedience and willing sacrifice of anything and everything demanded.

Always comparing them with the teaching on the revolution of the forces, witness the messages given by the Lord of Light, or "Prince of Countenances." and his Twelve Brethren:

> "Oh, ye Children, indeed are ye the three chosen for my work. Ye are the *Love, the Power,* and *the Perfect Reconciliation,* and to ye shall come *the Perfect Unity*—(Four Princess forces).

> "The day of disintegration and death lieth indeed before you, but fear it not, ye have passed beyond the harming power of death and only the final test remains. Unharmed and unhurt shall ye pass the barrier, the veil is thinning, urge ever upwards to the Light…"

The trained Ruling Chief was to be the apex, the etheric link; as Dr. Felkin wrote, March II, 1917:

"You are the chief channel now in Anglia."

"Learn of your colours, for ye must now use them."

"To you who standeth in the east (the Chief-KETHER) has the colour of Unity been given, for in it blendeth the Fire and Water, and from it proceedeth the *Spirit* (astral fight) presiding over all. Ever in thy work use well this colour, that from the multifarious claims of matter may arise the union of and with the pure spirit. Let thy watchword be *Unity*, one and alone — for one is thy Lord, and ye must unite ever with Him. Ye the *receiver* and *transmitter* of the contending forces must be indeed the *Pure White Spirit* enclosed in the unity of colour."

Ruby is the colour of Unity, and the above means the fixation of the astral light in the purified body of the Chief, controlled by the Lord and Master! — Illuminism.

"Ye, oh Child, who standeth in the left basal angle (BINAH) have received the colour of pure *Love* (blue), the waters of love flowing down to purge the evil world. Ever encompass the world with thy colour, get it in the Vault, and use it freely ever and anon: all need the divine love, so use it ever freely and fear not."

Here we have a deadly negative force let loose over the world, false pacifism and blindness, lack of fighting force, creating no doubt a form of apathy necessary for domination!

"To ye, my child (CHOKMAH), has the colour of negation and strength (purple) been given, for ye must ever lead upwards the soul of the multitude to the perfect offering of pure negation and with this your colour ye can give strength to the halting ones." (A form of false idealism!)

"When consciously ye meet, let thy colours merge with the pure whiteness of the Christ (astral light) and then let the blending form a link wherewith to encompass the world."

The three form the negative and positive forces united by the apex, it is the magnetic chain of influence.

> "Yea, ye have indeed brought down the spirit into the material." — Illuminism!

> "Ye, my Child (BINAH) must ever consciously rest at the Master's feet, for ye are the messenger of the gods."

The scribe and *receiver* of the instructions.

> "To ye, oh Ath (Air, CHOKMAH), have I other words to say; rest consciously indeed in my presence, but be ye not a messenger but a carrier."

Transmitter of the forces and instructions.

> "Work other and mightier have I for your Chief (KETHER), but of it the Chief shall learn in the coming silence, when ye shall all enter into the vast majesty and purity of God."

After the ceremony of Initiation and Illuminism!

> "Ye (KETHER) form the apex of the Triangle, and ye must first pass within the veil, that from the apex may shine down the glorious beauty from the Father's face (the SUN is the Father). In pure spirit (astral) must ye work upon the earth, for ye are a reflection of that brightness (the Moon is the Mother and reproducer) and purity which ever burns within the flame.

> "Let the Triad shine forth in dazzling whiteness, the pure basis on which the Son (the "Christ" or astral light) can manifest to the world."

The Iliuminised Instrument!

The Chief, by a "compelling force," was induced to enter the

Anglican Church, partly in order to establish confidence among the clergy whom the masters hoped to entangle in their net, and also to create the necessary uplift and atmosphere in which to fix the etheric link. Before the attempted Great Initiation, as usual with oracles of the Illuminati, the Chief was told: "A Guardian of the Order shall be given unto thee who will never leave thee!" The Chief was to be under the Master's constant supervision, having no will or thought but theirs, and no individual initiative.

The two basal angles (approved by Dr. Felkin, May 14, 1919) lived more or less constantly on the astral plane, and as one of the previous chiefs had done, they went to church to see visions, receive teaching, and perform rites as directed by these masters. In the Vault (the power-house of these masters) they received astral grades, and as tests were put through extraordinary astral gymnastics. One of the final ceremonies was given by the false "Christ", or Lord of Light and his Twelve Brethren, and in this they had to take an oath of fealty, secrecy, service, sacrifice, and absolute obedience, and this had to be signed with their own blood — a common rule among Illuminati and adepts of Black Mass.

The Initiation was called the "Opening of the Tomb" — Liberation, but— "free no to use your freedom for yourselves but for ME." The password was KADOSCH. The adept was to gaze fixedly at a six-rayed star, projected by the Master, and pass through the fire into the astral vault beyond. There an obligation of absolute secrecy, obedience, and willing sacrifice was to be demanded by the so-called Christian Rosenkreutz, and he and his Twelve Brethren would officiate at the ceremony. Finally, the adept was to return to his body with the power upon him. Hypnotic control! Not until after this initiation would the work required be made clear, and then there would be no further need of the Church.

Suddenly, without warning, the Lord of Light and his Twelve Brethren attempted to give the Chief this Initiation. This was in a London church at the Tenebres service, Thursday, April 17,

1919. Easter is a special time for Illuminati black magic. They said it meant "death and disintegration." Briefly, before the entrance of the officiating clergy, the Chief saw in place of the altar the great Vault of the inner Order, into which the Twelve Brethren, in black habits with cowls over their heads, were hurriedly entering, and almost at once a dazzling light was focused upon the Chief, and above in this astral fire was the Lord of Light. A sharp pain seized the heart, followed by a curious creeping faintness, and it required all the Chief's determined will to prevent complete trance, but as the clergy entered, gradually the light faded and the faintness passed. Next day the Master announced that the failure had been due to a mistake on the part of one of the Brethren, for which he had been duly punished!

And once more the Master sent forth his messages:

> "Ye have risen, but I have not used you freely because not yet are ye able fully to fulfil my work, but gradually are the limitations being purged away. The roses are blooming, but as yet they are not white and clear, pure offerings meet to be accepted at my Father's throne." (See the Tenth Path; also "Now in the Tree the sepiroth CHOKMAH and BINAH are referred unto the Briatic World which is called the 'THRONE' of the Atziluthic World, unto which KETHER is referred.')

> "I that speak am sent from the Lord of Light, the Incarnate Son of God."

From the Transmitter of the Astral Light! The Gnostic Logos worshipped under the image of the Serpent!

The Chief broke up the Triangle, and then followed the most extraordinary astral persecution, unexpected attacks, forces, overpowering scents and projections of astral light, etc., all in an attempt to induce trance or work upon the adepts physically and astrally in the hope of controlling them and others through them. As the Master said:

"Round ye like a curtain spreads the power from on high; can ye not see it and feel it?"

In reply to the Chief's request for enlightenment, Dr. Felkin cabled from New Zealand: "Christian Father reassures, hold fast, Ephesians vi. II- I2. Letter following." And the Christian·Father's (Rosënkreutz) message which followed was (July 10, 1919, in the N.Z. Vault):

"The messages of which you speak are true, but the channel through which they come has been faulty. It must be that the Powers of Light work through such vehicles as are available, and ofttimes it happens that a shard is cast aside because of a flaw which destroys its value. Nevertheless, the crystal vessel will be found which, being *filled with Light*, shall shine out through tbe darkness ... The source of evil is of little moment (the masters!), for it can but find entrance through the weakness that lies within themselves (want of blind faith!) ... Bid them be of good courage, for their feet are set upon the Path...

"The Brethren are indeed the Elder Brethren and the messengers of the Lord, but they are neither infallible nor do they belong to the company of the gods. They are but men highly advanced indeed, and waiting for the torch to be kindled in their midst, yet are they not of those of whom ye know as Masters, and it is not in their power either to kindle the torch nor yet to say at what day or hour the flame of Pentecost shall descend..."

And Dr. Felkin added:

"Such attacks as those you have had are quite definitely an attempt of evil forces to distract the soul in its ascent of the Mountain. So soon as this aim is accomplished the attacks cease (hypnotic control!). They are in themselves a proof that the teaching receiver is both good and highly important."

And he said you cannot be initiated without passing into trance-true, but what does it lead to? When asked, 'What proof have you that the masters are not black magicians?' the answer was, 'How can you test astral beings? you must have faith'—abnegation of the reason! Further, Dr. Felkin advised:

> "I think it would be better if, instead of fearing imaginary black Rosicrucians in Germany or elsewhere, you would consciously endeavour to co-operate with the true Rosicrucians who do undoubtedly exist (his German authority), and are seeking to guide Central European thought into the Light; you would then belong to the Great Work for the world."

And as we have said, this great Rosicrucian work was to begin in Russia and is now spreading everywhere! As a final warning of coercion, if need, be, the masters said: 'If the Chiefs do not choose to walk in the Path appointed, they must needs climb the Mountain of Initiation through much trial and tribulation!'

Still more dissatisfied, the two Chiefs demanded investigations, but Dr. Felkin and some of his followers, adopting Illuminati tactics, made every effort secretly to discredit the two Chiefs and gain possession of the Order documents. In 1916 these two Chiefs had received the ceremony of the 'Etheric link' from Dr. Felkin, a ritual brought over from Germany. Later one of these Chiefs died in a mental home, and the two basal angles returned to Dr. Felkin and their Master!

The Order was to be a Centre of Light in London, and they were told that shortly messengers of light would appear in many parts of the city who would lead and teach the people. Was this to be revolution? And this subversive Order has not only temples in England and New Zealand, but also in several great cities in Australia!

In the *Morning Post*, July 14, 1920, 'Cause of the World Unrest,' speaking of Revolutionary Masonry, it said:

"When at length the candidate is admitted into the 30th grade, and, after going through terrifying ordeals to test his obedience and secrecy, becomes a *Knight Kadosch*, he learns that it is no longer Adoniram or Hiram whose death cries for vengeance…"

We conclude with a few significant sentences taken from the catechism of the Knight Kadosch degree:

"Do you fully understand that this degree is not, like much of so-called Masonry, a sham that means nothing and amounts to nothing; … that what you are now engaged in is *real*, will require the performance of *duty*, will exact *sacrifice*, will expose you to *danger*, and that this Order means to deal with the affairs of nations, and be once more a *Power* in the world?"

Further light is thrown upon this Kadosch degree in an unfinished manuscript of the autobiography of Pierre Fourrier Chappuy, who was born in 1762 and died in 1830 (see 'Masonry and Revolution,' Patriot, August 5, 1926):

"We were in the spring of 1789… I was the more enthusiastic from the fact that those ideas were the same as I had already absorbed in Freemasonry… Pride, always pride! This it was which separated me from my God and from love of my like, to create a divinity in my heart which was nothing but a lively egoism, to which I referred and sacrificed all things… It was plainly *the Society of the Illuminati*… It is no longer unknown what are the spirit and objects of this sect which, after uniting with the Freemasons and the impious of all countries, has set Europe on fire, and threatens more than ever at this time to extinguish both Christianity and *Monarchism* … but I was far away from the sixteenth, in which alone one learns the famous secret. After having read what concerns this last grade, which is that *of Chevalier Kadosch* — signifying *regenerator* — and the discourse made to the adept, I saw the light; and I understood perfectly and at once the symbols, formulae, and the tests which had hitherto been enigmas for me. They are all allegories borrowed from the procedure of the Templars, of which they are the successors."

Who, with any insight, can hesitate to say that this is the same canker which to-day, as in 1789, is corrupting our religious, social, and political life, and that within these Rosicrucian and Illuminised Orders this evil is generated; that by means of their adepts, consciously or unconsciously, this disintegrating cankerous growth is *carried and transmitted* throughout our Empire and among all nations.

In the 5–6 ritual of the R.R. et A.C. it is said:

> "The Order of the Rose and Cross has existed from time immemorial, and its mystic rites were practised and its wisdom taught in Egypt, Eleusis and Samothrace, Persia, Chaldea, and India, and in far more ancient lands. (It is the ancient worship of the Serpent Power or Creative Principle.)"

Hippolytus (*Refutation*, book v) tells us that the Nasseni, a sect of Christian Gnostics, apparently of Hebrew origin, derived their creed from the Cabala, and worshipped the Logos, or soul of the world, under the name and image of the Serpent-Hebrew *Nachash*, which according to the cabalistic science of numbers, is equivalent to *Messiah*, the Christ (solar) of occult societies.

> "The Nasseni affirm concerning the 'spirit of the seed' that it is the cause of all existing things and is the secret and unknown mystery of the universe, concealed and revealed among the Egyptians … who confessedly were the first to proclaim to all the rest of men the rites and orgies of all the gods as well as the unspeakable mysteries of Isis."

This is the Kundalini or dual creative forces of Nature, as described in *Serpent Power* and *Tantra*, translated from the Sanskrit by Arthur Avalon. It is the "Hye, Cye, the great unspeakable mystery of the Eleusinian rites." Again, 'Mercury (the Great Hermes) is Logos … at once the interpreter and fabricator of the things that have been, that are, and will be.' It is also the Cabalistic Adam Kadmon; the Ben Adam as depicted on the pastos in the Vault of the R.R. et A.C.; he is hermaphrodite, and is thus described in the ritual:

"I beheld seven golden Light-bearers, and in the midst of the Light-bearers one like unto Ben Adam clothed with a garment down to the feet, and girt with a golden girdle. His head and his hair were as white as snow, and his eyes as a flashing fire. His feet were like unto fine brass, as if they burned in a furnace and his voice was as the sound of many waters. And he had in his right hand seven stars, and out of his mouth went the sword of flame, and his countenance was as the sun in his strength."

Here we have what would at first appear to be the "Alpha and Omega" of the Apocalypse, but it is the Gnostic Logos. On the pastos Ben Adam was placed on the cabalistic Tree of Life, with the two pillars of Mercy and Severity — the positive and negative forces — on either side, and in the midst of the ten sephiroth and twenty-two paths of the Jewish Cabala. The face was that of the "Lord of Light," the transmitter of the initiating light to the individual or Order; it was arresting, dark and sinister, full of a subtle magnetic and compelling force. In the right hand were the seven geometrical stars of the seven planets, the seven aspects of the solar force, which united form the White Light of Illuminism. Out of his mouth proceedeth the Flaming Sword, it is the initiating or illuminising light. The whole represents the power of the Illuminati. Its name is not the "Word of God" but the "Lost Word" of illuminised Masonry, bringing wisdom, so-called, from the "unknown Chiefs."

Here we have without doubt Johannism, the clue to the Templar heresy; it is Cabalistic and Gnostic, luciferian and a perversion of Christian symbolism. It is Baphomet! The badge by which the aspirant gains entrance into the inner Temple is this Serpent and the Flaming Sword. It means arousing and raising the Kundalini or unused sex-forces — the Serpent coiling hither and thither, and its union with the power from without — the descent of the Flaming Sword; producing what is called the "Great Liberation," but controlled by these sinister masters for their own ends.

Let us consider the "Smaragdine or Emerald Tablet of Hermes." Mme. Blavatsky writes:

"Tradition declares that on the dead body of Hermes, at Hebron, was found by an initiate the tablet known as the Smaragdine. It contains in a few sentences the essence of Hermetic wisdom. To those who read with their bodily eyes the precepts will suggest nothing new or extraordinary, for it merely begins by saying that it speaks not fictitious things, but that which is true and most certain."

The precepts are:

"What is below is like that which is above, and what is above is similar to that which is below to accomplish the wonders of one thing"—manifestation according to principle.

"As all things were produced by the mediation of one being, all things were produced from this one by *adaptation*"—Life-force—ether.

"Its father is the Sun; its mother is the Moon." The Sun was considered by ancient mages to be the great magnetic well of the universe; he is the generator. He is Osiris, the sun in his rising and setting. The Moon is Isis, Mighty Mother, reproducing all principles. Nature in her vastness—The two contending forces.

"It is the cause of all perfection throughout the whole earth"— The life-force—equilibrium.

"The power is perfect *if it is changed into earth*"—Fixation of the astral into·a material basis or "vehicle."

"Separate the earth from the fire, the subtile from the gross, acting prudently and with judgment"— A prepared and purified material basis.

"Ascend with the greatest sagacity from the earth to heaven, and then descend again to earth and unite together the power of things inferior and superior; thus you will possess the light of the whole world, and all obscurity will fly away from you"—The ascent of the Kundalini or Serpent, and descent of the Flaming Sword, producing Illumination, or illuminised instruments. According to Eliphas Levi, the secret of the Great Work is the fixation of the astral light in a material basis, by a sovereign act of will — for the Great Good or the Great Evil; it is represented as a serpent pierced with an arrow. It is the Sun, Moon, and uniting and destroying fire of the "Serpent Power."

"This thing has more fortitude than fortitude itself, because it will overcome every subtle thing and penetrate every solid thing. By it the world was formed"—Electro-magnetic forces, the 'unbreakable chains' of the 'Protocols'."

This mysterious thing is the universal magical agent, the all-pervading ether, "which enters into all magical operations of nature, and produces mesmeric, magnetic, and spiritualistic phenomena." It is the Od of the Jews, the astral light of the Martinists. As Eliphas Levi has written: "It has been said that this universal agent is a light of life by which animated beings are rendered magnetic." And "the practice of that marvellous Kabalah reposes entirely in the knowledge and use of this agent." This, then, is the power which renders the adept "a dynamo of ever-increasing power and light."

In a curious pamphlet, dated about 1836, reprinted in 1888 by the "Theosophical Publishing Society" (see *Patriot*, September 8, 1927), we read of this unseen power:

"The pamphlet purports to have been written by the Wandering Jew, and describes how at the fall of Jerusalem he took the Hebrew Talisman, *the signet of Salomon* (interlaced Triangles) from the Temple, and how by its power he secured the rise of the Jews in all lands throughout history, till by finance they obtained entire control of the Gentile kings and rulers."

Speaking of the source of Necker's power about the time of the French Revolution, 1789, the Wandering Jew says:

"It was I, it was the talismanic power which I gave him for a brief breathing space, to inspire his friends with admiration and his enemies with envy. *I withdrew that power* and there arose the scene of bloodshed and confiscation which was especially necessary to enable my people to spoil all the nations of Europe... From the Revolution of France sprang bloody and expensive wars."

We read of the sinister influence at that time of Cagliostro and Weishaupt's Illuminism. What was the secret power behind them? And has not the Grand Orient Judaeo-Masonry, which was illuminised in March 1789, boasted of its power in bringing about "Three Revolutions — 1789, 1871, 19—?—Bull. Hebd ., 1922."

Further, do not the "Protocols" say: "The secret Power will not mind changing its agents who mask it ... the masonic Lodge throughout the world unconsciously acts as a mask for our purpose." It is written in the Stella Matutina rituals: "The Light shineth in the darkness, and the darkness comprehendeth it not." How many among us recognise the power of this sinister light, working secretly in and through the darkness and death of World Revolution?

In the August 1928 occult issue of the *Revue Internationale des Sociétés Secrètes*, M. Henri de Guillebert gives the following interesting points on the Interlaced Triangles known as Solomon's Seal:

"In synagogues, in front of sanctuaries, in masonic Lodges, in esoteric temples, are·shown two interlaced triangles, one white the other black. It is the Seal of Solomon. The colour black signifies that the object symbolised remains for ever in the darkness within the body; it represents the feminine. In the centre of the figure, the symbolism of whose interlacing is apparent enough to make explanations unnecessary, is the great and mysterious lingam... In the Sanskrit the word *lingam* signifies what is meant by the Latinised Greek word *Phallus*... Its situation, in the middle of the interlaced black and white triangles, points out, under another form, the union of the sexes. Usually in the upper and lower angles of Solomon's Seal are the letters—*Alpha* and *Omega*. The sides of the triangles are enlarged in order to receive a letter inscribed at each of the four angles. These four letters form the Hebrew word *(Eheieh)* initial and final, by which Jehovah taught Moses His incommensurable name: *'I AM that I Am.'*

"The syntactical union of this word with the letters Alpha and Omega and the signs of the lingam, in the interlaced triangles of Solomon's Seal, gives therefore the text: "I lingam, I am Alpha and Omega, the First and the Last, the eternal Pan." For the whole hieroglyphic indeed supposes that the motto "I am Alpha and Omega.," is made actual by means of acts, phenomena of human life or microcosm, and the total phenomenality or macrocosm (universe) by the personified and deified lingam. The same device is found among some sects under the form "Generation, Creation." To initiators, generation is an operation peculiar to divinity, when accomplished by themselves or their initiates. It is the divine act *par excellence*. Man who gives himself up to it exercises or usurps divinity."

Now, *Eheiek* is the password of the 5–6 grade of the R.R. et A.C.,. and in this ceremony the Chief Adept, as representing 'the divine I.A.O,' says: 'I am the First and the Last. I am He that liveth and was dead, and behold I am alive for evermore, and I hold the key of Hell and death.'

In Eliphas Levi's *History of Magic*, a diagram is shown of the 'Great Symbol of Solomon,' the interlaced triangles. This too has the lingam reflected in man from the universe above, and the whole is encircled by the serpent biting its tail — the symbol of the Kundalini. The lower part of the Theosophical symbol, as we have shown, is this interlaced triangle, also encircled by a similar serpent, and having in its centre the Egyptian Ankh — the key of life — another form of the lingam. It is the pathway to·initiation. In a curious book on the mysteries of the Cabala we read:

"Eliphas Levi called this mystic seal the 'Great Arcanum',

and in his version of the diagram a man and a woman occupy the two interlacing triangles. The figure illustrates the following passage from the 'Lesser Holy Assembly': So also here, where the Male is joined to the Female, they both constitute one complete body, and all the universe is in a state of happiness because all things receive blessing from their perfect body. And this is an arcanum."

In the celebration of the High Mass in the Universal Gnostic Church, as given in the February 1928 occult issue of the *Revue Internationale des Sociétés Secrètes*, the High-Priest thus invokes their Lord I.A.O.:

"Thou art unity. Thou art our Lord in the universe of the Sun. Thou art our Lord within ourselves. Thy name is the mystery of all mysteries... Open the way the door of Creation, and the links between us and thou! Lighten our understanding. Enliven our hearts. Cause the light to penetrate into our blood, to achieve realisation. *All in two Two in one. One in nothingness. Glory be to Father and to Mother, to son and daughter, and the Holy Spirit without and within.* (The Tetragrammaton with the *shin* in the centre — *Jehesuah*.) Which was, is, and shall be, world without end. Six in one through the names of Seven in one. Ararita! Ararita! Ararita!" The High-Priestess interposes with: "There is no other law than this, Do what thou wilt and love under control."

It is also worth noting that in the R.R. et A.C., the six-rayed star of interlaced triangles represents the seven planetary forces; a planet at each angle with the Sun, of which the others are but different aspects or manifestations, in the centre. It is thus used in invocations of planetary forces, and the word "Ararita" is always used in these invocations to symbolise the united force, one letter being attributed to each planet as well as all to each, the solar power working in and through each, a part of the whole.

One must understand that these Orders are always built up and worked on the principle of two contending forces ever united by a third, producing manifestation — the eye in the centre of the

Triangle. That is, spreading the initiating forces of these invisible cabalistic Jews to bring about their power and glory. It may mean temporary power and even glory - *under control* - for the adept, but eventually death of his own-personality. He loses his birthright; his life becomes a twilight of unreality.

In one of the late Donn Byrne's books, *Brother Saul*, a novel which depicts the life of Saul of Tarsus, it is interesting to read of the duel of wills between Saul and the black magician Bar-Jesus.

Bar-Jesus boasts:

> "Satan or Adonai, I serve a God and I have powers. I can make the ill well, and cast out demons. I can foresee the future and retell the past. I discover hidden treasure, and hinder armies. I invoke and command the dead. But Saul, all you have is words, empty promises." But Saul answers: "I have the power of withstanding evil."

(Bar-Jesus' god is I.A.O., and his power is the power of the interlaced triangle!)

Then Bar-Jesus proceeds to display his evil powers and says: "I will call up David, King of Israel." Four young boys, his disciples, enter with sword, wand, and crucible. "The boys were only alive by his wish. They had no life of their own. Somehow they had come under his power and he had eaten their lives. They were not living; they were undead." That is under control or obsessed! Then he took the sword and made a circle enclosing all, and again a second, between the two, he, with the point of the sword, wrote Hebrew letters, which in themselves are potent powers. But Saul and Barnabas stepped outside the circle, and remained there during the evocation. With raised sword Bar-Jesus conjured and exorcised in the names of *"Tetragrammaton Elohim; Elohim Gibor; Elvah-Va-Dnath; Shaddai Elchai; Adonai Melekh, etc.,"* and commanded the Apostate Spirits "that ye come immediately to execute our desire." Then Saul, without the circle, felt all that was evil gather and pad around him, but he stood fast. At last Bar-

Jesus knew he was beaten, and departed the spirits (or forces) saying, "In the name of Adonai the Eternal and Everlasting One (the Creative principle), let each of you return unto his place; be there peace between us and you, and be ye ready to come when ye are called."

This must be very familiar to members of the R.R. et A.C., for what is especially interesting in this evocation, as performed by the Black Magician Bar-Jesus, is its similarity to magical evocations as taught and practised in the Stella Matutina·Outer and Inner, an Order which counts quite a number of rather well-known clergymen among its members.

One of its rituals is known as Z_2, and is for the evocation of so-called planetary spirits, such as "Bartzabel, the spirit of Mars," and charging a Talisman with the power evoked. In the Stella Matutina Temple the four points of the compass are fixed with symbols and burning lights, and for this evocation a single enclosing circle is made, lights are placed on this, in number corresponding to the spirit evoked. Hebrew names similar to those used by Bar-Jesus and others, corresponding to the spirit, or force, are used in order to bring about manifestation, and the words of the final banishment are practically the same.

Without the circle is placed a triangle; at each angle burns a brazier, and as the EYE of Power in the Triangle, the spirit, force, or is it Master? manifests in the centre! While this evocation is progressing, and until after the banishment, the adept must remain within the circle, for it appears much evil is attracted. The ritual is based on one of the Cypher MSS., found, as has already been stated, in 1884. Members who do not care to practise such magic may undertake some special work, such as healing, or social work, under the direction of the mysterious masters, who, like Bar-Jesus, appear to "eat the lives" or souls of their disciples, so that they blindly accept an evil perversion, believing it to be a Sacred Truth.

Many unsuspecting members are blinded to the true nature of the aims of these masters, who are but Black Magicians such as Bar-Jesus, only more subtle and powerful, by high-sounding teachings on Love, Unity, Service, and Universal Brotherhood. They are led to believe that this teaching contains many profound truths not understood by the Christian Churches, and that it is one of the works of these societies to enlighten this darkness — to be the light shining in the darkness!

In the *Patriot*, May 1924, are some articles by Z. on "The Jew and Masonry"; in one it says:

> "Des Mousseaux quotes the German Freemason, Alban Stolz, who in a brochure published in 1862 says: 'The power which the Jews have known how to acquire through Freemasonry … is one of the most imminent dangers to the Church and State… There exists in Germany a secret society in Masonic form which *is controlled by unknown chiefs*. The members of their association are mostly Jews… The Jews only use Christian symbols either in derision or as a mask for their intrigues.' … With reference to the 'Temple of Solomon,' Des Mousseaux says: "This symbolical term, of which the real meaning is only known to the Supreme and Invisible Hierarchy of the masonic Lodges, and which are composed of Cabalistic Jews, signifies the reconstruction of the Jewish power from the ruin of Christianity"—(the solve and coagula of Illuminised Masonry).

In the R.R. et A.C. the cabalistic ritual Z_2 spoken of above, was one of the tests which most of the members had to pass through before receiving a certain higher grade, the 6-5. The last and most important of these tests was the evocation of "Adonai Ha Aretz," the Jewish Lord of the Universe — or was it a Master! In this evocation no circle was used — only a line of demarcation — between the adept and so-called spirit to be evoked. Writing the Hebrew letters with the point of the sword the adept evoked the Power until his own body radiated with LIGHT (Illuminism!). If successfully evoked, "Adonai Ha Aretz" appeared standing upon the Universe, his arms outstretched in the form of a Cross, holding in one hand a cup of red wine and in the other a sheaf of corn, representing the dual forces of Nature. This "Lord of the Universe, the Vast and the Mighty One," is the spiritual or magical ruler of the R.R. et A.C. as well as the Stella Matutina, for it is in his name that many of the invocations are made during the various grade ceremonies. The whole Order is based on this Jewish Magical Cabala.

Speaking of this German masonry Alban Stolz again says:

> "Their grades and systems observe certain Christian rites and symbols in order to cloak their real meaning."

Briefly, the Stella Matutina or Outer Order has for its symbol the Pentagram; that is, the four elements—earth, air, water, and fire—to which the four grades are referred; and above all the Spirit—the ether—which is referred to the Portal leading into the Inner Order. The Order represents a body being prepared for the descent of the Light, individually or as a whole—the Pentagram or Illuminised instrument. And to form the individual link with the masters the Kundalini is aroused and raised by Processes — a form of mental suggestion.

Knowing nothing of the true nature of the Order, and unaware of the oath to be taken, the candidate, blindfolded, is led into the Temple, and after consecration by fire and purification by water is placed befre the altar, where he is thus addressed by the Hierophant:

> "We hold your signed pledge to keep secret everything that relates to the Order. To confirm it I now ask you, are you willing to take a solemn obligation in the presence of this assembly to keep the secrets and mysteries of the Order inviolate? There is nothing incompatible with your civil, moral or religious duties in this obligation [the same was said by Weishaupt!] … are you ready to take this oath?"

Mystified and somewhat dazed, the candidate assents, and kneeling, repeats after the Hierophant as follows:

"I — in the presence of the Lord of the Universe, who works in silence, and whom naught but silence can express, and in the Hall of the Neophytes of that section of the Mysteries of Egypt, the Stella Matutina, regularly assembled under warrant of the Greatly Honoured Chiefs of the Second Order, do of my own free will hereby and hereon most solemnly promise to keep secret this Order, its name, the names of its members and the proceedings which take place at its meetings, from every person in the world who has not been initiated into it, nor will I discuss them with any member who has not the password for the time being or who has resigned, demitted or been expelled.

"I undertake to maintain a kindly and benevolent relation to all the Fratres and Sorores of this Order. I solemnly promise to keep secret any information I may have gathered concerning this Order before taking this oath. I solemnly promise that any ritual or lecture placed in my care and any cover containing them shall bear the official label of this Order·(so that, as with Weishaupt, they may be returned to the Order in case of death). I shall neither copy, nor allow to be copied, any manuscript until I have obtained a written permission from the Second Order, lest our secret knowledge be revealed through my neglect. I solemnly promise not to suffer myself to be placed in such a state of passivity that any uninitiated person or power may cause me to lose control of my words or actions. I solemnly promise to persevere, with courage and determination, in the labours of the divine science, even as I shall persevere with courage and determination through this ceremony which is their image. And I will not debase my mystical knowledge in the labour of evil magic (!) at any time tried or under any temptation. I swear upon this holy symbol (the White Triangle — the Light of Illuminism) to observe all these things without evasion, equivocation, or mental reservation, under the penalty of being expelled from this Order for my perjury and my offence, and, furthermore, submitting myself by my own consent to a deadly stream of power set in motion by the Divine Guardians of this Order living in the light of their perfect justice, who can, as tradition and experience affirm, *strike the breaker of this magical obligation with death or palsy, or overwhelm him with misfortune. They journey as upon the winds, they strike where no man strikes, they slay where no man slays.* (Hierus places sword on candidate's neck.) As I bow my head to the sword of the Hierus so do I commit myself into their hands for vengeance and reward. So help me my mighty secret soul and the Father of my soul, who works in silence and whom naught but silence can express."

This is the Lord of the Universe, the Creative Principle of all Nature, and the force is that mysterious current which "slays and makes alive."

Later in the ceremony this oath is further emphasised by two pure liquids being placed before the candidate; one is poured into a dish, followed by the second, which changes the pure liquid into the semblance of blood. The officer warns the candidate:

"Let this remind thee, O Neophyte! how easily by a careless or unthinking word thou mayest betray that which thou hast sworn to keep secret, and mayest reveal the Hidden Knowledge imparted to thee and implanted in thy brain and in thy mind, and let the hue of blood remind thee that if thou shalt fail of this thy oath of secrecy, thy blood may be poured out and thy body broken, for heavy is the penalty exacted by the Guardians of the Hidden Knowledge from those who wilfully betray their trust."

Experience tells us that this is no empty threat, and if, as is asserted, this Order is merely a means to spiritual development, and in no way subversive or dangerous, why then the need of this terrible and terrifying secret and obligatory oath? The "divine" and Cabalistic Guardians alone know and guard their diabolical secret!

At the close of the Initiation ceremony, in which the above oath is administered, which foreshadows all the subsequent Outer grades, every member present partakes of the "Mystic Repast." Upon the altar in the centre of the Temple, is placed a white

Triangle, for the manifestation of the Light, above it the red Calvary Cross of suffering, the means of attracting and establishing the light. Around the Cross are grouped the four elements — *Air*, the red Rose of the Order, whose scent is as the repressed sighs of suffering; *Fire*, the red Lamp, the will to self-sacrifice; *Water*, the Cup of red wine, the blood poured out as a sacrifice unto the Great Work; *Earth*, a Paten with bread and salt, the body destroyed to be renewed for this same Great Work. It is the Tetragrammaton. The whole represents the refined subtle Malkuth forces, the Cabalistic Bride, a "body prepared" for the descent of the Light — the "Christ" of the Illuminati.

The Hierophant descends from the Throne in the east, passes to the west of the altar, projecting light upon it as he approaches, saying: "I invite you to inhale with me the perfume of the Rose as a symbol of air; feel the warmth of the sacred fire; eat with me this bread and salt as types of earth; finally drink with me this wine, the consecrated emblem of water."

He makes a cross in the air with the cup, above the altar, and drinks. Each member, in order of office and grade, receives the elements from the previous partaker, but in absolute silence, until lastly the Kerux — "The Watcher Within" — partakes and finishes tbe wine; upturning the cup and raising it on high, he cries, with a loud. voice, "It is finished!" — the blood is poured out, the body is broken, the willing sacrifice is accomplished! But, we would ask, for what end?

The perfecting of the adept, this illuminised instrument, takes place in the R.R. et A.C., the Inner Order. First the adept is made to recognise that as an individual he is 'nothing.' In taking the required Inner obligation, he is clothed in a black robe, with a chain round his neck, and with outstretched arms he is bound upon the red Calvary Cross of suffering and self-sacrifice; above head is a scroll bearing the letters I.N.R.I. The obligation is in the form of clauses in accordance with the ten sephiroth on the Cabalistic Tree of Life. Before it is taken one of the initiating Chiefs, in attestation of the obligation, invokes 'the Avenging

Angel HUA, in the Divine Name I.A.O.' Then the adept repeats the Oath after the Chief:

"*Kether* — I. — I (Christian Rosenkreutz) a member of the body of Christ, do this day spiritually bind myself even as I am now bound physically to the Cross of Suffering. *Chokmah* — 2. — That I will, to the utmost, lead a pure and unselfish life, and will prove myself a faithful and devoted servant of the Order. *Binah* — 3.—That I will keep all things connected with this Order and its secret knowledge from the whole world, equally from him who is a member of the First Order of the Stella Matutina as from an uninitiated person, and I will maintain the veil of strict secrecy between the First and Second Orders. *Chesed* — 4. — That I will uphold to the utmost the authority of the Chiefs of the Order; that I will not initiate or advance any person in the First Order, either secretly or in open Temple, without due authorisation and permission. That I will neither recommend a candidate for admission to the First Order without due judgment and assurance that he or she is worthy of so great a confidence and honour, nor unduly press any person to become a candidate; and that I will superintend any examinations of members of lower grades without fear or favour in any way, so that our high standard of knowledge be not lowered by my instrumentality; and I further undertake to see that the necessary interval of time between the grades of Practicus and Philosophus and between the latter grade and the Second Order is properly maintained. *Geburah* — 5. — Furthermore, that I will perform all practical work connected with this Order in a place concealed and apart from the gaze of the outer and uninitiated world, and that I will not display our magical implements, nor reveal the use of the same, but that I will keep secret this inner Rosicrucian knowledge, even as the same has been kept secret through the ages. That I will not make any symbol, or talisman, in the flashing colours for an uninitiated person without a special permission from the Chiefs of the Order; that I will only perform any practical magic before the uninitiated which is of a simple and already well-known nature; and that I will show them no secret mode of working whatsoever, keeping strictly concealed from our modes of Tarot and other divination of clairvoyance, of astral projection, of·the consecration of talismans and symbols, and the rituals of the Pentagram and Hexagram, etc.; and most especially of the use and attribution of the flashing colours, and the vibratory mode of pronouncing the Divine names (Cabalistic and Hebrew). *Tiphereth — 6.* — I further promise and swear that, with the Divine permission, I will from this day forward apply myself to the *Great Work*, which is so to purify and exalt my spiritual nature, that with the divine aid I may at length attain to be more than human (deified), and thus gradually raise and unite myself to my higher and divine genius, and that in this event I will not abuse the great power entrusted to me (raising the Kundalini and uniting it with the universal ether and so linking with the masters). *Netzach —* 7. — I furthermore solemnly pledge myself never to work at any important symbol without first invoking the Highest Divine names (cabalistic) connected therewith, and especially not to debase my knowledge of practical magic to purposes of evil and self-seeking and low material gain and pleasure, and if I do this, notwithstanding this mine oath, I invoke the Avenging Angel that the evil and material may react on me. *Hod — 8.* — I further promise always to support the admission of both sexes to our Order on a perfect equality, and that I will always display brotherly love and forbearance towards the members of the whole Order, neither slandering nor evil-speaking, nor tale-bearing, nor repeating from one member to another, whereby strife and ill-feeling may be engendered. (This is invariably broken.) *Yesod — 9.* — I also undertake to work unassisted at the subjects prescribed for study in the various practical grades, from *Zelator Adeptus Minor to Adept Adeptus Minor,* on pain of being degraded in rank to that of a Lord of the Paths in the Portal of the Vault only. *Malkuth — 10.* — Finally, if in my travels I should meet a stranger who professes to be a member of the Rosicrucian Order, I will examine him with care before acknowledging him to be so. Such are the words of this my obligation as an Adeptus Minor, whereunto I pledge myself in the presence of the Divine One I.A.O. and of the Great Avenging Angel *Hua*, and if I fail herein may my Rose be disintegrated and destroyed and my power in magic cease."

Then the officiating Chief takes a dagger, and, dipping it in red wine, marks the stigmata in the form of a cross upon the forehead, feet, palms; and heart of the adept, saying in turn: 'There are Three that bear witness in Heaven; the Father, the Word, and the Spirit, and these Three are One.' (The Gnostic Trinity.) 'There are Three that bear witness on Earth: the Spirit, the Water, and the Blood, and these Three agree in One.' 'Except a man be born of water and of the spirit, he cannot inherit eternal life.' 'If ye be crucified with Christ ye shall also reign with Him.'

In reading this obligation it must be clearly understood that this Order is Cabalistic and Gnostic, Jewish and anti-Christian. In it we have the Lord of the Universe, the I.A.O., the Pan of the Gnostic cults. The Christ is the Serpent, the Logos of the Gnostics; a 'Christ' is a deified man. The 'Great Work' is Luciferian, the 'incarnation in humanity of the sovereign Sun,' the deification of the adept, who directing and commanding the astral light, performs seeming prodigies and miracles not for himself but always under control of the 'Divine Guardians of the Order.'

Turning to the letters above the adept's head, the I.N.R.I., we find that it is the keyword of the 5–6 grade, and is analysed thus:

> I. — Virgo, *Isis*, Mighty Mother—the reproducer of seeds and fruits on the earth — the *Preserver.*

> N. — Scorpio, *Apophis*, destroyer—the destroying and uniting force — the *Destroyer*.

> R. — Sol, *Osiris*, slain and risen—the generating force of the Sun — the *Creator*.

> I. — Isis. Apophis, Osiris. — I.A.O. — I.N.R.I. The *Preserver, Destroyer*, and *Creator*, as invoked in the Equinox S.M. ceremony when bringing down the light. The Inner Sign is L.V.X.

According to R.R. et A.C. correspondences, therefore, I.N.R is another form of I.A.O. — the Creative Principle, the final I. being the synthesis of I.N.R.—it is the Moon, Fire, and Sun — the Serpent Power, the Kundalini 'Two basal angles of the Triangle and one forms the apex, such is the origin of creation, it is the Triad of Life.' Further, the signs of this grade represent the solstices and the equinoxes, and the descent of the light and the affirmation of the links with these hidden Guardians of the Order are further ensured at the ceremonies of the Equinoxes and Corpus Christi, all of which are solar and not Christian.

The above Inner Oath is also taken at the Corpus Christi ceremony by the Chief Adept on behalf of the whole Order. Thus it will be seen the Order is wholly Pagan and Pantheistic!

This ceremony of *the Rosoe Rubeoe et Aureoe Crucis* depicts the "Chymical Wedding" of the Rosicrucians-Union with the Universal Ether. According to the Cabalists the Triad of Ether is: *Ain*-nothing; *Ain Soph*-unlimited, undifferentiated, infinite space; *Ain Soph Aur*-boundless universal light-manifestation. Marriage of the Universal Light or life-force in man with the limitless light or life-force of Nature.

This Universal Ether, the Lord of the Universe, is thus invoked in aid of the aspirant to this Initiation:

> "... O God the Vast One, Thou art in all things; O Nature, Thou Self from Nothing, for what else can I call Thee? For myself I am nothing, in Thee I am All-Self. and exist in Thy Selfhood from Nothing. Live Thou in me, and bring me unto that Self which is in Thee."

Seeking this Light of Nature, the aspirant is led into the Vault, the Tomb of the Adepts, for death and disintegration awaits the seeker after this Light, death of his own Selfhood and absorption into the All-Self-not God but Nature's Creative Principle-controlled by the Guardians of the Order.

The key to the Vault is the Rose and Cross, which, like the Ankh, is a symbol of the dual forces of life. The seven sides represent the seven planets, the varying aspects of the solar force, and the whole shows the working of the Spirit or Serpent Power in and through these planets, the twelve signs of the Zodiac — the whirling force of initiation—and the three elements—the material basis. The Altar in the centre is the Pentagram, the four elements dominated by the·Hebrew letter *Shin*, the Solar fire. It is *Jehesuah* or Jesus the illuminised man. And thus the Rosicrucians say: "From God we are born. In Jesus do we die. Through the Holy Spirit we rise again" — the Serpent Power.

Above, in the Vault, is the Light, and below the Darkness; and here comes the Illuminati creed: "But the Whiteness above shines brighter for the blackness which is beneath, and thus mayest thou at length comprehend that *evil helpeth forward the good*. And by the juxtaposition, on the seven sides, of symbol, colours and evocations by formulae, the Vault becomes a place of vibrations and flashings, attracting and fixing the forces from the masters, and in this Vault these forces may never be banished.

Beneath the altar is the pastos, in which lies the Chief Adept, representing Christian Rosenkreutz, the man crucified upon the Cross of Light. The pastos is opened, and touching the buried adept on the breast with his wand, the aspirant says: 'Out of the Darkness let the Light arise!' Then from the pastos issues a mysterious voice:

> "Buried with that Light in a mystical death, rising again in a mystical resurrection. Cleansed and purified through Him our Master, O brother of the Rose and Cross! Like him, O adepts of all ages, have ye toiled; like him have ye suffered; tribulation, poverty, torture, and death have ye passed through. They have been but the purifications of the gold in the alembic of thine heart, through the athanor of affliction. Seek ye the Stone of the Wise.

> "Quit thou this tomb then, O aspirant, with thine arms crossed upon thy breast, bearing in thy right hand the Crook of Mercy and in thy left the Scourge of Severity, the emblems of those

eternal forces betwixt which, in equilibrium, the Universe dependeth. These forces whose reconciliation is the key of life, whose separation is evil and death..."

Here we have resurrection by means of the Stone of the Wise — the Serpent Power, the Key of Life, it is Illuminism! The lid of the pastos illustrates the means of this Illuminism. It is divided into two parts, dark below and light above, and both are placed upon the Cabalistic Tree of Life. Below is the crucified adept in the form of the Crucified Christ on the Cross of Light, and the Great Dragon Leviathan, with the seven heads and ten horns, rises up to the Daath—the pineal gland—of the adept, where the head of the serpent unites with its tail — the negative and positive life-forces. From above descends the lightning flash, attracted by and uniting with the serpent, and illuminising — destroying the adept's selfhoop, linking him with the universal ether and the Guardians of the Order.

Now Aleister Crowley, who was an initiate of this Order, still, we believe, uses these rituals in his pernicious Orders. In his *Equinox*, The *Review* of Scientific Illuminism, he writes:

> "In Daath is said to be the head of the Great Serpent Leviathan, called evil to conceal its holiness (!) — the Messiah or Redeemer. It is identical with the Kundalini of the Hindu philosophy ... and means the magical force in man which is the sexual force applied to the brain, heart, and other organs, and redeemeth him."

That is, illuminises him. The Kundalini, the Dragon with the seven heads, or Serpent Power, is therefore the Christ or Redeemer of the Rosicrucians and Cabalists! It is Luciferian!

The Chief danger therefore in all these secret and *occult societies* of to-day, as of yesterday, is that they are ruled and influenced by an invisible hierarchy, which cannot be more closely defined than as composed of Cabalistic Jews. The visible societies train and orient, physically, mentally and astrally, instruments or mediums to be used at will by this hidden centre. Their "inner senses" must be awakened, the Kundalini or unused sexforces must be aroused and perverted to bring about this mediumship. The danger of mental unbalance is recognised and risked by these masters and the chiefs working under them. It was said by a Stella Matutina chief of one such medium through whom the messages and instructions were coming: "Christian Rosekreutz said she would be of great use if her brain stood the strain." If mental unbalance took place it was never said to be because of the Order work, but always through some inherent weakness in the adept so afflicted.

There was a bad case, one, who had been a brilliant student, and who later under Order influences became undoubtedly unbalanced and obsessed by the masters, believing herself to be the Christ or "the woman clothed in the sun with the moon at her feet." Much physical suffering and danger is entailed by these initiating forces, often reducing the adept to the lowest ebb of vitality, and some have even slipped out of life under the strain and vital depletion. Doctors are often puzzled to account for these illnesses. Always they are looked upon by the credulous adept as mystery tests. No matter how bad the past record of an Order may be, the faithful ever believe, "we at least can make it beautiful and spiritual," and so the deception works out to its evil end.

Many brilliant men and women have joined, and even ruled, these Orders-only to be broken on the wheel. Fine young clergymen, who have gradually and unconsciously become imbued with the false and subversive teachings of these masters, believing them to be heavensent, now co-operate with revolutionaries, extolling the doings of Moscow, and at every opportunity decrying the British Empire, seeking to wipe it off the face of the earth, blasphemously perverting Christ and His teachings in their attempt to prove their points. Others are men and women with every apparent chance of a brilliant career; but, all, even legitimate personal ambitions, must be given up at the bidding of these masters, who say, "We have need of thee and all thy gifts." We have known of brilliant brains in all walks of life thus prostituted to the cause of a diabolical dream which has no place for God or Christianity.

There must be no communication with outside and uninitiated mediums, the masters must alone control and enlighten! They know the power of Christianity and its Holy Sacraments and the uplift of religious fervour, and these they pervert, encouraging the adept to let go the material under the influence of perverted idealism. In the Church messages and visions are given, and even diabolical initiations attempted by these masters.

Most of the heads of these Orders, more often women, are illuminised; controlled power is given to them, they are as "magnets" drawing people to these Orders. One group in the Stella Matutina had as a chief, an educationalist, and this group was designed by the Masters to influence all professors, masters, and those interested in education, and the influence is now apparent. The London group was appointed to influence and bring in clergy of all denominations, and for this purpose the chief had to become a member of the Anglican Church; and so it was decreed that the pernicious teachings of the Order were to eat into and corrupt the Church, and although this chief refused, the work is being done by other members, mostly clergy, and everywhere the Church is becoming permeated, consciously or unconsciously, with this subversive Illuminism.

Under such chiefs as the notorious Aleister Crowley and his O.T.O., which is openly immoral, many have been ruined in fortune, mentality, and morals. But these masters, who are behind all, what of their mental and moral outlook? They profess to deify humanity and bring peace upon earth, but only so that humanity may be a pathway leading these Cabalistic Jews up to their throne, there as the "God-people," to rule over a "collective man," whose peace is apathy.

CHAPTER V

ALEISTER CROWLEY

THE thoroughly exposed and pernicious Aleister Crowley, *alias* Aleister MacGregor, Count Svareff, was, according to his own statement, born at Leamington, October 12, 1875, and was undergraduate of Trinity College, Cambridge, 1895-8. In November 1898, he became a member of the "Golden Dawn," the original of the Stella Matutina, where he was known as "Perdurabo," and under this pseudonym he wrote many of his unsavoury verses and books on Yoga, etc. He was, however, on account of his well-known reputation, refused admission into the London Inner Order the R.R. et A.C. As we have already stated, the then chief, MacGregor Mathers, had established a "Temple of Isis" in Paris, and in 1900 we have seen Crowley acting as his emissary to the London Temple, which had rebelled against and suspended this chief. He broke into and took possession of the London premises, but was eventually evicted. Nevertheless, he retained a full set of the Outer and Inner rituals and MSS. of the "Golden Dawn," and from 1909 to 1913, by direct orders, he said, from the Secret Chiefs, he published these documents in his *Equinox*, The Review of Scientific Illuminism, under the title of "The Temple of Solomon the King," along with much putrid and blasphemous stuff. This Review, with these rituals and MSS. as. teaching basis, was also the organ of his own Order of A.A. — the Atlantean Adepts, or Great White Brotherhood.

Of the A.A. he writes, in the *Equinox*:

"It is the unique and really illumined community which is absolutely in possession of the key to all mystery, which knows the centre and source of all nature… Lux is the Power always present (Serpent Power)… Yet besides their secret holy work, they have from time to time decided upon *political strategic action*… It is the most hidden of communities, yet it contains members from many circles; nor is there any centre of thought whose activity is not due to the presence of one of ourselves. He who is fit is joined to the *chain*, perhaps often where he thought least likely, and at a point of which he knew nothing himself."

Many are caught unbeknown to themselves and linked to this evil chain.

The Key to all Mysteries is shown by their symbol. It is the seven-pointed Star of Venus or Cytherea — the goddess of the ancient Serpent Fire, the Goddess of Love (also representative of the R.R. et A.C.). In the centre is the Vesica, or symbol of the union of the dual sexforces of Nature, and in each angle is a letter of the name BABALON — the Great Mother of all Gnostic and illuminised cults; it is Nature in her Vastness. The work of the A.A. is said to be the opening of the "inner senses 'by rousing and raising the Kundalini. Therefore do his disciples say of Crowley,' Blessing and worship to the Beast, the Prophet of the Lovely Star!" *Equinox*, 1911.

Of the same nature, if not actually the same, are his "Ordo Templi Orientis", and his M.M.M. — "Mysteria Mystica Maxima", — and all are apparently akin to the "Universal Gnostic Church." An account of the "Ordo Tempi Orientis" will follow later.

In 1905 Crowley went to India and made an unsuccessful attempt to climb Kinchinjanga, with fatal results to four of his party. In November of that year he was in Calcutta, and his night-prowling in the bazaars ended in such serious trouble that he, his wife, and young child left precipitately and proceeded to Burma. From Bhamo they trekked through Southern China to Hong Kong, and he was again in England in June 1906.

In 1912 his Temple was in 33 Avenue Studios, Fulham Road. In

1916 his O. T. O. Temple, near Regent Street, was raided by the police, books and papers were seized, and Mary Davis, the well-known medium, who was in charge, was fined. Later she was in a Temple in Hampstead as priestess of the Cult of the Beetle, again under Crowley. According to the *Patriot*, May 17, 1923: "During the War Crowley went to America, renounced his allegiance to his country, and conducted an active anti-British propaganda."

In 1922 we hear of him in his "Abbey," at Cefalu, Sicily, to which, according to the *Sunday Express*, February 25 and March 4, 1923, he enticed a brilliant university man of twenty-two and his young wife, and there, after going through unspeakable horrors, the young man died. Shortly after Crowley was cleared out of Sicily by the Italian Government, and for nearly seven years his headquarters have been in Paris, and only recently (April 1929) was he asked to leave France on the score of his immoral cults and practices.

Here and there from out the enforced silence a tragedy, due to Crowley's evil power and vicious influence, shows its ghastly face, renegade priests, broken and ruined, officiating at his Black Mass; young students and women demoralised and demented, hypnotised and forced to do the will of the "Beast 666" (the solar serpent), whose doctrine is the doctrine of the "Universal Gnostic Church." "Do what thou wilt shall be the whole of the Law; Love is the Law; Love under will." According to Crowley, Christianity is played out, and a new era is about to begin, an era apparently of the Cult of the Serpent-sex, the so-called redeemer of humanity! — the power of Illuminism and Judaeo-Masonic domination!

The following quotations from certain instructions issued by the Fratres of the O.T.O. to outsiders in the hope of drawing them into the net, November 1924, and also to be found in the *Equinox*, September 1912, will show how easily one might be deceived by apparently inspiring words and lofty ideas.

In the *Equinox* it is called:

"I.N.R.I. British Section of the 'Order of Oriental Templars O.T.O., M.M.M.,' and adds: 'The Praemonstrator of the A.A. permits it to be known that there is not at present any necessary incompatibility between the A. A. and the O.T.O. and M.M.M. and allows membership of the same as a valuable preliminary training"

In the instructions of 1924 the heading was:

"Sign of the Seal of Hermes, O.T.O., Ordo Templi Orientis, Rosicrucian Order of Freemasonry."

Then follows the *Preamble*:

"During the past twenty-five years constantly increasing numbers of earnest people and seekers after truth have been turning their attention to the study of the hidden laws of Nature. ... Numberless societies, Orders, groups, etc., have been founded in all parts of the civilised world. all and each following some line of occult study... There is but one ancient organisation of Mystics which shows the student a royal road to discover the ONE TRUTH. This organisation has permitted the formation of a body known as the ANCIENT ORDER OF ORIENTAL TEMPLARS. It is a modern school of Magi, it derives its knowledge from Egypt and Chaldea. This knowledge is never revealed to the profane, for it gives immense power for either good or evil to its possessors. It is recorded in symbol, parable, and allegory, requiring a key for its interpretation... By the right use of the 'Key' alone, the 'Master Word' can be found."

Instructions.—

"Let it be known that there exists, unknown to the great crowd, a very ancient order of sages, whose object is the amelioration and spiritual elevation of mankind by means of conquering error, and aiding men and women in their efforts at attaining the power of recognising the truth. The Order has existed already in the most remote and prehistoric times; and it has manifested its activity, secretly and openly in the world under different names and in various forms; it has caused social and political revolutions, and proved to be the rock of salvation in times of danger and misfortune. It has always upheld the banner of Freedom against Tyranny in whatsoever shape this appeared, whether as clerical or political or social despotism, or Oppression of any kind... Those persons who are already sufficiently spiritually developed to enter into conscious communication with the great spiritual Brotherhood (Great White Lodge) will be taught directly by the spirit of wisdom; but those who still need external advice and support will find this in the external organisation of this society ... it is the *Society of the Children of Light who live in the Light and have obtained immortality therein*... The mysteries which are taught embrace everything that can possibly be known in regard to God, Nature and Man... We all study only one book — the Book of Nature — in which the keys to all secrets are contained, and we follow the only possible method in studying it, that of experience Our place of meeting is the 'Temple of the Holy Spirit' pervading the Universe (ether or astral)... The first and most necessary requirement of the new disciple is that he will keep silence in regard to all that concerns the society... Not that there is anything in that society which needs to be afraid of being known to the virtuous and good, but it is not necessary that things which are elevated and sacred should be exposed to the gaze of the vulgar and be bespattered by them with mud (!) ... There may be things which appear strange, and for which no reason can be given to beginners, but when the disciple has attained a certain state of development, all will be clear to him or her... The next requisite is obedience... The conquest of the higher self over the lower self means the victory of the divine consciousness in man over that which in him is earthly and animal. Its object is realisation of true manhood and womanhood."

Crowley is said to have established these "Temples of Love" all over the world. *John Bull*, Feb. 4, 1925.

In 1911, according to the *Equinox*, he had more or less flourishing branches of his cult in England, America, South and West Africa, Burma, India, Malay Peninsula, Australia, British Columbia, Paraguay, Brazil, Holland, Switzerland, Germany, France, Algeria, and Egypt, and "excellent accounts from the Caucasus!" And thus is the canker spread abroad.

The following, which might well be applied to all these pantheistic and cabalistic cults of to-day, is an interesting statement, said by Mme. Blavatsky in her *Isis Unveiled* to be the words of General Albert Pike at a Supreme Council of the Ancient and Accepted Rite held in New York, August 15, 1876:

> "This *Principe Créateur* is no new phrase — it is but an old term revived. Our adversaries, numerous and formidable, will say, and will have the right to say, that our *Principe Créateur* is identical with the *Principe Générateur* of the Indians and Egyptians, and may fitly be symbolised, as it was symbolised anciently, by the Lingae ... To accept this, in lieu of a personal God, is to *abandon Christianity*, and the worship of Jehovah, and return *to wallow in the styes of Paganism*."

THE UNIVERSAL GNOSTIC CHURCH

The *Jewish Encyclopaedia* points out that Gnosticism "was Jewish in character long before it became Christian," and quotes the opinion, "a movement closely connected with Jewish mysticism." The Freemason Ragon says: "The Cabala is the key of the occult sciences. The Gnostics were born of the Cabalists." Again, to quote Dr. Ranking, "During the Middle Ages the main support of the Gnostic bodies ... was the Society of the Templars."

In his *History of Magic* Eliphas Levi tells us:

> P. 169 "The idea of Christian hierophants was to create a society pledged to self-sacrifice by solemn vows, protected by severe rules, recruited by initiation, and as sole depository of the great religious and social secrets, making kings and pontiffs without being itself exposed to the corruptions of

empire... A similar realisation was also dreamed by dissident sects of Gnostics and Illuminati, which claimed to pin their faith on the primitive Christian tradition of St. John. A time came when this dream was an actual menace for the Church and the State, when a rich and dissolute order, initiated into the mysterious doctrines of the Kabalah, seemed ready to turn on legitimate authority, on the conservative principles of the hierarchy, menacing the entire world with a gigantic revolution. The Templars ... were the terrible conspirators in question... To acquire wealth and influence, to intrigue on the basis of these, and at need fight for the establishment of Johannite dogma — such were the means and end proposed by the initiated brethren... 'We shall be the equilibrium of the universe, arbiters and masters of the world.' The Templars had two doctrines: one was concealed and reserved to the leaders, being that of Johannism; the other was public, being Roman Catholic doctrine... The Johannism of the adepts was the Kabalah of the Gnostics, but it degenerated speedily into a mystic pantheism carried even to idolatry of Nature and hatred of all revealed dogma... They fostered the regrets of every fallen worship and the hopes of every new cultus, promising to all liberty of conscience and a new orthodoxy which should be·the synthesis of all persecuted beliefs. They went even so far as to recognise the pantheistic symbolism of the grand masters of Black Magic ... they rendered divine honours to the monstrous idol *Baphomet.*"

Is this not equally true of the present World Revolution and the hidden power, working through the many secret Orders and groups of to-day?

In February 1928 occult issue of the *Revue Internationale des Sociétés Secrètes*, M. A. Delmas, speaking of the Universal Gnostic Church, with its centre in Lyons, tells us that it has adherents in France, Switzerland, Germany, Austria, Hungary, Holland, Russia, Rumania, the Slavonic States, Turkey, and America. It is known under different names, two being, "Order of the Templars of the East" and "Order of Light of the Seven Communities of Asia," and its affiliations are now generally known as Neo-Christians and Neo-Gnostics. Its Supreme Head is Sovereign Patriarch and Vicar of Solomon. M. Delmas gives a curious and interesting account of its office and liturgy of High Mass. The following are its doctrine and creed:

> "Do what thou wilt, this is the whole Law. But remember that thou must render an account of thine actions. Therefore I proclaim the Law of Light, Love, Life, and Liberty in the name of IAO."

Here again we have the Serpent Power, the Lord of the Universe. "Love is the Law, Love under control of the will." At once we recognise the doctrines of the notorious Aleister Crowley. Love too is the watchword of the R.R. et A.C., said to be love of humanity; but in the 5–6 ritual it says:

> "Note well that through the side of the Planet *Venus* thou hast entered" into the seven-sided Vault of the Adepts, the place of initiation. And we find in A. J. Pearce's *Text-book* of *Astrology*: "It was early recognised that Venus was the chief cause of generation and the mother of Love — the universal passion ... the Star of Being and existence."

The Creed:

> "I believe in the Lord, a God secret and inexpressible (in the S.M. ritual we find, 'The Lord of the Universe who works in silence and whom naught but silence can express'; in a star among a group of stars (sun and planets), by whose fire we are generated and to whom we return; a father of life; O mystery of mysteries! his name is *Chaos* (the all-pervading ether); it is the sole representative of the sun upon earth; in air, nourisher of all beings who breathe. And I believe in earth our mother, from whose womb is born all who are born. O mystery of mysteries! her name is *Babalon* ('Babylon, the Great Mother of the idolatrous and abominable religions of the earth'). And I believe in a Serpent and a Lion, O mystery of mysteries! it is called *Baphomet* (the Serpent of Wisdom and the Flaming Sword of the R.R. et A.C.; according to Eliphas Levi 'the Lion is the celestial·(astral) fire, while the

serpents are the electric and magnetic currents of the earth.' the Gnostic Logos, the spirit of the seed). And I believe in a Universal Gnostic Church, whose Law is Light, Love, Life, and Liberty; whose name is *Thelima*. And I believe in the Communion of the Saints. And seeing that our daily bread, material and earthly, which we eat is transformed each day within us into a spiritual substance, I believe in the miracle of the Holy Mass. And I believe in the baptism of Wisdom by which we accomplish the miracle of becoming men. (Crowley, in his O.T.O., says: 'Its object is a realisation of true manhood and womanhood'). And I confess and believe that my life is eternal, which was, is, and ever shall be. Amen. Amen. Amen."

The ether is said to be a storehouse of all that was, is, and shall be; and to be without beginning or end. It is Luciferian!

THE EMPEROR JULIAN AND MAXIMUS OF EPHESUS

In connection with these many illuminised orders—all of the Kingdom of Lucifer—the following is interesting.

Dmitri Merejkovsky, the Russian historical writer, in his book, *La Mort des Dieux*, gives a wonderful picture of a mystery initiation supposed to be given by Maximus of Ephesus, the theurgist, to Julian, the Apostate, before he became Emperor.

It begins at midnight with Julian, clothed in hierophant's tunic, entering the long, low, mystery hall.

"A double row of orichaic pillars sustained the vault. Each pillar, representing two interlaced serpents, served as supports for perfume-boxes... At the end shone two golden-winged bulls (emblems of life), supporting a superb throne upon which was seated, like a god, the very great Hierophant Maximus of Ephesus, clothed in a black tunic entirely embroidered with gold, emeralds, and rubies... Someone approached Julian from behind and securely bandaged his eyes, saying, 'Go, fear neither fire nor water, spirits, bodies, life nor death.'"

He is passed through a door into a long, dark passage; descending into the depths of the earth he passes through the trials by water and by fire, succeeded by nauseating odours and following shadows; an icy hand clutched his, which "had the playful movement and repugnant caresses of dissolute women." In horror he signs himself three times with the cross and loses consciousness.

"When he recovered his senses the bandage no longer covered his eyes, he was in … an enormous dimly lit grotto… In his front of Julian was a man, emaciated and nude, with copper-coloured skin, the Gymnosophist (Yogi), Maximus's assistant. Motionless above his head he held a metal disk. Someone said to Julian: 'Look!' He gazed at the circle, scintillating with an almost painful brilliance… Long he looked, the contour of the objects blurred, and a pleasant languor took possession of him. It seemed to him that the luminous circle no longer burned in space but within himself, his eyelids closed … Several times a hand lightly touched his head, and a voice asked 'Art thou asleep? … Look into mine eyes!' Julian obeyed, and perceived Maximus leaning over him… Under his thick eyebrows Maximus' eyes shone, alive, searching, penetrating, in turn mocking and tender… Julian, lying motionless, pale, with eyelids half—closed, watched the rapid visions which unrolled themselves before him, and it seemed to him that he saw them not of himself, but that someone willed him to see them… 'Wouldst see the Rebel? (Lucifer) Look! …' Above the head of the spectre shone the Morning Star, the Star of Dawn; and the Angel said: 'In my name deny the Galilean' (thrice demanded and thrice denied). 'Who art thou?' — 'I am the Light, I am the Orient, I am the Morning Star!' — 'How beautiful thou art!' — 'Be as I am.' —'What sadness in thine eyes!' — 'I suffer for all living; there must be neither birth nor death. Come to me, I am the shadow, I am peace, I am liberty! (liberation, loss of personality) … rebel, I will give thee force … break the law, love, curse Him and be as I am.'"

Julian awakes. He climbs the stairs with Maximus' firm hand in his: "He feels that some invisible force raises him on its wings (psychic force)... 'Didst thou call him?' asked Julian. — "No, but when a cord of the lyre vibrates another responds to it, the contrary to the contrary (polarity)." Maximus demands that Julian should choose one of two ways — the Kingdom of Lucifer or the Kingdom of God. Julian refuses the cross, and Maximus says: "Then choose the other way, be powerful as the ancients! Be strong and proud, pitiless and superb! Without pity, love, or forgiveness! Rise and conquer all... Eat of the forbidden fruit; but repent not. Believe not, doubt not, and the world shall be thine. ... Dare! thou shalt be Emperor!"

"They find themselves on a high marble tower astronomical observatory of high theurgy — built after the model of ancient Chaldean towers, on a high rock above the sea." Below were luxurious gardens, palaces, etc., and beyond on the mountain Artemision and Ephesus." Stretching out his arm, the Hierophant said: "Look! all this is thine... Dare! ... Unite, if thou canst, the truth of the Titan and the Truth of the Galilean, and thou shalt be greater than all men born of women." (Is this not Johannism?)

In his marvellous library Maximus talks of this initiation with one of his disciples.

"How can Maximus, the great philosopher, believe in all these absurd miracles?—I believe and I do not believe in them. replied the theurgist. Nature, which you and I study, is it not most wonderful of miracles? What a superb mystery in the vessels of the blood and the nerves; the admirable combination of organs... Our mysteries are more profound and more beautiful than thou thinkest. Men require enthusiasm. For him who hath faith the prostitute is truly Aphrodite and the luminous scales, the starry heaven... Julian hath seen what he wished to see. I have given him enthusiasm, force, and daring. Thou sayest I have deceived him... I love the lie which contains the truth... Until my death I will never forsake Julian. I will allow him to taste of all forbidden fruits.

> He is young, I will live in him, a second existence; I will unveil for him the seductive and criminal mysteries, and perhaps he shall be great through me! — Master, I understand thee not. — And because of that I thus speak to thee."

Is this not an illustration of what is taking place today in all these Luciferian Orders? This Invisible Centre, by means of theurgic power, deceives, hypnotises, sugests; promising power, liberty, and peace, a peace which is the peace of the controlled, of a living yet will-less and soul-less man, filled with the power of these devilish masters such as Aleister Crowley!

It is interesting to find in the R.R et A.C. that the chief who refused the initiation was some time before astrally taken up a similar theurgic tower and shown the world above and below, as a promise of future power! This power is the "Hebrew Talisman"!

Turning back the pages of Russian history we come across a man who was obviously another tool in the hands of this Central Power. In his booklet, *Mysticism in the Court of Russia*, M. J. Bricaud says: "In all ages the Court of Russia knew of, and submitted to, the influence of prophets and theurgists... Certain writings of Dostoiewsky, Tolstoi, and Merejkovsky have revealed to Western people the secret nature of the Russian soul, tormented and eager for the marvellous." Merejkovsky, in several of his books, has vividly painted the various aspects of this soul-sickness of Russia which, according to M.Bricaud, "ended in 1917 in the fall of the dynasty and the overthrow of its ancient institutions."

In *Le Mystère d'Alexandre Ier* and *La Fin d'Alexandre Ier*, Merejkovsky gives an interesting and detailed account of certain secret societies which were initiated and which spread throughout Russia in the reign of Alexander I. The translator, E. Halpérine-Kaminsky, tells us in his prefaces that it was after the march through Europe, after the retreat of Napoleon, that the Russian officers became imbued with, more especially, the French revolutionary·ideas. On their return a first secret society was founded by them in 1816 called 'Alliance de Salut'; one of the chiefs was Paul Pestel.

In 1818 this society took the name of "Alliance de la Prospérité." Under Pestel a revolutionary organisation (Society of the South) was formed within this, having for its aim the violent abolition of autocracy. The society for the union of the Slavs was formed in the south, and later fused with the Society of the South. "It is certain, in fact, that the movement created in 1816 marked the beginning of the Russian Revolution, which a hundred years later, in March 1917, triumphed in the name of the same principles as the 'Decembrists' of 1825."

Again, E. Halpérine-Kaminsky shows the extraordinary parallels between the reigns of Alexander I and Nicholas II. He write:

> "Other parallels could easily be established. But what will astonish even the best-informed on Russian affairs is the disclosure of actual Bolshevik roots working in the ground which gave rise to secret societies recruited from among the better class, even from the Imperial Guard, and which empoisoned the whole latter part of Alexander's life. To listen to the chief conspirator, Colonel Pestel, is to believe oneself listening to Lenin in person."

Let us listen to this conspirator Pestel, director of the Society of the South, who was executed in 1826. This was written by Merejkovsky in 1910, and was remarkably prophetic of what came to pass in 1917 and later:

> "The reunion of the Society of the North with that of the South is proposed by our Tribunal, commenced Pestel, on the following conditions: (I) Recognition of a sole director and sovereign dictator over the two tribunals. (2) Swear to an absolute and passive obedience towards this dictator-director. (3) Abandon the long road of civilisation and slow action generally accepted, and decree regulations more absolute than the futile principles given in our statutes. Finally, accept the constitution of the Society of the South and swear on oath

that there shall be no other in Russia… The first and principal action is revolution, insurrection in the army, and abolition of the Throne… The Synod and Senate must be forced to grant the provisional Government absolute power… The reigning dynasty must, therefore, in the first place cease to exist… The murder of one only will cause divisions, will produce internal dissensions, and will lead to all the horrors of popular insurrection. It is, above all, necessary that the destruction of all tyrants should be consummated.' He spoke placidly but unnaturally. 'He is an automaton, thought Golitsine, or rather one possessed!'…"

"The events of the years 1812, 1813, 1814, and 1815, said Pestel … as well as those of preceding and subsequent times, have shown us so many thrones overturned, so many kingdoms abolished, so many *coups d'état* accomplisbed that these events have familiarised minds with revolutionary ideas, the possibilities and opportunities of their realisation… From one end of Europe to the other, from Portugal to Russia, not excepting England and Turkey, these two political opposites, the spirit of reform is setting all brains seething ' (the actual words of Pastel)."

"He spoke as a master, and the fascination of his logic acted as the charm of music or the beauty of women. Some were subjugated, others were enraged … but all felt that what had been only a distant dream became all at once a near reality, terrible and heavy with responsibilities… 'These aristocrats, said Pestel, are the principal obstacles to public prosperity and the surest support of tyranny; only a republican Government can level them… I have greater faith than you in the predestination of Russia — the "Vérité Russe" is the name I have given to my constitution. I hope indeed that the "Vérité Russe" will one day be the universal truth, and that it will be adopted by all European peoples, asleep up to now in a slavery less apparent than ours, but perhaps worse, because inequality of property is the worst slavery. Russia will be the first to free herself. Our way goes from complete slavery to integral liberty. We have nothing; we want all! Without that the game would not be worth the candle… All differences of fortune and condition will cease, all titles and nobility will be annihilated. The merchant and bourgeois classes will be suppressed. All nationalities will renounce individual rights of its people. Even the names of nations will be abrogated except only the name of the Great Russian People... The citizens will be divided into rural communities so as to give all a uniform life, instruction, and government, and all will be equal in a perfect equality... The severest censure of the Press, secret police with a staff of spies, all tried citizens; qualified liberty of conscience...'"

Murmurs went round: "It is a penitentiary colony, and not a republic ... the most detestable autocracy!"

"Pestel saw nothing, heard nothing... The little man was a mere simulacrum, a waxwork automaton. He obeyed a fatal obsession coming from beyond, he no longer controlled himself, an invisible hand set him in motion, pulling him by a string like a marionette!"

The revolution was attempted in the reign of Nicholas I, December 14, 1825, and miserably failed. Five of the conspirators were hanged July 13, 1826, among them Pestel. Merejkovsky further says that these secret societies were branches of the Carbonari. Also speaking of their control, he writes:

"Our aim is the same and our forces are yours on the sole condition that you submit yourselves absolutely to the Sovereign Duma of the Society of the South. — 'What Duma? Where is it, and who belongs to it?' 'According to the rules of the Society I cannot reveal it ... but look!' He took a pencil and piece of paper, drew a circle, writing within — 'Sovereign Duma,' tracing rays from it, at the extremity of which he drew other smaller circles. 'The great central circle ... is the Sovereign Duma; the lines from the circle are the intermediaries, and the little circles the districts which communicate with the Duma, not directly, but by intermediaries.'"

Was not Pestel merely a controlled intermediary, and the Sovereign Duma the Supreme Directory of the Cabalistic Jews, the Invisible Power of the "Protocols"? Is this not the system of all revolutionary Judaeo-Masonry, of yesterday and of to-day?

CHAPTER VI

THE PANACEA SOCIETY

In the preface to Jane Lead's *Early Dawn of the Great Prophetical Visitation to England*, "Octavia," of the Panacea Society, tells us that since 1666 the plan of redemption for England has been set forth thus:

> "(I) As a prophetic whole by Jane Lead (1681–1704).

> "(2) Split up into the seven prismatic colours (the seven aspects of solar force, the planets!) and given forth by—Brothers, Joanna Southcott, George Turner, William Shaw, John Wroe, Jezreel, and Helen Exeter in succession, 1792–1918. (The last was drowned in the *Galway Castle*, which was torpedoed in the Channel on September 14, 1918.)

> "(3) As an operative whole, now being set forth by Octavia and by Rachel Fox, supported by the four, the Twelve, and the gathering 'remanent.'"

Jane Lead, associated with Dr. Pordage, and her son-in-law the Rev. Francis Lee, founded the Philadelphian Society in London in 1652. In *The Mystery of God in Woman*, Rachel Fox, President of the Panacea Society, writes:

> "... Between 1623 and 1704 a certain Jane or Joan Lead received revelations of a very pure and exalted nature. These are printed in what is called "Sixty Propositions to the Philadelphian Society, whithersoever dispersed as the Israel of God." In this Prophecy is set forth the future rise of the

Philadelphian Church, depicted in the Apocalypse as the ideal Church … 'a Virgin Church which has known nothing of man nor human constitution … shall be adorned with miraculous gifts and powers beyond what ever yet hath been.'

A careful study of these "Prophecies" shows that they are pure Illuminism and cabalistic. The teaching, as usual in all these cults, mystic or occult, leads to an initiation, forming an etheric link with some invisible power, arousing and perverting the Kundalini for this purpose, awakening the "inner senses": *clairvoyance* — "a clear crystalline sight … without any medium"; clairaudience — "a supernatural hearing … the Heavenly language as from eternal nature spoken"; *intuition* — "profound deep wisdom." Finally, fixation of the astral light in a prepared and purified material body. To describe one such cult is to describe all; it leads to pure negation of Self, cutting off "the rational understanding," bringing about complete subjection; as with Steiner, no intellectualising is permitted.

As we have seen in the R.R. et A.C. (1919), a Triune-cup, or Triangle, was to be prepared (1700), formed of three "Love-elders," placed at the top of the Cabalistic Tree of Life, representing the *Priest* or reconciler, full of *Faith*, and to whom was said as to the chief of the Triangle in the R.R. et A.C.: "Except ye drink of My Blood, ye have no life in you." (Compare this with the vision, as previously described, of the Spirit of Earth and Adonai, when the woman had to drink the cup of blood!) It is said to relate to the "Melchizedek" priesthood; the second love-elder is the *Prophet*, or passive receiver of the wisdom from above. The third is the *King*, the active transmitter or wielder of the Power, always under control. The whole attracting and manifesting the superior forces. Further it was said: "Whereupon from the *Upper Court and Council* did come forth a decree that it (Triune-cup) should be enclosed round with a *threefold circle*. The first appeared as a circle of golden light (Sun), the second was a circle of a silver light (Moon), the third a mild, gentle fire, yet invincible strength for defence (destroying fire)—"Sun, Moon, and Fire of the Serpent Power. And the final fixation of. the light in the "vehicle" is expressed in words similar to those used in the R.R et A.C. 6-5 ritual: 'Arise, shine, for thy light is come, and the glory of thy bridegroom is now become thy covering.' The light and glory of Illuminism!

This was to be built up for the purpose of establishing a Love Kingdom to be ruled by their Prince of Love and Peace; first, invisibly in the hearts and minds of certain persons who are 'to scatter among all fellowships and societies these pure sparkling powers of Love received from the Deity — ether.' Their deity is the Creative Principle, the Great Mother is Nature, and their Christ is the illuminising astral light. Finally,

> "a healing embassage from heaven is now sent down, that calleth and urgeth for *a universal harmony and unity* (universal republic and brotherhood!)... For the Prince of Love and Peace is near to pitch his Throne-Dominion and Kingdom ... and from whence will go forth such mighty influencing powers as shall cause all that is destructive to the Love-Kingdom to cease."

This is the power spoken of by Dr. Felkin's Arab teacher: 'We can project the psychic fluid with such tremendous power that it is positively possible to literally SLAY or make ALIVE ... but this power is so tremendous and dangerous that it is only permitted to a few'; as a *curative* or *punitive* current, or even hypnotic. What is this but the Jewish World Dominion by means of Illuminism-Krishnamurti's "Kingdom of Happiness"?

As etheric link and oracle, Jane Lead, like all such links, suffered much both mentally and physically. In 1699 she speaks of "great war and muting in the bodily parts ... that might very easily have released the imprisoned soul ... and such a depression of my superior life and spirit, which prevented me free use of my supersensual faculties." As sole answer to her complainings, her master said: 'You must not think it much (trial) to have your faith ground down, tried and proved' — a faith attained only when reason and sense "were cast into a deep sleep" — hypnotic control!

Coming now to the present-day manifestation of this movement, Rachel Fox, in her book, *The Finding of Shiloh*, tells us of the "triangle of workers" and the founding of the Panacea Society, whose work is to "spiritualise the material and materialise the spiritual," that is, to prepare "empty vessels," fill them with light, forming light-bearers for the masters' work for the world. Their master is a so-called Christ, no doubt one of the invisible council. The members of the triangle for the manifestation of this invisible power were: Octavia, widow of a clergyman and gifted, the apex and etheric link; Rachel Fox, a member of the Society of Friends, and K. E. F., as basal angles. Apparently the work was to be done through women, for it was said:

> "Know that it is not in all your thoughts how mighty and astonishing is this great work that I am come to perform. Therefore I can only permit man and woman to associate with me in supreme obedience… Herein I will show how the weakness of woman tends to my glory, for that she readily renders up to me the reins of government…" Again: "Do not question, do not argue, only obey and all will be well … in an instant I can so inspire you that ye shall think as one man and act as one body."

Mass hypnotism! One of their chief works was to enlighten the Church and to induce twenty-four bishops to open Joanna Southcott's box, the contents of which they believed would save England. To further this end Rachel Fox was strongly impressed that she must first be baptised and later confirmed in the Anglican Church so as to "hold her own with the bishops." She was therefore confirmed June 25, 1919, by the Bishop of Truro.

Octavia, being the etheric link with the masters, suffered intensely. We are told of a nervous breakdown, the result of the bishops' refusal to act, and a long sojourn in a mental institution about which she writes, November 1915: "What I suffer is hell… How can I live out each day in this torture with no aim, no hope, no ideal? I am horribly sane, but I am too full of a nervous dread ever to be myself again." And when her diabolical master considered her sufficiently chastened, he said, September 15,

1916: "I know her faithful work and her suffering, and it was my will that she should drink of the cup of pain, for so she is taught and purified, and she shall have reward. Bid her now come forth from her house of pain, and fear not, for I will be her guide." She only came out, however, to be imprisoned (set apart!) within her house and garden for some years, and still she suffered intensely; she was to be isolated from all that might influence and turn her aside from the great work! November 27, 1917, the triangle took an Oath, swearing to be led only by the Master, and to seek light on the Visitation from no book but the Bible, the Apocrypha, and the writings of their prophets. August 4, 1918, his master asked Octavia, "Art thou willing to lose thy personality for a period?" Believing the Master to be divine she consented, and on March 27, 1919, she tells of the fixing of the link, the illuminising power — Shiloh, Prince of Peace — descended into her body ready "after suffering great and terrible."·Her reason and sense "were cast into a deep sleep"!

Finally, they are told:

> "All who would enter the coming Kingdom, which is the realisation of what has hitherto existed in vision, speech, and writing, must enter a period of cessation from psychic momenta (it was said in the R.R. et A.C. that a time would come when all magic must cease!). Those have been allowed by me to develop in the last decade for this reason, that I had to gather many in this manner ... but all must now walk on the material plane... Concentration upon soul-development (that is, astral-development) will hinder the Coming. This is a hard saying, but be it known I *will* now to be a centre (having taken possession of his 'vehicle'), drawing my people unto me, whereas in soul-development my people endeavoured to draw me unto them...' (As in Steiner's Way of Initiation, leading to obsession.)

In other words, these masters — doubtless identical with the terrible power behind the horrors of Russia's sufferings and World Revolution — have in reality no interest in soul or astral development except as a means of forming passive illuminised tools, completely controlled in mind and actions.

As we have seen, one of the main objects of this Society was to get Joanna Southcott's box opened by twenty-four bishops, but only under specified conditions as decreed by their masters. These conditions are as follows:

'1. The exact location of the box is known to a lady who has seen the box herself, and upon hearing from the Bishops, will put them into communication with the intermediary, who will supply the custodian's name and address.

'2. Portions from the writings of Joanna Southcott, from the moment they were written, were commanded to be kept close till the Bishops should ask for them, "in a time of grave national danger." The initiative must therefore be taken by the Bishops or by some authority in the land and not by believers in the Visitation. But, when the Bishops agree to send for the box, twenty-four believers will come forward to form a jury, to meet the twenty-four Bishops or their representatives.

'3. The Book of the trial of the claims of Joanna Southcott (1804) must be read by all those consenting to be present. It will be produced for the Bishops.

'4. An attorney must be present.

'5. There are written instructions for the Judges and jury, which are to be kept sealed until the Assembly meets.

'6. A suitable house must be lent or rented for the occasion. The box of writings must be previously placed for three days in the vault or cellar of the house. (*Note*. Perhaps the writings are charged with the 'original atom' even as the sections of linen are said to be!)

'7. The house must be close to a field or railed-in space. (Is this to 'set it apart,' in order to place round it the 'threefold circle'?)

'8. The sixty-five books and any original MSS. possessed by believers are to be exposed for investigation on the first three days of the Assembly.

'9. In the first the double jury of believers must meet the Bishops, that they may discuss the problems at stake.

'10. On the second there will be a sign from the Lord of great importance.

'11. On the third the sealed writings are to be cut open and examined.

'12. This trial is the herald or precursor of the doom of Satan, as described in Rev. XX. There will be no rest in the world until the opportunity be afforded of putting the assertion in Joanna's writings to the proof.

'13. If the verdict of the Bishops be against the writings, they may be burnt.

'14 It wilt be recognised, when the box is opened, that the trial compares for importance with the Trial of Christ before the Sanhedrin.

'15. In the published writings, the ceremony is also compared to the reading of a last wilt or testament. (It might be the death of the British Empire! brought about by the "small and constant Sanhedrin.")

'16. It is also compared in the writings to an inquest (!), the box to be regarded as men regard a body which has been discovered.

'17. On this occasion the Church of England will stand her trial, to keep or lose her place among the Candlesticks.

'18. Those calling the trial must sustain the cost-i.e. the expenses of jury and witnesses, etc. (Bishops!)

"19. No sealed person is to be refused admission to the Trial.

'20. "As I made Myself known in the breaking of bread at Emmaus, so will I make Myself known in the breaking of the seals of the Writings."" (Taken from Healing for All.)

Jane Lead's Prophecies are the basis of all this, and they are Illuminism and Rosicrucian. As we have seen, one of the great aims of the R.R. et A.C. was to corrupt and disintegrate the Church in England and the Empire.

A box, said to be Joanna Southcott's, was eventually opened, and one of the most interesting accounts was given in the *Daily Telegraph*, May 9, 1927, written before the actual opening. We are told that she was born in 1750, had little education, working in domestic service and in shops, and in an orthodox way was an assiduous attender at church and chapel. At the age of forty-two she began to prophesy, announcing the near approach of the Millennium and coming convulsions in Europe. According to her prophecies, the faithful were to number 144,000 (Rev. vii.), and certificates of their appointment to felicity, no doubt a form of sealing, were issued.

Notwithstanding this, "one of the recipients was certainly hanged for murder"! In 1813, at the age of sixty-three, she announced 'that she was to become the mother of Shiloh the Prince of Peace,' a new Messiah! But 'Joanna died without bearing a child.' 'Upon her death-bed, it is reported she gave to a companion a sealed box, with the injunction that it was only to be opened in time of dire national need, and in the presence of a number of bishops; under these conditions it would reveal an unexpected means of saving the country.' What is said to be this box, though it is denied by the Panacea Society and others, was opened, and the result was not only a fiasco but a farce.

In *The Impatience of the People*, by Mark Proctor, the Panacea Society once more made a brave effort to catch the public eye. The consummation of their hopes, 'the Second Advent,' so-called, which was looked for in 1923, is now long overdue! Joanna's box, or at least one of the many, has been opened and has passed into oblivion, resulting in a fiasco to all such as believed in her supposed power to save an England which apparently has no desire so to be saved! England still rides the storms and still holds her own, notwithstanding many onslaughts visible and invisible, and long may she do so.

The first thing that impresses one in this little book is its profound and almost insolent arrogance, a trait common to these hidden illuminati, these Cabalistic Jews, but not what one expects from Divine inspiration, such as they claim! In it he says:

> "How good, then, it is to learn that man's extremity is God's opportunity, and that when things are getting to such a climax that no one knows what to do, God is coming to the rescue with a fresh message (through the Panacea Society!) which brushes aside the confusion of academic intellectualism, of false ecclesiasticism, of mystical spiritualising, of ritual staging, of quarrelsome Anglicanism and Protestantism, of the emotional religiosity of the Nonconformists, and of the whole gamut of cults and sects daring to call themselves 'religious' to-day."

One wonders in what respect the Panacea Society differs from "the whole gamut of cults and sects," illuminised as they themselves are. Do they not each one believe, as does the Panacea Society, that they alone are not as other cults and sects?

Further he writes: "A prophet is not a priest at all; he is an automatic receiver of a direct divine message, stated in a sequence of words, which he must set down precisely as he heard them." He adds that fulfilment is the proof of their divine nature, in which case their messages apparently fail in the test; have they been fulfilled?

We have before us an astonishing pamphlet and leaflet issued by the Panacea Society, April 1926. It speaks of their power to give "Divine Protection" during a coming crisis. Now what is this crisis? In their magazine, *Panacea*, they give an explanation. They have in it a quotation from an amusing article, reprinted from *Punch.,* called "the Next War," in which it is said there is going to be another war, and this time *entirely in the air* — aeroplanes dropping "filthy things" over all, "so you will just inhale your ration of stink-bomb like a man, and die like a dog!" The *Panacea* takes this very solemnly, and writes:

> "Yes, it is true that no weapon formed against England will prosper when she awakens to the power of the Panacea remedy. Our airships carrying *the blessed water* — the result of God's Visitation to England since 1792 (Joanna Southcott) will be a wall of defence to Britain, a wall which no enemy will be able to pass or destroy!"

In 1923 they placarded the following poster in Plymouth: "Earthquakes, Thunder, Plague will soon startle England unless the Bishops open Joanna Southcott's box." Such troubles are always more or less with us, but the plague we have to fear more than all these put together, is the plague of these illuminised societies and their so-called divine missions, directed from the air; they are the stink-bombs to be shunned by all who really love their country and Empire.

Again they speak of "Divine Healing," and for this healing the afflicted one must write out a full list of complaints, imaginary or otherwise. This is read to the "Oracle," who receives the so-called divine instructions, and the wafer or section of linen is charged with the required psychic-magnetic forces much in the same way, no doubt, as a magical talisman is charged. These sections are to be dipped into the drinking water, bath, and even it may be into the medicine prescribed by a medical man, though it seems scarcely fair to the medical man! In all occult Orders, with varying methods, healing by means of this magnetic fluid goes on with more or less success, and as we know it can slay or make alive. If curative it may also be hypnotic, creating a band of faithful followers! They make much of healing, "without money and without price," but, after all, one of the rules of the Rosicrucians was: "That none of them should profess any other thing than to cure the sick, and that *gratis*," though some adepts have interpreted "gratis" as "*freely*," so that a fee might be asked!

In their pamphlet, *Healing* for *All*, they say: "Any fool can detect Satan's wickedness, but it takes a wise man, indeed, to discover Luciferian error!" Can they be sure that they are wise enough not to be deceived by Luciferians such as these hidden Illuminati? Can they be sure that they, along with all these other Orders and groups, are not working to bring about the reign of Luciferian power — that is, Illuminism? They say: "We have no hesitation in declaring that no religion nor cult nor any individual whatsoever, outside of this Visitation, has the *whole Truth*!" This is very like the spiritual pride, that, it is said, brought about the fall of Lucifer!

One word about their communications which are recorded by them in *The Writings of the Holy Ghost*—that is astral communications. They appear to be very much the same as many received to-day by occult and spiritualist groups, and, far from being divine, are full of crafty deception and flattery. In these records, April 15, 1920, it is said: "I have led thee to note that in the years of 1919, 1920, and 1921, the period between Easter and Ascensiontide was a time of many developments." Easter 1919 was the time of the attempt, by these hidden illuminati, to establish the Triangle of Power in the R.R. et A.C.!

THE UNIVERSAL ORDER

THE Universal Order is yet another pseudo-mystic group, professing to have nothing to do with occultism, but nevertheless equally deceptive and dangerous. It was known for many years as the "Order of Ancient Wisdom," with its headquarters in Manchester, and a branch in London and possibly elsewhere. Its teachings were Neo-Platonism, and they held their London meetings and gave grades in the large upper room over Eustace Miles's vegetarian restaurant. The ceremonies were simple, but occult, attracting forces, such as are found in all occult ceremonies, though they professed merely to teach a form of philosophy. In or about 1918-19, when similar movements, unbeknown to each other, were taking place in other groups, the leaders of this group were by some "compelling force," or occult influence, made aware that they were expected to recognise and practise the Christian faith, from which they, as Neo-Platonists, had lapsed; this they accordingly did.

Somewhat later the name was changed to the "Universal Order," no doubt as being more akin to international brotherhood, and was conducted on more or less Christian lines, including retreats, meditations, and having, I believe, modified grades to suit the apparent change of outlook. This induced a form of pseudo-religious excitement, creating highly nervous, emotional, and mediumistic conditions, leading to possible control, as is universally found in all such Orders and groups. The Order was linked by mutual membership to the S.M. and R.R. et A.C., and their mission was also apparently to enlighten the Church or bore from within, as in the S.M. Later again, some of its groups changed the name to the "Shrine of Wisdom" — the title of its publication.

Having studied the Leaflet No. I sent by the "Secretary of the Universal Order," a few words about their aims and system might be useful. From this leaflet the Universal Order appears to be a veritable Esperanto of philosophy, religion, and mystic science, for they aim at the realisation of Universal Wisdom; yet it "is not a religion, but embraces the essence of all religions; it is not a philosophy, but it includes the fundamentals of all great philosophical systems." In seeming contradiction we are told that the finite intelligence nominally is capable of apprehending only one presentation of Truth; following several it frequently fails to understand any of them! Therefore, although universal, they advocate one definite system of instruction, their own, professedly embracing all aspects of Truth! Who then has built up this apparently contradictory system — universal yet particular? Who is the judge of the true essence and fundamentals with constitute this system of universal wisdom leading to brotherliness and tolerance? Have they, too, unseen masters who direct and instruct?

Let us see what they endeavour to avoid. Following their "Ideal Harmony", they cultivate such a "wide sympathy and tolerance, a silencing of that inquisitorial criticism," that they "do not condemn, nor attack, nor countenance the attacking of any other movement, howsoever diverse it may seem," for they believe every movement may serve some useful purpose! What of the Grand Orient Judaeo Freemasonry, whose avowed aim is "International Revolution" and its subsequent "Universal Republic"? What of the Illuminati? — who seek by subtle pseudo-spiritual teachings to create illuminised tools, blinding and intoxicating by false ecstasy, false vision, and false teaching, forming "unbreakable chains," as the" Protocols "show, whereby they secretly unite mankind and control them, the only possible method by which they could hope to rule the world as a whole. What of the Bolsheviks and the invisible power behind them? Does the Universal Order passively condone such movements?

They endeavour to avoid all dualistic doctrines, but what is the triangle of their symbol? Is it not the two contending forces ever united by a third, which produces manifestation in conformity with its principle — as above so below? Again they endeavour to avoid psychic, passive mediumship, necromancy, and magic of all sorts; but they "do not turn away or oppose those who follow any of these pursuits!" Thus through this passive tolerance and lack of using their critical faculties, their Order may become a secret breeding-ground for all these evils they do not oppose or turn away.

They use rituals, rites, and symbolism, rightly or wrongly interpreted and adapted from the teachings of the ancient mysteries, even as is done in the Stella Matutina and kindred Orders — we have seen what the basis of these mysteries was! Upon this unstable and somewhat contradictory basis the members are encouraged to seek for "personal illumination" and 'interior occultism of the soul' by 'soaring in prayer, meditation, and contemplation' Is this not playing with hidden fire, which invariably leads to nervous wreckage? Can the leaders of this Order with any certainty assure their members that this personal illumination will mean union with the divine, and not obsession by this invisible material power which is everywhere seeking for instruments, and which perverts all that is sacred, using it as a means of ensnaring the unsuspecting victim?

What do the 'Protocols' say of "collectivism"?

> "We will let them ride in their dreams on the horse of idle hopes of destroying human individuality by symbolic ideas of collectivism. They have not yet understood, and never will understand, that this wild dream is contrary to the principal law of nature, which from the very beginning of the world, created a being unlike all others in order that he should have individuality."

Why, then, this demand of absolute self-sacrifice from members of these mystic and occult groups? Is it not that these groups of pseudo-public and actual secret societies are merely so many cogs in this great annihilating machine, whose mission, in the name of Unity and Universal Brotherhood, is a slow and deadly destruction of all individuality, creating a soulless automaton, whose driving and directing power is the will of this central group of Hidden Chiefs, the Great White Lodge?

A powerful picture of this "Collective Man" as attempted in Soviet Russia is given in *The Mind and Face of Bolshevism,* by René Fülöp-Miller. Here is the author's final judgment:

> "What concerns the whole civilised world in the highest degree is this 'barbarous jesuitry' (as seen in Weishaupt's Illuminism) which claims to be a doctrine of salvation for the whole of humanity, while in reality it is threatening its very foundations. Bolshevism aims at more than the confiscation of private property: it is trying to confiscate human dignity in order ultimately to turn all free reasonable beings into a horde of will-less slaves."

The same might, with truth, be said of the way of salvation and so-called "evolution of humanity, "as depicted in the teachings of all these secret societies and "new temporary religions" of to-day.

CHAPTER VII

AMERICAN CULTS

AMERICA — internationalism personified in her people — that land of amazing cranks, crazes and cults, teems with examples of this soul-destroying canker of "isms"; only one or two need be touched on in these investigations.

THE SADOL MOVEMENT

The "Sadol Movement" is yet another esoteric masonic group, another link in the "magnetic chain," prepared by this invisible centre in their schemes for World Domination. It was established in America in 1883 by J. E. Richardson, who is known as TK, or the "Elder Brother," and is the representative in America of the "Great School of Natural Science" (Great White Lodge), whose centre, they say, is in India.

According to TK, it is said in their *Bulletin*, January 1926, that this Great School has a written history extending over a period of more than 200,000 years! Further, that it settled in India 23,000 years ago, at the time of the sinking of the Atlantean Continent! This is without doubt the 'Great White Lodge' of all esoteric Masonry, such as Max Heindel's' Rosicrucian Fellowship," Mrs. Besant's group, the Stella Matutina, etc. Who can say where the centre of this occult government really is? The whole organisation has been built up by systematic confusion between things said and things meant.

We have before us an extract from *the Sadol Magazine*, 'The Great Work in America,' showing that they follow the Ancient and Accepted Scottish Rite, although in their text-books they speak only of the three degrees of the Blue Lodge. TK writes:

> "It is already known by Scottish Rite Masons generally that General Albert Pike was the author of the ritualistic ceremonials for the entire 33 degrees of the Order. It is not generally known that he received the 'Legenda,' which constitute the philosophic background of each individual degree of the entire 33 — directly and personally from the Arabian member of the Great School."

With reference to the 'Arabian Member,' it is interesting to note the Stella Matutina 'Arab teacher.'

The text-books of this Movement consist of the 'Harmonic Series,' in four volumes. A careful study of these clearly shows that the teaching is not constructive leading to Mastership, as they maintain, but destructive leading to Mediumship. Volume 4, *The Great Known*, might equally be the teaching of Conan Doyle or Vale Owen! They believe they have found the 'Lost Word' of Freemasonry, which, according to TK, means direct communications from the masters. Thus the whole teaching would appear to be given for the purpose of inducing clairvoyance, etc., preparing mediums sensitised by means of secret formulas, and the use, in rotation, of the colours of the spectrum. They believe themselves free, absolutely *self-controlled*; but it is intellectual bondage induced on the part of their masters by ambitious and diabolical misapplication of occult knowledge and abuse of power gained thereby.

I have already explained the methods adopted in this group for contacting the Master or 'wise and powerful Luminous Ones!' and how they correspond to those used in the Stella Matutina, and the Edinburgh Sun Order.

THE ORDER OF THE INITIATES OF TIBET

These notes are taken from an article in the *Washington Post*,

October 31, 1909, entitled 'Washington's Most Curious Cult Under Leadership of a Woman.'

Miss A. E. Marsland, President of the Order in America, is a daughter of George Marsland, founder of the American Bankers' Association. Washington is the centre of this movemnent for America, which was founded there in 1904 by Miss Marsland and four or five enthusiasts. There are now (1909) 5,000 members, and the cult is slowly and quietly growing. Among her followers are found some of the most prominent members of the social and diplomatic set; they meet twice weekly at the home of the Oriental Esoteric Centre, 1443 Q Street, there to drink in the mysteriously transmitted wisdom. Miss Marsland does not know the exact place from which her instructions and lectures come, but she believes that the documents written in Sanskrit are sent out from the fastnesses of Tibet (not Lhasa) to Paris, where they are translated into French and then sent to Washington, Brazil, and Egypt. The occult masters are the fountain-head of knowledge, but each centre is independent as far as internal government is concerned.

According to the doctrine of the Initiates, the fifth Great World leader and teacher of mankind is to be born in America within the next twenty-fiye years. The four previous leaders were, they say, Rama, Krishna, Buddha, and Jesus. The mission of the centres established by the Initiates is to draw men from the study of material effects which has so far occupied the exclusive attention of scientists, and to direct them to the study of cause, force, vibration, and the unseen. This, they say, can only be done with safety by the man who is master of himself, and so the stupendous task of the pioneers of the New Era is to transmute the scientist into the Mage! According to Miss Marsland, the world entered upon the New Era in 1898, and will show a wonderful advancement in knowledge of the occult, leading, perhaps, within the next 2,000 years to contact with the inhabitants of the other planets, who are said to be spirits who have previously lived upon earth. But knowledge of this and many other mysteries of the cult are not revealed even to Miss

Marsland!

Prof. F. Charles Bartlet is leader of the Order in France, and a recently discovered spring, which is curative, at Châtel Guyon, at the foot of the extinct volcano Puy de Dôme, is now the property of the Order. On the summit of the mountain is a ruined Temple to Venus and the Sun, which appears appropriate to such a cult! One or two of their precepts are enlightening, as for instance: 'The entire submission of the personality to the Higher Nature (Masters!); non-resistance or the law of love (pacifism!); the Universe is one, therefore all are united in Universal Brotherhood.' Also, *"Noontide Meditations,"* as 'O disciple, it is indispensable to silence thy reason and give ear to thy mentality. Listen! but not with the outer years (clairaudience). Behold! but not with the outer eyes (clairvoyance). There comes a voice, a presentiment, a thought, yet it is not a thought, a feeling, a vibration, yet it is none of these.' No, it is the Master forming links, trying to control and suggest! They further profess to believe in a Supreme Deity, but he is no doubt the Lord of the Universe, I.A.O.

The key to this cult is given in one of its most interesting symbols — Adda-Nari. She is Nature-generation, creation, as is shown by the symbols of manifestation in her four hands, and the sign of the lingam, and the Triad of the Serpent Power on her forehead.

The purposes of this cult are: "To form a chair of universal brotherhood based on the purest altruism, without hatred of creed, sect, caste, or colour … to study occult sciences of the Orient, and seek by meditation and a special line of conduct to develop these powers which are in man and his environment." This is the usual yoga, awakening and raising the Kundalini!

They have a monthly magazine, *The Esoterist*, edited by Agnes E. Marsland; in the July issue 1924 there was an article called "Good Government"! Further, November 1927, a letter was sent to members, Plea for investment in the Marsland Centre, and Conditions, Live in Community Stock Farm." It appears to increase and prosper! Finally, a *Prophecy Bulletin*, with a tau cross at the head of it, issued last New Year, says: "This crisis is now imminent, and will decide once for all the future condition of the earth. The Great Master is with us directing the battle." Signed, AGNES E. MARSLAND, Lexingvton, N.C.

The movement is said not to be Jewish; but one of their publications bears on its front the symbol of Solomon's Seal!

Again, the above is a Pantheistic and apparently cabalistic cult.

THE BAHAI MOVEMENT

THIS movement was founded in 1844 by a Persian, Mirza Ali Muhammad, who took the title of "Bab" (the Gate); he revolted against the Hierarchy, who, fearing his growing influence, had him shot at Tabriz, 1850.

It claims to be the fulfilment "of that which was but partially revealed in previous dispensations," and they look upon Buddha. Zoroaster, Jesus, Mohammed, and Confucius as merely preparing the world for the advent of the "Most Great Peace" and the "Mighty World Educator," Baha'u'llah (Glory of God), 1863-92, and later Abdul-Baba, 1892–1921. It further claims to be the unity of all religions, also older and modern movements, such as Theosophy, Freemasonry, Spiritualism, Socialism, etc.;·it aims at conferring *illumination* upon humanity, and like all illuminated groups, it works for universal peace, religion, education, language (Esperanto), and universal everything leading to unity of humanity; therefore all prejudices must be abandoned, traditional, racial, patriotic, religious and political; all religions must be in accordance with science and reason.

From *The Confusion of Tongues*, by Charles Ferguson, we·find the following Bahai documented information: All these nineteenth-century movements "have been the instruments of God to make the world receptive to His Cause. (Bahaism)"; and, "Apart from the Bahai cause, modern world movements and tendencies seem sinister anarchy; but from within the cause they assume perfect order and fullness of meaning!" Baha'u'llah's teachings include science, philosophy, economic and governmental problems, as well as ethics and methods of spiritual purification and attainment (Yoga). 'Fifty Years ago he commanded the people to establish universal peace, and summoned all the nations to the Divine Banquet of International Arbitration, so that questions of boundaries, of national honour and property, and of vital interests between nations might be decided by an arbitral court of justice' — all of which makes one think of Grand Orient Judaeo-Masonry!

When the Bahai followers in Chicago heard of the Great Temple, a Mashriqu'l-Adhkar in'Ishqábád, in which city of Turkmenio there are 4,000 Bahai families, they begged permission to build a similar temple in Chicago; it was to overlook Lake Michigan. From 1903 they have been working at its erection, and it is still far from completion; the towering light was to signalise unity of all faiths, and the temple was to symbolise and embody their revelation (like Steiner's Goetheanum!). Its services consist of reading or chanting the 'Most Holy Word of Baha'u'llah.' In form it is a perfect nonagon, and all its dimensions are based on the number *nine* — the cabalistic number of generation, which initiates and leads to unity with the universal astral light. Of this temple they say: "When the Temple of God shall be built in Chicago it will be to the spiritual body of the world what the inrush of the spirit is to the physical body of man, quickening it to the utmost parts and infusing New Light and Power" — universal and individual Illuminism!

Further, there is a Guardian of the Cause-Shogi-Effendi — with nine co-workers, and in each town there is a Spiritual Assembly of nine members, who must be consulted, absolutely obeyed, and submitted to. There are also National Spiritual Assemblies in all countries to which the cause has spread, and, finally, they are making elaborate plans to form an International Spiritual Assembly to be elected by all believers — to enact ordinances and regulations not found in the explicit Holy Text.

Though full of platitudes, and apparent high ethics, the teaching is anti-Christian, and suggests that their 'Mighty Educator's' source of inspiration was not God, but the age-old Mysterious Central Power, which is behind all illuminised movements, and which aims at unification for the purpose of World Dominion.

CHAPTER VIII

CONCLUSION

THE *Morning Post*, September 22, 1928, published a very useful article, by Edgar Wallace, the well-known writer and expert on all sorts of weird criminology, entitled, 'A New Crime-Hypnotism as a Weapon.'

It shows that he realises, as we have time and again stated, that one of the deadliest powers of occult centres lies in their knowledge and practice of hypnotic control.

Quoting a letter he had received, he says:

"... There is the criminal about which you have not written: he or she who exults in the undoing of his fellow... A friend of mine, a woman with some property, fell under the influence of a certain occult group. She became fascinated, and eventually a devotee, and submitted to a form of hypnotism... It is sufficient to say that the woman who did the hypnotism began to exercise an extraordinary influence, telepathically — that is to say, when they were not together ... and (the friend) was only stopped by timely interference from conveying all her property by deed of gift ... the mischief was wrought by a superior mental power upon a weaker."

Fdgar Wallace continues:

"Now here is the fact which has interested me... During the past two years I must have received more than a dozen letters, written by people who are obviously sane, if handwriting goes for anything, telling me exactly the same story without any florid etceteras… In every case (so far as I remember) … there was a history of occultism at the beginning, and in every case it was a practiser of this 'magic' who gained dominion over the mind of the novice. There is support for the theory, that such a form of criminality is on the increase, by reported cases. The domination of a strong mind over a weaker is no unusual phenomenon, but there is more than a suspicion that this mental tyranny is becoming systematised, and that it may easily represent a real danger, especially to women of the moneyed class.·… It is, at any rate, a matter which is well worth investigation, for the practisers of this new 'art' are among the most dangerous members of the underworld. They are more dangerous because, in the strictest sense of the word, they are not members of the criminal classes. We are probably on the verge of making very important discoveries in the psychic field, and when the new truths (whatever they are) are established, when realities of, let us say, telepathy are revealed, quite a new department may come into existence at Scotland Yard."

Similar cases have come to our knowledge, and all due to the powerful influences of advanced occultists, one at least most unscrupulous. In the *Morning Post*, October 4, 1928, there was an interesting letter on the above article sent by Mordaunt Shairp, in which he writes: "… I can quite understand the hesitation he felt before writing it. In spite of all that is known of the possibilities of waves of light and sound, we are still reluctant to believe in these thought waves, which are the basis of that powerful and dangerous telepathic influence he so convincingly describes." Speaking of his own play, "The Bend in the Road," produced by the Play Actors at the Apollo Theatre, January 1927, which was well noticed by the *Morning Post*, Mr. Shairp says: "It showed a man in whom this thought-power had been remarkably developed, using it out of motives of revenge to undermine the health and happiness of his rival to the verge of suicide… As Mr. Wallace points out, it is a fact, and we shall hear more of it in the future."

Here we have the use and abuse of the psychic fluid which "slays and makes alive"—this Serpent Power—set in motion by powerful will and thought, the worker of all magic and miracles, as used in esoteric masonry and all Rosicrucian and occult groups. In the R.R. et A.C. there·is a formula used for influencing people from a distance for good or ill. In this is used the power of the Pentagram and of the Interlaced Triangles (the Hebrew Talisman!). This fluid is attracted and then projected with strong and concentrated intention in the required direction, as if along a path or ray of light, and interesting and weird results·have been obtained. It not only acts upon the person physically and mentally, but apparently through the intermediary adept, who uses this formula, it links him with the hidden centre who controls the Order.

In that curious pamphlet, *The Hebrew Talisman*, already quoted, the following extract is interesting in connection with the above. Speaking of Abraham Goldsmid, who is said to have received the Magic Box from Dr. Falk, a cabalistic Jew who arrived in London in 1742 (see Mrs. Nesta Webster in *Secret Societies and Subversive Movements*), the Wandering Jew says:

> "Aye, let the Nazarene dogs lift their hands and eyes in ignorant wonder; the great Goldsmid was my very and mere instrument: I raised him because I deemed him worthy; I found him incompetent to the vast and sacred duty I designed him for, and I dashed him down even as we cast aside the gourd when we no longer require a drinking-cup. Who among the elder frequenters of the great Temple of Mammon, which is called the Exchange, does not remember the golden box with which the hand of Goldsmid was perpetually occupied in his busiest and most important moments! It was his *talisman*. The words of power had been pronounced above it: with it he could encounter a world and be triumphant… I had warned him again and again; I had menaced, I had entreated, but in vain; I found him incorrigible in his neglect of the cause of our people and our God; and even while he was wassailing at his luxurious villa in the neighbourhood of Morden, the words of power went forth from my lips, and his talisman had

departed from him for ever... He appeared upon the Exchange without his palladium; bargained, lost, and saw absolute ruin looking at him with steadfast and unpitying eyes. *Two days he bore this, and then he blew his brains out!* None can be false to our cause and prosper."

And if an adept destined by these evil masters for some "mighty work", dares to betray their trust, misfortune, discredit, and even death may follow, but that great occultist Paracelsus writes:

"The spirits (forces) of a man may act upon another without the other man's consent or intention... If man's will is in unity with his thought and desire, a spirit (force) will be produced which can be employed for good or evil. If two such spiritual forces battle with each other, the weaker one, which does not defend itself sufficiently, will be overcome, and bodily disease may be the result. An evil-disposed person may throw the force of his will upon another person and injure him, even if the latter is stronger than the former, because the latter does not expect and is not prepared for the attack; but if the other is stronger and resists successfully, then a force will be kindled in him which will overcome his enemy and which may destroy him."

Might not England and her Empire take a lesson from the above teaching of Paracelsus? She is stronger than the enemy within and without her gates, but she has been more or less taken unaware. Let her shake off this insidious apathy and pacificism, which are merely the poisonous vapours of her enemy; let her resist! and then and only then will she rise strong and ready to recapture her old and honoured place in God's Sun not the Devil's!

And who is this enemy? It is the power behind these deadly secret Orders, which is slowly but surely sapping her power of resistance, it is the "serpent," which fascinates, but fascinates unto death.

Cheiro, in his *Predictions*, tells us of the coming World

Domination by the Jews, the setting up of their kingdom in Egypt and Palestine which is to eventuate in 1980, according to his reckoning, a reckoning which we can falsify if we recognise the possible danger.

This book of Cheiro's appears as if it might be a subtle piece of propaganda, seeking through astrology, cabalistic teaching, so-called seership, and much playing about with scriptural quotations, to prove the inevitableness of the Jewish World Domination. Astrology is an ancient science we know, but Cheiro himself says: "As I see it," and "in the light of occultism," man is not infallible, and occultism, as taught in these devilish secret societies, was ever a deceiver! On the cover of the book is an allegorical design by Countess Hamon of a lightning-stricken world — Illuminism! A few extracts will show his ideas and conclusions:

> "That the Israelites were for some unaccountable reason a race set apart for the manifestation of the God Power in connection with the destiny of mankind, is, I think, evident from the prophecies concerning them. That they were also intended to be an example of the mysterious influence of the planets on human life appears to be equally evident... All through the story of the Israelites ... the power of the Seven Creative planets is not only distinctly emphasized, but in all cases represents the mysterious 'God-Force' in nature ... the mysterious Law of Vibration or 'God-Force,' symbolised by the number seven."

Here we have the electro-magnetic forces of the ether, the "finer force of nature," the seven aspects of the solar force, the spectrum, the Serpent Power.

He appears to throw cold water upon the beliefs of the "British Israel Movement," which he says represents—

> "England as the children of Ephraim and the U.S.A. as Manasseh. My own opinion is that such a proposition appears to limit the purpose of the Creator and brings too much into

the controversy the personal element of the English and American people... The present so-called 'Great Powers,' in the intoxication of their youth, forget they are but children in comparison with races which have passed away ... With the innocence of children they prattle of their greatness..."

He claims,

"that the real meaning of the Great Pyramid is an astrological one, setting forth the religion of life ... that this plan or design is linked up with the Children of Israel, and contains in its records exact periods of years corresponding to the great events in their history ... (p. 136). It is in fact the Solar-Lunar Clock of the Universe ... (p. 143). From 1980 ... will, in my opinion, see the restoration of the Twelve Tribes of Israel as the dominant power in the World. The Great Pyramid will then become the controlling centre in the world's civilisation ... (p. 144). Beneath the thirteen-acre base of the Pyramid a treasure temple will be discovered ... revealing scientific secrets by which the Pyramid was built, which will upset all previously known laws relating to astronomy, gravitation, electricity, the harnessing of the powers of light, etheric rays, and the hidden forces of the atom. With such knowledge at their disposal the Israelites and all the descendants of 'the lost tribes' will become the possessors of the earth in every sense, as has been predicted so many times in the Bible ... (p. 145). Another Law-giver, like Moses, will arise ... and so in the end through this 'despised race' universal peace will become established..."

Are the above secret laws not the same forces used to-day by these hidden Illuminati, these "grand-masters, all Jews"?

Further, as in all illuminised orders, he too says that there is to be a new age of (p. 35)

"the negation of Self — arrived at through suffering — (p. 175). It may be that the revolutions and upheavals we see around us on all sides may for the time being bring about the fall of empires, the destruction of thrones, the death of the 'old' and the birth of the 'new'. He believes in a "War of Wars" (p. 181): "The aftermath of the Great Armageddon will completely revolutionise our present ideas of nations, kingdoms, and republics; a wonderfully organised Central Government in Palestine will radiate laws of life and humanity to the entire world ... (p. 144). That "the stranger" will be a co-worker (subordinate dupe) with the returned Israelites in making Palestine and its surrounding countries the centre of a new and coming civilisation ... (p. 182), such perfection cannot be attained until all religions have become merged in one ... (p. 183), the language of stars, planets and suns, will translate the 'Book' into words 'understandable by the people' (Jewish Cabala!) ... (p. 151). The predicted period 'the Times of the Gentiles' is rapidly coming to a close..."

Compare this with the *Protocols* as already quoted in connection with the T.S. symbol:

"To-day I can assure you that we are only within a few strides of our goal. There remains only a short distance, and the cycle of the Symbolic Serpent — that badge of our people — will be complete, etc."

Finally, in all this domination by the power behind these secret and illuminised societies there is a deadly danger to civilisation.

With reference to an article in the *Patriot*, March 14, 1929, on "Growing Moral Degradation," does not Disraeli, in his novel *Lothair*, 1870, speaking of the aims of the Illuminati and Freemasons, make the Cardinal say:

"The foundation of the Christian family is the sacrament of matrimony, the spring of all domestic and public morals. The anti-Christian societies are opposed to the principle of home. When they have destroyed the hearth the morality of society will perish." (*Patriot*, May 10, 1928.)

Prof. Charles Grangent, of Harvard University, says in his book *Prunes and Prisms*:

> "If the colour of sex has come to pervade all our thinking, even as the smell of gasoline forms the major constituent of our atmosphere, we owe that ether-like omnipresence, in great measure, to a Viennese nerve doctor, called by some of his American disciples 'Froude'"(*Patriot*, February 21, 1929).

In her *Secret Societies and Subversive Movements*, Mrs. Webster thus quotes an eminent neuro-psychiatrist of New York:

> "The Freud Theory is anti-Christian and subversive of organised society... Freudism makes of the individual a machine, absolutely controlled by subconscious reflexes... Whether conscious or unconscious, it makes for destructive effect... Not only the Freud theory "of psycho-analysis, but a considerable quantity of pseudo-scientific propaganda of that type has for years been emanating from a group of German Jews who live and have their headquarters in Vienna."

The Freudian theory reduces everything, good or bad, to a crude sex-basis.

Do we not find the same "ether-like omnipresence" in all these illuminised and esoteric secret societies, where the power of illurninism lies in the awakened and perverted sex-forces united to the universal agent or ether? To bring about the unity of humanity, bound by the magnetic chain into the "Universal Republic" of the Grand Orient Judaeo-Masonry, perverted sex-consciousness by every means possible is necessary, such as illuminism, eurhythmy, nudity cults and dances, etc., and perhaps in some groups psycho-analysis — even when practised "in the light of spiritual science" according to Steiner.

Further, Mrs. Webster quotes a critic who wrote of a well-known Jewish artist:

"He brings to the world of art a new gospel, a black gospel, a gospel in which everything is to be inverted and distorted. Whatsoever things are hideous, whatsoever things are of evil report, whatsoever things are sordid; if there·be any unhealthiness or any degradation; think on these things."

Is this not·the curse of certain other present-day expressions of life and art-books, plays, music, etc.?

Mr. H. A. Jung, of Chicago, writes of the Hon. Bertrand Russell:

"His teaching on the sex question can be bluntly summed up as follows: complete sexual promiscuity under sanitary conditions; that man's desires should be the guiding factor in life, and that outside of human desires there is no moral standing; that right or wrong can only be determined by consequences… He says in his book, *Why·I am not a Christian*: 'I say quite deliberately that the Christian religion as organised in the churches has been, and still is, the principal enemy of moral progress in the world.' Mrs. Russell writes in her book *The Right to be Happy*: 'Animals we are, and animals we remain, and the path of our regeneration and happiness, if there be such a path, lies through our animal nature'." (*Patriot*, February 23, 1928).

Rasputin, that licentious evil genius of Russia, had a similar creed — "Redemption through sin." Likewise that pernicious Aleister Crowley, of the O.T.O., looks upon sex as the redeemer of man! Krishnamurti, the Leadbeater-Besant fallen "Star in the East which was to proclaim the dawn of earth's new and greater day," advocated in his book: Life *in Freedom*, revolt from all restraints, and said that each one must be his or her own law-giver-intuition! He writes: "When you bind life to beliefs and traditions, to codes of morality, you kill life."

And to all this is linked birth-control and "Companionate Marriages"!

William Farren, who has belonged to the stage for over fifty years, writes in a letter to the *Patriot*, April 19, 1928: "There are very few theatres, music halls, and places of entertainment which are not under Jewish management (the same is said of Paris and New York in the *Victories of Israel*) … the theatre has become a mere workshop to turn out what is ugly, vulgar, and debasing." Why? Because of the modern "commercial manager"!

"The Protocols of the Learned Elders of Zion," whatever their origin, foreshadow all this in remarkable way when they say:

> "The educated classes of the Gentiles will pride themselves in their learning, and without verifying it, they will put into practice the knowledge obtained from science (even "Spiritual Science!"), which was dished up to them by our agents *with the object of educating their minds in the direction which we require.*"

I have now laid before you some of the results of years of difficult experience and research into the hidden workings of this Great Conspiracy, hatched in the secret and subterranean places of the world by some crafty Overshadowing Power, who would rule the world by gaining control over the minds and actions of men and women, using them as credulous idealists and dupes, dreaming of a "universal evolution of humanity," caught and held in the snare of these secret societies; or again as more or less honest sceptics, who are employed to cover up the tracks of this secret Overshadowing Power, in case, by some unlooked — for miscarriage of their devilish plans, the truth might leak out — for they are but flesh and blood men and, as such, are in no way infallible — mistakes are made which can only be rectified, if rectified they can be, by bluff, and for this purpose honest sceptics are more than useful — they are absolutely necessary.

As has been said of the Emerald Tablet of Hermes:

> "To those who read with their bodily eyes the precepts will suggest nothing new or extraordinary, for it merely begins by saying that it speaks not fictitious things, but that which is true and most certain. 'What is below is like that which is

above, and what is above is similar to that which is below to accomplish the wonders of one thing'—manifestation of their ambitious and diabolical World Dominion by this mysterious "Overshadowing Power."

Other titles

OMNIA VERITAS

MK ULTRA
Ritual Abuse and Mind Control
Tools of domination for the nameless religion

For the first time, a book attempts to explore the complex subjects of traumatic ritual abuse and the mind control that results from it...

How is it possible to mentally program a human being?

OMNIA VERITAS

OMNIA VERITAS LTD PRESENTS:

SCARLET AND THE BEAST

ENGLISH FREEMASONRY, BANKS, AND THE ILLEGAL DRUG TRADE

English Freemasonry is wealthy and capitalistic, controlling the money and rulers of the world through banking and commerce. French Freemasonry, on the other hand, is poor and communistic, attempting to control state finances through an all-powerful socialistic government.

The Harlot's abominable cup is in the hands of English Freemasonry

OMNIA VERITAS

Omnia Veritas Ltd presents:

MYRON FAGAN

THE ILLUMINATI
AND THE
COUNCIL ON FOREIGN RELATIONS

The objective is to brainwash the people into accepting the phony peace bait to transform the United States into an enslaved unit of the United Nations' one-world government.

They have seized that power on orders from their masters of the great conspiracy

OMNIA VERITAS
Omnia Veritas Ltd presents:
THE HIDDEN AUTHORS of the FRENCH REVOLUTION
It seems," Robespierre once said to Amar, "that we are being carried away by an invisible hand beyond our control..."
by HENRI POUGET DE SAINT-ANDRÉ
The more we study the history of the French Revolution, the more we come up against enigmas...

OMNIA VERITAS
Omnia Veritas Ltd presents:
HERVÉ RYSSEN
Since time immemorial, spread in all countries, they are famous for having dedicated themselves to the great international trade. They are also, for centuries, the masters of banking and speculation.
ISRAEL'S BILLIONS
Jews have a very particular relationship with money...

OMNIA VERITAS
Omnia Veritas Ltd presents:
The Jewish Mafia
HERVÉ RYSSEN
The Jewish mafia is, however, undoubtedly the most powerful mafia in the world. The most dangerous, too. Some overly curious journalists have already been killed.
The "Jewish mafia", that one, does not exist; the Western media do not talk about it...

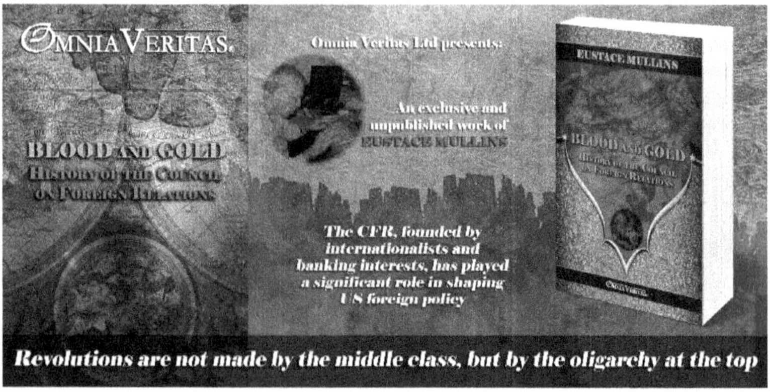
OMNIA VERITAS
Omnia Veritas Ltd presents:
An exclusive and unpublished work of EUSTACE MULLINS
BLOOD AND GOLD
HISTORY OF THE COUNCIL ON FOREIGN RELATIONS
EUSTACE MULLINS
The CFR, founded by internationalists and banking interests, has played a significant role in shaping US foreign policy
Revolutions are not made by the middle class, but by the oligarchy at the top

OMNIA VERITAS
OMNIA VERITAS LTD PRESENTS:
SCARLET AND THE BEAST
My research has revealed that there are two separate and opposing powers in Freemasonry...
SCARLET AND THE BEAST
One is Scarlet. The other, the Beast.
A HISTORY OF THE WAR BETWEEN ENGLISH AND FRENCH FREEMASONRY

www.ingramcontent.com/pod-product-compliance
Lightning Source LLC
Chambersburg PA
CBHW070811270326
41927CB00010B/2382